The Roots of Polarization

Chicago Studies in American Politics

A series edited by Susan Herbst, Lawrence R. Jacobs, Adam J. Berinsky, and Frances Lee; Benjamin I. Page, editor emeritus

Also in the series:

Additional series titles follow index.

The Roots of Polarization

From the Racial Realignment
to the Culture Wars

NEIL A. O'BRIAN

THE UNIVERSITY OF CHICAGO PRESS   CHICAGO AND LONDON

The University of Chicago Press, Chicago 60637
The University of Chicago Press, Ltd., London
© 2024 by The University of Chicago
Published 2024
Printed in the United States of America

33 32 31 30 29 28 27 26 25 24   1 2 3 4 5

ISBN-13: 978-0-226-83454-2 (cloth)
ISBN-13: 978-0-226-83456-6 (paper)
ISBN-13: 978-0-226-83455-9 (e-book)
DOI: https://doi.org/10.7208/chicago/9780226834559.001.0001

Library of Congress Cataloging-in-Publication Data

Names: O'Brian, Neil A., author.
Title: The roots of polarization : from the racial realignment to the culture wars /
    Neil A. O'Brian.
Other titles: Chicago studies in American politics.
Description: Chicago ; London : The University of Chicago Press, 2024. |
    Series: Chicago studies in American politics | Includes bibliographical
    references and index.
Identifiers: LCCN 2023054070 | ISBN 9780226834542 (cloth) | ISBN
    9780226834566 (paperback) | ISBN 9780226834559 (ebook)
Subjects: LCSH: Polarization (Social sciences) — United States. | Culture
    conflict — Political aspects — United States. | Abortion — Political aspects —
    United States. | Public opinion — Political aspects — United States. | United
    States — Politics and government — 20th century. | United States — Emigration
    and immigration — Political aspects.
Classification: LCC JK1726 .O37 2024 | DDC 306.20973 — dc23/eng/20240110
LC record available at https://lccn.loc.gov/2023054070

♾ This paper meets the requirements of ANSI/NISO Z39.48-1992 (Permanence of Paper).

This book is dedicated to Sarah and my entire family, old and new.

Contents

Introduction

O n April 10, 1975, Massachusetts Democratic Senator Ted Kennedy stood on the Senate floor and "bored in constantly" at a legislative amendment from Republican Senator Dewey Bartlett. The issue at hand? Bartlett's amendment prohibited federal Medicaid funds for abortion services (Lader, undated memo A; Hunter 1975). Kennedy's actions caught abortion activists off guard. "The attack on Bartlett was led, surprisingly enough, by two Catholic Senators who had stayed aloof from [the] issue before—Kennedy of Massachusetts and Muskie of Maine," Lawrence Lader, founder of the then-nascent National Abortion Rights Action League (NARAL) wrote (Lader, undated memo A). Robert Lynch, who led the US Catholic Bishops' organized efforts to ban abortion, was just as upset by Kennedy's actions as NARAL was pleased. Lynch interpreted Kennedy's actions as a clear message that Kennedy had finally decided not to endorse any attempts "to change the current status of abortion-on-demand" (Lynch 1975a, 1974a).

While fights between Democrats and Republicans over abortion politics are commonplace today, Kennedy, like other Democrats (and Republicans), had not yet taken a clear position on abortion in the early 1970s (Wolbrecht 2000). Lynch and other Catholic leaders wondered what prompted Kennedy's about-face in 1975.[1] Catholic leadership learned, from Kennedy's staff, "that Senator Kennedy is convinced that a majority of the Massachusetts citizenry support his position of acceptance of [*Roe v. Wade*]" (Lynch 1975a). Kennedy had taken a private poll, and his pro-choice abortion position, which he worried might hurt him in a heavily Catholic state, did not affect his standing among the electorate (Hehir 1975). "Only if we can demonstrate that [Massachusetts voters oppose Kennedy's abortion stance] will we be able to move Senator Kennedy

to a position of at least neutrality," Lynch concluded. But as Kennedy's
internal polling suggested, this would prove difficult. A 1976 exit survey
showed that 72% of Massachusetts voters believe a woman should be able
to have an abortion (CBS/NYT Exit Poll 1976). Furthermore, "Kennedy's
leadership . . . [on] abortion," Lawrence Lader mused, "coupled with his
strong stand on Boston school integration, seems to portend a major bid
for liberal support, perhaps the signal for his re-entry into the 1976 campaign." In a matter of years, Kennedy had transformed from being publicly
indifferent on the issue of abortion to being "the leader of abortion [rights]
forces in the Senate" (*New York Times* 1980).

While this vignette focuses on Ted Kennedy and his position on abortion, it is illustrative of a broader transformation of the political parties that
has long interested academics, journalists, and other political observers:
issues like abortion that had been nonpartisan came to define intense party
conflict of the 1980s and 1990s.

This book explores why the party coalitions—which once held overlapping and diverse views on issues like abortion or gun control—polarized on
these and effectively every other major culture war issue in the latter part
of the twentieth century. By "culture war" issues, I mean the non-economic
domestic issues that have animated political fights in recent decades: gun
control, abortion, the environment, immigration, gay rights, and women's
rights.[2] On each of these issues, Democrats moved leftward, Republicans
moved rightward, and intraparty divisions, common in the 1970s, all but
disappeared.

I argue that the 1960s racial realignment—referring to the moment
when the national parties polarized on civil rights—was a defining moment
for contemporary party polarization across other nonracial culture war
issues. The parties were able to sort as they did on issues like abortion and
gun control in the 1980s and 1990s because the parties in the electorate had
already sorted on civil rights in the 1960s. By sorted, I mean that Democrats
adopted what we now consider to be liberal positions and Republicans
adopted what we now consider to be conservative positions. This is the central thesis of this book: partisan divisions on now-salient culture war issues
are connected to and constrained by the electoral coalitions that formed as
a result of the 1964 racial realignment (prior to 1964, the national parties
held similar positions on civil rights).

At the root of this transformation is a long-standing feature of US public
opinion: ordinary voters who hold more conservative racial views also hold
more conservative views on a range of other social issues including abor-

tion, guns, and gay rights. These linkages date to the earliest public opinion polls and, important for this book's argument, precede the national parties staking divergent positions (or in some cases, any position) on these now-salient issues. While scholarship shows that people who are conservative on race hold other conservative positions in the present day, the fact that these same patterns of public opinion date to the earliest opinion polls, some of which go back to the 1930s, has been overlooked.

These preexisting issue connections meant that when racially conservative Democrats, disaffected by the growing racial liberalism of the Democratic Party, started entering the GOP, they quietly brought their conservative positions on other culture war issues with them. In other words, the racial realignment, although about civil rights, redistributed the issue preferences of other policies across partisan lines as well. This is despite issues like abortion or gun control being largely or completely absent from the political agenda at the time.

To be sure, polarization on these issues did not occur only because of the racial realignment, but the racial realignment altered the partisan distribution of public opinion on other culture war issues, which in turn shaped the behavior of politicians and activists in the decades that followed. Absent a racial realignment—in a world in which the parties held overlapping positions on civil rights and cleaved only along economic lines—it is not clear whether the parties would have sorted on issues like abortion or gun control in the manner or to the extent that they did.

This book's argument breaks from an existing literature on political parties, which contends that party sorting and polarization on culture war issues is a "top-down" process driven by interest groups, politicians, or the media (e.g., Aldrich 2011; Bawn et al. 2012; Carmines and Stimson 1989; Layman and Carsey 2002; Adams 1997; Noel 2013). This existing scholarship, which collectively serves as a leading theory of US political parties, argues that elites or activists determine which side of an issue the party will take a position on, and then voters eventually follow along. These theories argue that because abortion and gun control were nonpartisan issues when polarization was at its low point, either party could have been the anti-abortion or pro–gun control party and that the eventual partisan alignment was the result of contingent choices made by politicians and activists. Voters played a peripheral role, this scholarship contends.

The Roots of Polarization: From the Racial Realignment to the Culture Wars shifts the focus back to voters, and it argues that the policy preferences of the mass public are fundamental for understanding the transformation of the contemporary party system. In doing so, this book offers new insights on old theories of interest groups and social movements (e.g., Key 1942; McCarty and Schickler 2018; Krimmel 2017; Proctor 2022). While existing literature focuses on the role of interest groups for party positioning on issues, less work explores why interest groups enter one party and not the other. I argue that the racial realignment, by shaping the parties' coalition of voters, constrained interest groups to which party they could join. To return to the example of Ted Kennedy, many pro-life groups pressured Kennedy and other Democrats to pick up their cause. But these groups eventually found more support in the conservative wing of the GOP that had been rapidly growing since the early 1960s.

Likewise this book calls into question the role of party leaders as opinion makers who had the ability to pull the party in one direction over another in polarization's formative years. At least on highly salient issues, politicians staked positions that reinforced what their (potential) constituency desired. For example, Kennedy's prominence in the Democratic coalition meant his public support for abortion reform shaped public opinion among liberal Democrats. But this messaging did not appear out of nowhere; it was shaped by the perception and reality that for Kennedy, staking prochoice positions was an avenue to build or maintain his voter coalition at the state or national level.

Together, these findings offer a new frame for understanding how the 1964 racial realignment still shapes the party system today. Our current politics runs through partisan paths worn and re-worn over the last sixty years. Even at times when race has been less visible in political campaigns, the partisan divisions over race that arose in the 1960s are the roots of today's partisan culture wars.

A Primer on Twentieth-Century Party Positions

Today, we take for granted that a suite of cultural issues including civil rights, abortion, and gun control are bundled together in the party system and that each of these issues will receive at least some attention throughout the campaign cycle. But this has not always been the case. This section briefly outlines the evolving positions of the national and state parties, as well as other political elites, across non-economic issues that define the contemporary culture wars.

National Party Platforms

Between the 1930s and the early 1960s, the national parties held similar positions on civil rights, and partisan conflict in this era largely centered on government intervention in the economy. Party competition and coalitions were shaped by the New Deal economic policies created to combat the Great Depression of the 1930s. However, in 1964 (for reasons discussed in chapter 2), the incumbent Democratic President Lyndon Johnson embraced the civil rights movement while Barry Goldwater, the Republican presidential nominee, absorbed the conservative opposition. In a fairly short time period, civil rights and racial equality, which had crosscut party lines since the 1930s, had become a *central* feature of national partisan conflict. Democratic voters supported broader calls for racial equality while Republican voters opposed them. Parties in government and organization divided similarly. Political scientists refer to the moment the parties divided on civil rights as the "racial realignment" (a term I use throughout this book).

My core argument is that the parties splitting on civil rights pushed them to divide on other once-nonpartisan social issues like abortion or gun control, which at the time were largely absent from political conflict. In the mid-twentieth century, the national parties either lacked positions on now-salient culture war issues or held overlapping views on those issues. If you read a copy of the *New York Times* in the 1950s, you would see few articles about abortion or gun control, and those that existed made little-to-no mention of partisan conflict.

To get a broader sense of party conflict on culture war issues, figure 1.1 plots the net number of liberal and conservative sentences that address each culture war issue in the national Democratic and Republican parties' platforms between 1944 and 1996. Although the platform lengths vary, and tone cannot be captured by mentions, they paint a broad picture: the parties did not start taking consistent, differentiated positions on these issues until at least the mid-1970s.

Both parties first included brief language on gun control in their 1968 platform but had yet to divide on the issue; each party's respective platform *supported* gun control.[3] Perhaps surprisingly, Congress passed gun control legislation in 1968 with a higher percentage of Republicans supporting its passage than Democrats. Senators Eugene McCarthy, George McGovern, and Edmund Muskie—the Senate's leading liberal Democrats and national figureheads of the Democratic Party—did not vote on the legisla-

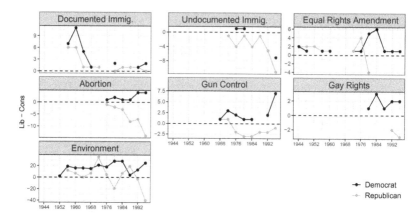

FIGURE 1.1. National Party Platform: Liberal/Conservative Issue Mentions. Each graph plots the difference in the total number of liberal sentences minus total number of conservative sentences in each party's national platform. To do this, I simply count the number of sentences in each party's platform that take a stand on the respective issue and subtract them. Higher values are more liberal. Republican Party plotted in gray; Democratic Party plotted in black. Platforms are from the UCSB American Presidency Project.

tion; a common maneuver to avoid taking a stand.[4] McCarthy said gun laws should not be passed under "panic conditions" (Karol 2009, 86). It was not until the mid-1970s that the national parties first diverged on gun control. On abortion, the parties first took diverging stances in 1976, although the language in each party's platform was carefully crafted to reflect the intraparty heterogeneity that still existed. And although Republican Gerald Ford was marginally to the right of Democrat Jimmy Carter in the 1976 presidential election, it would not be until 1980 that the two major presidential candidates meaningfully differed on abortion. In fact, the most prominent partisan advocate for liberalizing abortion laws in the late 1960s was Republican Nelson Rockefeller.

On gay rights, Democrats first included very brief language about protecting against discrimination based on sexual orientation in 1980, although the 1972 Democratic platform made a vague mention that "Americans should be free to make their own choice of lifestyles" without discrimination. The national Republican Party platform did not include language on gay rights or sexual orientation until 1992, at which point they adopted a conservative position.

While abortion, gun control, and gay rights were completely absent from the parties' platforms until at least the late 1960s, the issues of women's equality, immigration, and the environment did receive attention by the national political parties in the mid-twentieth century. However, the parties held overlapping views on these issues until the 1970s. For example, both parties included supportive language on the Equal Rights Amendment in their national party platforms between 1944 and 1976. In fact, the GOP in 1940 was the first party to endorse the Equal Rights Amendment. This makes its disappearance from the GOP's platform in 1980 all the more surprising.

On documented immigration, both parties supported liberalized immigration laws in the 1950s and 1960s. In fact, when Congress passed reform legislation that removed nation-based immigration quotas in 1965, a higher percentage of Republicans than Democrats in Congress supported this legislation. On undocumented immigration, the issue was absent from either party's platform until 1972, at which point Republicans included a single line in opposition.

With respect to the environment, both parties supported federal environmental regulations in the mid-twentieth century (Karol 2019, 12). While there were certainly exceptions—such as George H. W. Bush's passage of the Clean Air Act in the 1990s—by the late 1970s, Republicans were generally to the right of Democrats on environmental action.

State Parties

The Democratic and Republican state parties did not split much earlier than the national parties on culture war issues. Gamm et al. (2022) find that abortion and gay rights were absent completely from state party platforms until 1968 and 1972, respectively. When these issues did emerge, they did so gradually, and partisan lines were blurred. Democratic platforms in Massachusetts, Missouri, Rhode Island, and South Dakota adopted conservative abortion platforms throughout the 1970s while Republican parties in Michigan, New York, and Hawaii, for example, adopted liberal abortion platforms (Gamm et al. 2022, 20–21). On gay rights, Republicans did not mention homosexuality until 1978, and in 1980 just 25% of Democratic state party platforms endorsed gay rights.

Analysis of state party platforms by Hopkins, Schickler, and Azizi (2020, 2022) show that it was not until the late 1970s that state party platforms divided on gun control, and state party polarization on immigration did not appear until the late 1980s. Relatedly, Jake Grumbach's (2022) analysis of state-level party conflict shows that through the 1970s (at least), state policy

outcomes on abortion, immigration, the environment, LGBT rights, and
guns differed little between state governments controlled by Democrats
compared to state governments controlled by Republicans.

Public Intellectuals

Due to the centrality of national parties to an existing literature on parties
and public opinion, much of this book focuses on national parties and
their leaders (e.g., presidential candidates). However, it is worth noting
that thought leaders, on both the right and left, were also generally quiet
on culture war issues throughout the 1950s and 1960s. When conservative
thought leaders envisioned a new Republican Party, one that broke away
from the New Deal consensus and racial liberalism that defined much of
the midcentury Republican Party establishment, issues like abortion, gun
control, and gay rights were absent. For example, in 1963 William Rusher,
the publisher of William F. Buckley's conservative magazine, *National Review*, wrote a now-famous piece titled the "Crossroads for the GOP," which
argued that the GOP's path to winning national elections ran through the
South. Rusher and this article were enormously influential for building
modern conservatism in the Republican Party, yet Rusher's piece did not
mention abortion, guns, gay rights, or women's rights as issues to build this
coalition.

Barry Goldwater's 1960 book, *The Conscience of a Conservative*, a road
map for conservatism in the next decades, also did not mention abortion,
guns, gay rights, or women's rights. Likewise, Kevin Phillips's 1969 book,
The Emerging Republican Majority—which *Newsweek* called "the political bible of the Nixon era" and which was treated as a "blueprint" for
the modern Republican Party—also did not mention any of these issues
(Phillips [1969] 2014, xv).

In fact, conservative social activists who would later stand on the front
lines of the culture wars on abortion and gay marriage (often referred to
as the "New Right"), were routinely frustrated by conservative intellectuals for focusing on abstract economic principles rather than emerging
social issues that they believed would mobilize new voters. "The New Right
had always been different from the Old Right (a la William F. Buckley,
for example) because of its concern for the moral issues," a founder of
the culturally conservative activist movement recalled. "When mainline
conservatives were trying to decide whether abortion was an individual

freedom issue or not, the precursors of the New Right were introducing Human Life Amendments into Congress" (Marshner, n.d.).

One might imagine that conservative intellectuals, committed to reducing the role of government in everyday life, might oppose or feel conflicted about more government restrictions on abortion and gay rights. For example, in 1957, in their first article that took a stand on homosexuality, the conservative *National Review* supported a British commission that rescinded laws making homosexuality a crime. "What we want are fewer laws, not more," the article read (Lejeune 1957). Such an argument cropped up among activists, politicians, and thinkers on the political right for years (Proctor 2022). William Safire, a tremendously influential conservative intellectual, and James J. Kilpatrick, a very prominent and racially conservative commentator on the right, employed a similar libertarian logic at times (Safire 1974; Kilpatrick 1964). (Chapters 3, 6, and 7 discuss this further.)

In short, the issues that filled and divided the political world of the 1950s and 1960s were much different from what characterizes contemporary partisan and ideological conflict.

Voters

Finally, while the parties and political thought leaders' views crisscrossed partisan lines, partisan cleavages among voters in the mid-twentieth century were also blurred. Figure 1.2 plots partisan opinion, measured by partisan identification, in the 1950s and 1960s toward now-major culture war issues. Not only are the partisan divides on the issues small, on some issues Democrats have more conservative attitudes than Republicans. This might surprise some readers. Several broad factors underpin these trends. First, the white South and conservative Catholics, two very culturally conservative constituencies, still identified as Democrats in this era. Conversely, more socially liberal constituencies in the Northeast were still Republicans. Third, African Americans, who were heavily Democratic by the 1960s, held quite conservative views on abortion and gay rights.

As the next section discusses, the fact that Democrats and Republicans held similar views on now-salient culture war issues coming out of the 1950s is used by existing scholarship to argue that when the parties divided, the parties could not have been reacting to public opinion because public opinion was nonpartisan. This book argues that this is an incomplete picture: by the time abortion and guns became salient issues, southern white

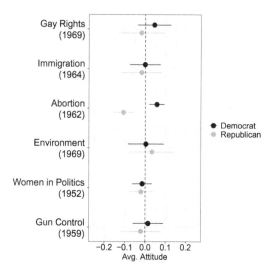

FIGURE 1.2. Public Opinion by Partisan Identification, 1950s–1960s. Each black dot represents the average position of Democratic identifiers and each gray dot the average position of Republican identifiers for each policy listed down the y-axis. Each variable is standardized to have a mean of 0 and a standard deviation of 1. Higher values reflect more conservative attitudes.

and conservative Catholic constituencies had already become unmoored from the Democratic Party because of its embrace of racial liberalism in the 1960s. This is despite these voters not yet identifying as Republican.

Party Positioning: Existing Scholarship

If issues like abortion once sat outside of partisan political conflict, how then did the parties develop the positions they hold today? One view of parties is that politicians, hungry to get elected and stay in office, will learn what their voters' positions are on issues like gun control or abortion and adopt those views to secure votes. Indeed, this concept rests at the center of representative democracy in the United States. In *Federalist*, no. 57, James Madison defends frequent elections to the House of Representatives as a crucial link ensuring that the elected few would pursue the interests of the many. Members of the House of Representatives, Madison wrote, will "anticipate the moment when their power is to cease, when their exercise of it is to be reviewed, and when they must descend to the level from which they were raised; there forever to remain unless a faithful discharge of their trust shall have established their title to a renewal of it."[5]

Yet a literature on political parties in the United States, which collectively stands as a leading theory of parties, argues that this overstates the role of voters in the United States. Rather than serving as agents of their constituents, this literature contends, politicians choose positions, perhaps at the behest of an activist and donor class, and most voters, who pay little attention to politics or lack strong positions on issues of the day, follow along. Thus, when new political issues emerge on the agenda or gain increased salience after years of being swept under the rug, party leaders, media figures, and activists—not voters—drive party positioning and change (e.g., Bawn et al. 2012; Carmines and Stimson 1989; Noel 2013; Layman et al. 2010; Miller and Schofield 2003; Aldrich 2011; and although somewhat more voter focused, Karol 2009). Achen and Bartels (2017) call the democratic ideal, one in which voters hold politicians and parties accountable, the "folk theory of democracy." While these theories do acknowledge voters, their conceptual contribution is that the mass public is not central for understanding the sorting or polarization of US political parties.

The contemporary focus on elite-centered theories of parties is rooted in Carmines and Stimson's (1989) theory of "issue evolutions," which argues that politicians drive party change. In an issue evolution, parties evolve slowly over time, and at critical junctures, party leaders stake their party's new position. On prominent issues, this new positioning then becomes a distinguishing cleavage between parties that trickles down to activists and finally voters: "Visible changes in elite behavior . . . realign the constellation of voter issue attitudes and party identifications to reflect earlier changes among the elite" (162).

A crucial implication of Carmines and Stimson's theory—which they apply to the 1960s racial realignment—is that either party's electorate would have been amenable to supporting the civil rights movement in the late 1950s. This flexibility of the mass public gave elites discretion to choose their position relative to the other party (Carmines and Stimson 1989, 179). Indeed, elite discretion distinguishes Carmines and Stimson's theory from the older realignment literature, which views voters as the driving force (e.g., Key 1959; Schattschneider 1960; Sundquist 1983). Scholars have argued that Carmines and Stimson's account also characterizes party positioning on abortion, defense spending, gun control, and the environment (e.g., Adams 1997; Lindaman and Haider-Markel 2002; Fordham 2007).

A second strand of elite-centered theories, which has become a "new conventional wisdom" (McCarty and Schickler 2018, 176), focuses not on politicians, but on interest groups and activists as the primary movers of partisan change (e.g., Layman et al. 2010; Bawn et al. 2012; Miller and Schofield 2003; Karol 2009). Although the details differ, these theories argue that policy activists work their way into the parties and push politicians to take non-centrist policy positions on their group's issue. Because parties need activists to knock on doors, raise money, and organize, these activists play an outsized role in party positioning.

A key contribution of this literature is the theoretical and empirical argument that parties are polarizing across many different policy dimensions at the same time (Layman et al. 2010). When activists concerned about new issues enter the party's coalition, existing activists update their position to align with the ascendant view. Consequently, parties and their activists are not polarized on one dimension, but across a series of dimensions (Layman et al. 2010, 328–29). The activists' non-centrist positions induce candidates in the parties' respective primaries to take non-centrist positions across multiple policies. This elite-created conflict is then eventually communicated to and absorbed by the mass public.

Bawn et al. (2012) come to a similar conclusion but focus on interest groups or "intense policy demanders," rather than just party activists. To receive a party's nomination, politicians must appeal to various policy-demanding groups in the coalition. Party positioning or change occurs when new policy-demanding groups work their way into the party, incentivizing candidates to adopt the group's position in order to gain a leg up in the party's primary elections. This collection of policy demanders not only defines the parties' positions, but defines the ideological space (Bawn et al. 2012, 575). This theory suggests that Democrats are pro–gun control and pro-choice because gun control groups and NARAL are both in the Democratic Party and recruit candidates who advance both groups' goals.

Collectively, this scholarship views party positioning across a variety of issues, either implicitly or explicitly, as a series of decisions made by political elites or midlevel actors. These top-down theories argue that elites or activists move first, and then voters, following the lead of their preferred party or candidate, belatedly tag along.

These theories have been immensely influential in political science's understanding of why the parties divided across once-nonpartisan issues like abortion or gun control. When polarization was at its low point in the 1960s and the parties either lacked positions or held overlapping views on issues, these theories suggest, many different coalitions could have potentially formed. For example, Carmines and Stimson's theory—which scholars have used to explain party positioning on civil rights, abortion, gun control, and defense spending—collectively implies that the reason Democrats line up to the left on each of these issues is the consequence of a series of unrelated decisions made by political leaders. On any one of these issues, Democratic leaders could have led the party to the right (e.g., Carmines and Stimson 1989; Adams 1997; Fordham 2007; Lindaman and Haider-Markel 2002). Likewise, Bawn et al. (2012) contend that Republicans are the pro-life party because anti-abortion activists worked their way into the Republican Party. Applying this process over various interest groups suggests that many different party coalitions could have emerged in the 1970s.

The argument that elites drive partisan divides has marshaled some compelling evidence. First, among ordinary people, there was no correlation between party identification and attitudes on abortion, defense spending, and civil rights until after party elites established clear positions (Carmines and Stimson 1989; Adams 1997; Fordham 2007). For example, panel A of figure 1.3 shows the long-term relationship between attitudes on issues of women's rights (e.g., abortion, the Equal Rights Amendment, women's role in society) and party identification. Scholars argue that when

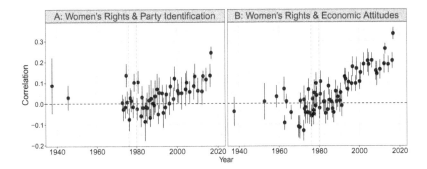

FIGURE 1.3. Correlates: Issues of Women's Rights. The left panel (A) plots the correlation between party identification and an index of issues of women's rights (including abortion rights, the Equal Rights Amendment, women's role in society). The right panel (B) plots the correlation between issues of women's rights and an index of economic attitudes (e.g., government guaranteed health insurance, taxation, etc.). The gray dashed lines roughly represent when the national parties divided on abortion (which the parties had already marginally divided on in 1976) and the Equal Rights Amendment in 1980. Data before 1972 are from the Roper Center for Public Opinion Research and the Louis Harris Data Center. Data after 1972 are largely from the ANES or General Social Survey. See chapter 3 for more discussion.

the national parties first divided on abortion in 1976 and the Equal Rights Amendment in 1980, national party leaders had a choice on whether to adopt a liberal or conservative position because the relationship between party identification and attitudes on issues of women's rights was effectively zero. Democrats (or Republicans) could have gone in either direction and cross-pressured a similar number of voters (e.g., Adams 1997; Karol 2009). Existing scholarship argues that polarization on abortion emerged because the national Republicans moved to the right, the national Democrats to the left, and the parties in the electorate followed along a decade later (Adams 1997). The belated emergence of a correlation between party identification is evidence of those trends.

The second broad piece of evidence used to suggest that voters did not drive partisan divides is that the relationship between attitudes on economic issues, which defined partisan conflict in the New Deal era, have historically had little relationship with other policy attitudes, such as abortion (Sanbonmatsu 2002, 60; Noel 2013; Layman et al. 2010, 328). Figure 1.3, panel B, shows the long-term relationship between attitudes on economic issues (e.g., taxation, government health insurance, etc.) and issues of women's rights. Not until the late 1990s do economic issues and matters of gender equality become consistently linked. Scholars argue that the national parties had a choice on which way to go on abortion in the 1970s because the relationship between economic issues—which defined New Deal party conflict—and abortion was effectively zero. This made positioning open-ended, so Democrats could move left or right and cross-pressure a similar number of voters along the economic cleavage. The trend in figure 1.3B suggests the parties divided as they did, and voters followed along two decades later.

These top-down views of party positioning are underpinned by a large body of literature on US public opinion, which argues that the mass public pays little attention to politics, lacks genuine attitudes on policies, and does not have a coherent "ideology" (e.g., Lenz 2012; Delli Carpini and Keeter 1996; Zaller 1992; Converse [1964] 2006). By ideology, scholars often mean that knowing someone's position on economic intervention in the economy is not informative of views on abortion or gun control (e.g., Kinder and Kalmoe 2017, 18).

To the extent that people do package issues together into ideologies, or have issue preferences at all, it "often [turns] out to be just a rather mechanical reflection of what their favorite group and party leaders have instructed them to think" (Achen and Bartels 2017, 12). This has crucial implications for parties because it enables interest groups or party leaders to have discretion to stake new positions when they become salient. The effect of elite-led partisan and ideological messaging offers a parsimonious theory for explaining contemporary sorting and polarization. If Democratic elites are telling voters to be pro-choice, pro-environment, and pro–gun control, it is simple to understand why Democrats are more liberal than Republicans—by following elite cues.[6] But as *The Roots of Polarization: From the Racial Realignment to the Culture Wars* shows, this is an incomplete picture.

Party Positioning: A New Theory

I argue that the racial realignment served as a critical juncture that constrained the positions parties could take on other, ostensibly nonracial culture war issues. The parties did not have nearly as much choice to position on issues like abortion and gun control as the extant literature suggests.

Social turbulence over race had begun to realign partisan coalitions, and this created a set of constraints on the party system that would have been absent had national partisan loyalties remained divided primarily along economic lines. The fact that people who identified as Republican or Democrat held overlapping views on abortion or gun control in the 1960s meant little in this era because civil rights was realigning the electorate: the number of Independent voters was high, and many people voted for candidates of the opposing party.

This book contends that the transformation of civil rights into a partisan issue had a profound impact on party sorting for other culture war issues for three reasons.

1. The Salience of Civil Rights

At the heart of this transformation is the 1960s racial realignment and the unique ability of civil rights to realign and define the party system. The national Democratic Party, by abandoning their position as the party of segregation—which had effectively locked the southern United States into the Democratic Party for a century—caused white southern Democrats to either move to the GOP or become disillusioned with the Democratic Party they had long called home.

This is a crucial point: Race is central because it is capable of realign-

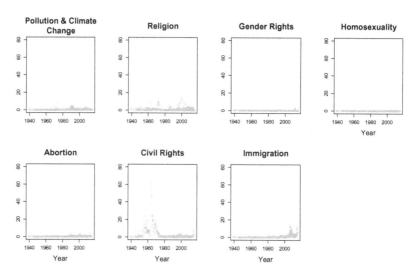

FIGURE 1.4. Most Important Problem, by Issue. Each point shows the percentage of people identifying an issue as the most important problem using open-ended questions. Data compiled from Heffington, Park, and Williams (2017).

ing the party system and moving a large bloc of voters from one party to another in ways that other culture war issues cannot. Sundquist (1983, 41) writes, "For an issue to shatter a party system and create a new one, it clearly must arise from a grievance that is both broad and deep, that a large number of people feel fervently about it." Not only were views toward racial issues widely held, but figure 1.4 shows that 61% of respondents, in open-ended response format in July 1964, ranked it as "the most important problem."

Framed differently, opposition to civil rights kept the South in the Democratic Party for a century. The national Democratic Party's switch on the issue freed the southern region to be open to appeals from the Republican Party. Whether other issues, such as abortion or guns, could have triggered such large-scale realignment is doubtful.

Compare the salience of racial policy to abortion policy, another deeply felt social issue: the high-water mark for respondents listing abortion as the most important problem in this dataset (using open-ended response format), which runs to 2015, occurred around the 2000 election and amounts to less than 3% of the electorate. While scholars have shown that voters change their party identification on the basis of abortion policy when it is salient to them (e.g., Carsey and Layman 2006; Killian and Wilcox 2008),

only a small number of respondents identify abortion as the most important issue. Even in 2022, when the Supreme Court repealed *Roe v. Wade*,
only 8% named abortion (using Gallup's open-ended response format) as
the most important problem in the months following the Supreme Court's
ruling (Newport 2022). Other issues central to the culture wars, tracked in
figure 1.4 — including gay rights, gender, and climate change — rarely rank
as the most important problem among the mass public.

2. Racial Issue Bundles

The second part of this transformation is a long-standing feature of US
public opinion: People who are more conservative on race have long held
more conservative views on effectively every other major culture war issue
including abortion, women's rights, gay rights, gun control, the environment, and immigration. These linkages date to the earliest public opinion
polls and persist even among respondents who know little about politics.
While the nature of issues have changed over time, the results are robust to the contours of the contemporaneous debate. For example, in the
1930s, survey companies asked about racial issues in the context of voting
rights and anti-lynching legislation, while in the 1980s they asked about
affirmative action and school busing. In each case, people who are on the
conservative side of the contemporaneous debate on race are more likely
to be on the conservative side of the contemporaneous debate on abortion
(favor more restrictions) or gun control (less gun control).

Important for this book, these issue linkages *precede* the national (and
state parties) from dividing on these same issues. This undermines leading
theories of parties, which argue that parties first adopt positions across
issues and then these issue bundles are belatedly absorbed by ordinary
voters. Existing scholarship overlooks that a prominent package of issue
bundles that emerged in the national party platforms by the 1980s had
existed in the mass public for decades prior.

Rather than these issue bundles being constructed by elites and passed
down to voters, I argue that a shared set of values underpins the linkage between conservatism on racial and other cultural issues (chapter 3
empirically explores elite-driven explanations, partisan and otherwise, in
polarization's formative years). Race and civil rights represent a prominent
dimension of social change in the United States. Among a midcentury
electorate that was largely white, views toward civil rights, women's rights,
and gay rights tapped into a similar underlying commitment to existing

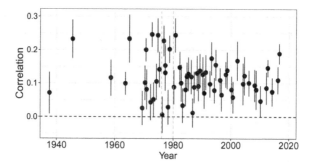

FIGURE 1.5. Issues of Women's Rights and Racial Attitudes. Graph shows the correlation between racial attitudes (as defined by attitudes on voting rights, busing, aid to minorities, etc.)
and broader questions of women's equality (abortion, women's rights more generally, willingness to vote for a woman president). Data are from the Roper Center for Public Opinion
Research and the Louis Harris Data Center. Data after 1972 are largely from the ANES or
General Social Survey; see chapter 3 for more discussion.

values, cultural traditions, and hierarchies. People hesitant of cultural
change around race also express hesitancy around change toward women's
rights, gay rights, or abortion. "Cultural conservatives tend to unite," a leading activist on the right wrote in the 1980s, around the idea "that society,
including government, must play an active role in upholding traditional
culture" (Lind and Weyrich 1987).[7]

To illustrate the enduring relationship between race and other policy
views, and its potential to influence party positioning, figure 1.5 plots the
long-term relationship between issues of women's rights and racial attitudes
(broadly defined to include civil rights, aid to minorities, affirmative action,
etc.), dating to 1937. If scholars only examined public opinion after the late
1970s, top-down theories would suggest that the reason conservative attitudes on issues of women's rights go with conservative racial attitudes is because party leaders had divided on both women's rights and civil rights by the
late 1970s, and voters were following the leader. Elite-driven theories would
also suggest that before the late 1970s, because the parties were not sending
clear signals on both issues, the relationship should fall to zero or fluctuate.
Yet a similar constellation of attitudes exists dating all the way to 1937. This
aligns much more with a bottom-up view, where trends first emerged in
public opinion, and then when abortion and the women's rights movement
became politically salient, a similar trend emerged among the parties, too.

This point is worth lingering on. Despite an intense interest in political
science on whether voters cluster issue attitudes together (see Kinder and

Kalmoe 2017 for an excellent overview), little work investigates whether the issue bundles that define elite conflict today existed in the mass public before parties and campaigns contested those issues. While, for example, a literature shows that people who are conservative on race are also conservative on women's rights in the contemporary era, no existing work shows that these issues were linked together in the mass public dating back to the 1930s. Figure 1.5 and the long-term trends shown in chapter 3 are crucial for understanding mass-elite interactions.

3. Racial Realignment's Cascading Effect

The third part of this transformation is how public opinion on this cluster of issues interacted with candidates and parties. I argue that when the parties divided on civil rights in the 1960s, these preexisting issue connections meant the parties in the electorate were also quietly dividing on a host of other culture war issues as well. I say quietly because abortion and gun control were not politically salient issues. But this is the central point: When these issues did become salient, abortion liberals were already predisposed to the Democratic Party because of their racially liberal attitudes while racial conservatives had brought conservative abortion attitudes to the Republican Party.

For example, southern Democrats and conservative Catholics—two constituencies central to the Democrats' New Deal coalition and that were quite conservative on abortion, gay rights, and gun control—had already left or felt uneasy with the Democrats' coalition of the 1960s because of the national party's highly visible position on civil rights. By the time gay rights, abortion, and gun control became contested political issues in the 1970s, many conservative Democrats were either already voting for Republicans or viewed as constituencies that could be easily peeled off from the Democratic Party. This pushed the parties apart, even while existing party identifications remained crosscutting. The strategy was further encouraged by the fact that while partisan identification remained largely unrelated to attitudes on abortion or guns until the 1980s, people voting for Republican presidential candidates generally held more culturally conservative attitudes than those voting for Democrats by the early 1970s. Furthermore, as chapter 5 shows, Democrats who defected to Goldwater in 1964 or George Wallace in 1968, already held very conservative positions on guns and abortion despite the lack of prominence of these issues in their campaigns.

It is worth lingering on this point: people changed their vote choice before their partisan identification. Figure 1.6 contrasts divides in opin-

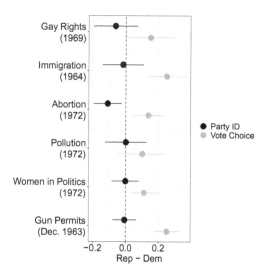

FIGURE 1.6. Attitudes by Vote Choice vs. Partisan Identification. Each point is the difference in attitudes between Republicans and Democrats measured by vote choice (gray points) and partisan identification (black points). I standardize each variable to have a mean of 0 and a standard deviation of 1. Positive values mean Republicans are more conservative on the given issue than Democrats. Graph shows that partisan divides emerged by vote choice prior to party identification.

ion by vote choice (vote for Democratic versus Republican presidential candidates) versus partisan identification (identify as Democratic rather than Republican) for six different culture war issues. Vote choice shows a much more clearly divided electorate than does partisan identification in the 1960s and 1970s. The fact that culture war issues correlated with vote choice by the 1970s pushed the parties to divide even while partisan identification reflected more limited (or no) divides.

While the initial effect of the racial realignment for partisan conflict on abortion, gun control, or immigration was perhaps modest, it engendered a set of electoral incentives that enabled interest groups and politicians to exacerbate the divides set in motion by the racial realignment.

Common Alternative Explanations and Clarifications

Throughout the book, I address many alternative explanations, but for clarity, the following section summarizes several counter-arguments and clarifications to guide the reader.

1. What about theories of elite partisan messaging? Empirical and theoretical work shows that when elites send partisan signals, voters update their prior beliefs (e.g., Lenz 2012; Zaller 1992; Converse [1964] 2006). I argue that elites can influence public opinion consistent with top-down accounts, but that elite cues are often endogenous to what elites perceive will be popular among their supporters (Zaller 2012, 571; Arnold 1992; Key 1961).

2. What about political messages sent by non-party elites? This book largely focuses on national political candidates, given the centrality of national parties to the parties' literature and the fact that they are, for many people in the formative years of polarization, the most visible political actors. However, chapters 3, 6, and 7 discuss public intellectuals in the media as a possible explanation for these issue bundles. As the discussion earlier in this chapter hints at, now-prominent culture war issues were largely absent from the pages of ideological magazines in the decades preceding the culture wars of the 1970s.

3. Can party sorting be reduced to a single moment? A skeptical reader might argue that the racial realignment did not cause polarization on these other issues; this was a complex process that emerged over many years. The core argument of this book is that the racial realignment altered the electoral environment and changed the behavior of political actors to do things they would not have done absent a racial realignment. If the white South and conservative Catholics remained in the Democratic Party, anti-abortion and pro-gun groups, for example, would have had an easier time mobilizing Democratic politicians. Worded differently, polarization on abortion or gun control compounded and built on events initially set in motion by the racial realignment. Interest groups, media actors, politicians, and current events have further exacerbated and locked in the existing equilibrium.

4. This argument rests on the fact that the parties polarized by civil rights first. What if the parties divided on abortion or guns first? Would this have similarly constrained the parties? Why not place those other issues at the center of this transformation? Part of what makes civil rights so central is because it was able to move a large bloc of voters from one party to another and, as an unintended consequence, redistribute preferences on other issues across partisan lines as well. Abortion, for example, could not have realigned the party system to the extent that civil rights did. This is what makes civil rights so important to this story; when the parties moved on civil rights, it created a ripple effect that other, even important issues, could not have. Civil rights had locked the South in the Democratic Party for a century, and its changing position in the party system caused the parties to realign.

Bundled in this conversation is a debate among scholars about whether economics, rather than civil rights, dislodged the South from the Democratic Party. Some scholars (e.g., Shafer and Johnston 2009; Lassiter 2006) argue that the growing wealth and suburbanization of the region or resistance to government intervention into the economy, not civil rights, generated southern realignment. In other words, portraying civil rights as the cause of southern realignment paints too simplistic of a portrait. However, recent work by Kuziemko and Washington (2018), discussed further in the chapters ahead, presents overwhelming evidence that economic issues were not the cause of southern realignment: John F. Kennedy's sudden turn toward civil rights in June 1963 caused an abrupt, almost astonishing downward shift in white southern loyalty to Kennedy and the Democratic Party. Furthermore, as other scholars have argued, southern white people's turn against the New Deal was not rooted in abstract hostility for government intervention in the economy, but the perception that the New Deal economic programs benefited minorities (e.g., Schickler 2016; Caughey 2018). This is true today as well (Gilens 1996; Mendelberg 2001).

5. All voters or white voters? The racial realignment had an uneven impact on voter allegiances. Among black voters, it cemented partisanship. African Americans by the 1960s voted overwhelmingly for the Democratic Party, and because of the party's position on civil rights and its salience to black voters, the party could take positions on other issues that were less popular among black constituencies (Frymer 2011). This is important because African Americans, despite being overwhelmingly Democrat by the 1960s, continued to hold quite conservative positions on issues like abortion or gay rights (Tate 1993). This meant that Democrats pursued abortion liberals without risking a (large) defection of black abortion conservatives going to the Republican Party.

Conversely, the racial realignment weakened partisan attachments among white voters; white conservative Democrats, upset at the racial liberalism of the Democratic Party, either moved to the Republican Party or became up for grabs. In many ways, partisan fights for voters on culture war issues were in pursuit of largely white voters unmoored from the Democratic Party (Frymer 2011, 9). This is one reason these issue bundles become constraining. Even Republican politicians who wanted to pursue African American voters on abortion or gay rights realized the GOP's position on civil rights presented a perhaps insuperable obstacle to making inroads among black voters. "Over the past three decades a great wedge of racism, real and perceived, has been driven between the black and conservative segments of American society," a conservative activist articulated. Conservatives cannot meaningfully appeal to black voters on abortion or school prayer if they "continue to turn our backs on this great area of immorality—racism" (Brand 1980). Thus even prominent Republican efforts to appeal to black voters on culture war issues were met with little success in the late twentieth century.

Finally, and with respect to the issue bundles themselves, much of the public opinion survey data are from samples that are overwhelmingly white, both because of the demographics of the mid-twentieth century and because surveys of this era underrepresented African Americans. However, black over-samples by the General Social Survey show that a similar cluster of issue bundles had emerged among black voters by the 1980s, too.[8]

6. What are "culture war" issues? Why focus on them? By "culture war" issues, I am referring to the non-economic domestic issues that have defined political battles in recent years such as abortion, gun control, gay rights, broader issues of women's equality, the environment, and, later, undocumented immigration. In the comparative literature in political science, these are sometimes referred to as post-material issues (Inglehart 1977). While the parties had long fought over and been divided on economic issues, abortion or gun control became newly partisan in the latter part of the twentieth century. This book is an effort to understand why the parties divided as they did on these issues. (While it is likely that the racial realignment also generated more polarization on economic issues as well, this book focuses on non-economic issues.)

To be sure, many culture war issues have an economic component: whether federal funds should be used to pay for abortions or providing welfare for undocumented immigrants are prominent examples. The crucial point here is that political players and activists in the 1960s and 1970s viewed culture war issues as distinct from the economic dimension and

that culture war issues could mobilize new voters into the GOP while conservative economic messages could not. While this might sound odd, the
white South was fairly liberal on populist economic programs in the 1960s
and 1970s. This posed a challenge for Republicans messaging economic
conservatism in the South (Kuziemko and Washington 2018). Republicans
needed new issues to appeal to these voters. As chapters 2 and 5 show, this
is what made the development of the culturally conservative appeals so
constraining.

Finally, when I refer to culture war issues in this book, I am referring to
ostensibly nonracial cultural issues. While civil rights and the ensuing fights
over busing or affirmative action are also generally considered culture war
issues, a robust literature has debated why the parties polarized on civil
rights, including whether it was a top-down process, discussed above, or a
more bottom-up process. A similar reexamination has not been applied
to less explicitly racial culture war issues that became salient in the 1970s.

Plan for Book

I have made efforts to make each chapter largely self-contained. However,
different chapters highlight different strands of the argument. Chapter 2
is largely theoretical while chapters 3 and 4 are more statistical, although
the text explains these analyses for readers not familiar with these meth-
ods. Chapters 6 and 7 are historical case studies of abortion politics and
immigration.

This book is organized as follows. Chapter 2 lays out the theoretical
mechanisms that place the racial realignment at the center of contemporary party sorting on other culture war issues. In addition to presenting the
theoretical argument, chapter 2 provides a history of the parties' shifting
positions on civil rights and the centrality of race for shaping the party
system. Chapter 3 then delves into the core empirical trend underlying
this book. Using historical public opinion dating to the 1930s, I present an
exhaustive analysis of issue linkages between race and other policy views.
These linkages date to the earliest public opinion polls and precede the
national parties dividing on these issues. This chapter shows that in polarization's formative years, people who lacked knowledge of where parties,
ideological groups, or their preferred media sources stood on political issues still packaged race and other views together.

Chapter 4 then turns to cross-pressured voters. What happens to people who hold racially liberal issue positions but conservative positions on another issue? I find that people update their nonracial views to match their racial views, but this does not consistently happen in reverse. This underscores a core point: racial attitudes, not party, was the core organizing force in this era. Next, I turn to the consequences of these issue bundles for partisan cleavages in the mass public. Chapter 5 finds that when southern conservatives exited the Democratic Party on account of civil rights to support the Republican presidential candidate Barry Goldwater in 1964 or third-party segregationist candidate George Wallace in 1968, these voters brought very conservative attitudes on abortion, gay rights, and gun control with them. *This happened without these candidates taking positions on these issues.*

Chapter 6 uses abortion politics as a case study to explore the consequences of the parties' shifting voter coalitions for the ability of interest groups to work their way into parties and for the parties to adopt issue positions on abortion. Chapter 7 then argues that the accelerating partisan divide on immigration that emerged prior to the 2016 election represents, to date, perhaps the longest legacy of the 1960s racial realignment. While the initial effect of the racial realignment on partisan conflict on immigration was perhaps modest, it created a set of institutions and forces that maintained and then eventually drove the massive immigration polarization of the 2010s.

Finally, chapter 8 draws parallels between parties in the United States and other parts of the globe; this chapter is an effort to contextualize the US party system and public opinion. The issue bundles observed in the United States are found in public opinion in many other countries.

Materials Used

To develop this argument, I use over eight decades of survey data, much of which has been underutilized by political scientists and some of which, to my knowledge, has not been used at all. The American National Election Studies, a US public opinion survey conducted every two to four years and widely used by political scientists, did not ask questions about abortion or gun control until the 1970s. Thus, the data from before 1972 comes from either the Roper Center for Public Opinion Research at Cornell University or the Louis Harris Data Center Dataverse, which is housed by the Odum Institute for Research in Social Science at UNC at Chapel Hill.

Much of the data after 1972 comes from the American National Election Study (ANES) or the General Social Survey because they consistently ask the same questions across time. Much of the data are cross-sectional, but chapter 4 relies on an old ANES panel that surveyed the same voters over a four-year time period between 1972 and 1976. Chapter 7 uses longitudinal data between 2011 and 2016 from the Democracy Fund Voter Study Group (2018) to analyze Trump voters before and after his rise to the national stage.

Chapter 8, which analyzes public opinion outside the United States, includes public opinion data from the World Values Survey (Inglehart et al. 2014), a 2006–2010 panel of Swedish voters (Holmberg, Oscarsson, and Statistics Sweden 2014), and the Chapel Hill Expert Survey, which asks area experts to place European parties on policy scales (Polk et al. 2017).

I complement public opinion data with archival research from eight different archival libraries around the United States. This archival work helps illuminate how politicians and activists viewed their political environment. Why did Nixon, Reagan, and eventually Ford pivot to the right on culture war issues? Why did pro-life activists, many of whom had preexisting ties to the Democratic Party, end up working more closely with Republicans?

This book includes archival work from the following: the Paul M. Weyrich Papers at the American Heritage Center in Laramie, Wyoming; the papers of the United States Conference of Catholic Bishops at the Catholic University of America in Washington, DC; the Paul M. Weyrich Scrapbooks, 1942–2009, and the William A. Rusher Papers, 1940–2010, both at the Library of Congress, in Washington, DC; the Conservative Caucus Papers at Liberty University in Lynchburg, Virginia; the Lawrence Lader Papers, 1956–1985, at the New York Public Library Archives in New York City; the Ronald Reagan Collections at the Hoover Institution Archives in Palo Alto, California; the Southern Baptist Historical Library and Archives in Nashville, Tennessee; and the Gerald R. Ford Presidential Library and Museum in Ann Arbor, Michigan. I also use digital collections, available online, from the Gerald R. Ford Presidential Library and the Richard Nixon Presidential Library.

The Racial Realignment and Politics Today

While much of this book focuses on the 1960s and 1970s, the racial realignment still shapes politics today. The ascendancy of Trump in the GOP cannot be abstracted from the racial realignment sixty years ago. Trump's tactics are the maturation of strategies that have been used and reused since the 1960s. Trump deployed immigration, race, and cultural issues to win the Republican primary and then to peel off culturally conservative but economically moderate Democrats in the general election. This, as the next chapters explore in more depth, has been in the Republican playbook since the formative elections of the 1960s and 1970s.

While the parties initially divided on cultural issues because they saw them as an opportunity to gain a leg up in elections, staking positions on abortion or gun control that fit with the party's orthodoxy is almost a prerequisite to secure each party's nomination today. Whether one can be a conservative abortion Democrat or a liberal abortion Republican and win national or even subnational primaries today is, at best, a challenging path. Between voters, donors, and activists, it is an uphill battle.

Consider a 2009 vote in the US House of Representatives on an amendment to the Affordable Care Act (i.e., "Obamacare") that banned government health insurance plans from paying for abortions. The Stupak Amendment, as it became known, was sponsored by *Democratic* Congressman Bart Stupak. Sixty-four Democrats supported the amendment, as did all 176 congressional Republicans. While congressional Democrats, as a party, were more liberal on abortion than congressional Republicans, the congressional Democratic Party still contained a modest conservative wing (Elving 2015).

However, the parties rapidly changed in the years to come. By 2015, only twelve of the sixty-four Democrats who voted for the Stupak Amendment in 2010 remained in Congress. Many lost in the Republican tidal-wave elections in 2010 and 2014. The few Stupak Amendment supporters who remained in office nearly all switched their abortion views. These pressures seemed to come from forces within the party. Ohio Congressman Tim Ryan moved left in 2015 as he geared up to run for the Democratic presidential nomination (Pitofsky 2019). Longtime Pennsylvania Congressman Mike Doyle, facing a primary challenge from the left, switched his abortion position in the lead-up to the 2020 congressional Democratic primary (Deitch 2020). Although Doyle forestalled the 2020 challenge, in 2021 he announced his retirement from Congress. Insiders speculated it was because Doyle's once-conservative district (previously represented by Republican presidential candidate Rick Santorum) was projected to move even further left after the decennial redistricting. Doyle, a moderate, would have had a difficult time defending his decades-long conservative abortion record to a liberal primary electorate (Perkins and Potter 2021).

This process resembles change that has been repeatedly building on itself since the 1970s. Conservative Democrats face challenges on the right in the general election and from the left in the primary. And even if elected, conservative members resided in a party where an increasing number of their colleagues disagree with them. Whether similar pressures would have existed had the pre–racial realignment Democratic Party remained intact, one in which southern and conservative interests held sway, is unclear. The effects of the racial realignment continue to shape politics today.

CHAPTER TWO

Theory

Racial Realignment and Contemporary
Party Sorting

In the 1970s, Republican and conservative operatives lamented that the GOP was dead. Before the 1972 election, a Nixon aide remarked, "The Republican Party is a last-place ball club. . . . [People who identify as Republican] are now only 22 percent of the vote" (Buchanan 1971). The Republican Party is "in worse shape than it has ever been before in its history," Senator Bob Dole exclaimed in 1975 (Apple 1975). And a syndicated columnist direly noted, "It is hard for me to see how the Republican Party can survive beyond 1976" (St. John 1975).

This dismay was well-founded. Even after the Great Depression became a memory, the New Deal economic policies of the Democratic Party remained popular. The Democrats' New Deal coalition, which congealed under President Roosevelt in the 1930s, put Democrats in the White House each year between 1932 and 1952, and Democrats held a majority in the House of Representatives in all but two Congresses between 1932 and 1994. "On economic issues alone, there cannot be elected a Republican Congressional majority," a Reagan staffer wrote his White House colleagues in the 1980s. "We cannot outbid the liberal Democrats on economic issues" (Blackwell 1982).

However, despite only a fifth of the population identifying as Republicans in the 1970s, conservative leaders noticed that a majority of people (with a preference) identified as conservative or said they preferred a conservative rather than liberal political party (Rusher 1975a, xiv; 1975b). How could Democrats, the liberal party, do so well in elections while a plurality identified as conservative? William Rusher, publisher of the conservative *National Review*, had a hunch. Fights over civil rights meant that "many elements of the old Roosevelt coalition now began to turn against Democratic liberalism and toward what we shall call, for want of a better term, 'social conservatism'" (Rusher 1975a, 26). This distinction was crucial to Rusher and other conservative organizers: "Americans identifying themselves as 'conservatives' cannot be construed as indicating sympathy with conservatism's post-Hoover economics" (Phillips 1974). Through the late 1960s and 1970s, this social conservatism expanded to include what *Fortune* magazine described as "personal deportment, social attitudes, [and] moral values" (qtd. in Rusher 1975a, xv).

Sensing opportunity, Rusher asked a simple question: "Might not a realignment of the parties be brought about, in which the 'conservative' values endorsed by so substantial a proportion of the population could find expression in a party specifically designed to express them?" (1975a, xvi). This socially conservative political force had been "struggling for political representation in America for nearly twenty years," Rusher wrote in his 1975 book (1975a, 100). Rusher and other politicos referred to this constituency of social conservatives as the "New Majority."

It was not obvious to contemporaneous observers, though, which party would move toward the New Majority constituency or if a third party might form. Coming out of the 1950s, civil rights was a nonpartisan issue among both voters and the national parties. Not until Goldwater's 1964 campaign did a Republican presidential candidate campaign on conservative civil rights messages. Other culture war issues that were emerging as Rusher wrote in 1975—like abortion, gun control, or gay rights—to the extent they were on the agenda, were also nonpartisan issues. Moreover, conservative activists and thinkers did not necessarily want to join the GOP: the Republican Party was not popular among voters, and many conservatives viewed the Republican establishment as effectively Democrats in all but name (Lowndes 2009).

Rather than pushing for a specific partisan alliance, conservative movement leaders such as Paul Weyrich, who played an instrumental role in building the conservative religious political movement of the 1980s, saw the sorting of the parties as a change of broader structural forces: "There is going on a certain amount of movement tending toward two parties—one liberal and the other conservative. . . . [W]e conservatives want the reorganization to evolve naturally—and this is of great importance—that is we do not expect nor want anyone, or any law, or anything to compel a reorganization" (Weyrich 1977).

This chapter presents a theoretical argument as to *why* the conservative bundle of culture war issues—like abortion, guns, and gay rights—became absorbed into the Republican Party rather than the Democratic Party, despite the fact that many of these issues crisscrossed party lines in the mid-twentieth century and despite partisan indifference among leading activists, politicians, and intellectuals.

The explanation for this puzzle lies in perhaps the most profound and polarizing cleavage in US politics: civil rights. Partisan divisions on race and civil rights that emerged in the 1960s created a set of constraints for party positioning on social issues like abortion or gun control in the 1970s and 1980s. At the root of this transformation is a long-standing feature of US public opinion that existed before the parties started dividing on culture war issues: people who are more conservative on race already held more conservative views on issues like abortion, women's rights, gay rights, gun control, the environment, and immigration. (Chapter 3 argues that pre-political values, not signals from political elites, underpin the enduring nature of these long-term connections between civil rights and other culture war issues.)

I argue that the racial realignment pushed the parties to divide on ostensibly nonracial culture war issues through two mechanisms. First, the racial realignment created Republican and Democratic primary electorates that diverged from each other not just on race, but on culture war issues like abortion or gun control as well. Many of the racially conservative Democrats who moved to the GOP because of civil rights also held quite conservative attitudes on other culture war issues, too. As Republican (Democratic) candidates realized that conservative (liberal) positions on these issues could be used to gain a leg up in the party's primary, candidates converged to these positions.

Second, Republicans, long the minority party, pursued racially conservative Democrats, already loosened from the Democratic Party on the issue of race, by making conservative appeals to them on other culture war issues like abortion or gun control—issue preferences these voters already held prior to the elite messaging of the Nixon, Ford, and Reagan campaigns. These reinforcing mechanisms drove the parties to separate on these previously nonpartisan issues and allowed interest groups, which fanned the flames of polarization, to enter the party coalitions that they did.

This chapter is organized in the following manner: I first start by discussing factors that drove the parties to polarize on civil rights. This section covers ground well-trodden by other literature, but I emphasize a feature crucial for this book's argument—throughout the 1960s and 1970s, conservative activists, thinkers, and politicians viewed winning the South, which had long been a Democratic stronghold, and other socially conservative voters as essential for the Republican Party to win national elections. To do this, these actors believed, they would have to pivot away from talking about economic issues, which had defined midcentury partisan conflict. This is because many white southerners had long supported the Democrats' economic platform and would continue to do so if elections remained about economic issues. Civil rights and the racial conflict of the 1960s presented an initial inroad to the white South and other racially conservative constituencies. By the 1970s and 1980s, abortion and guns reinforced the initial appeals of civil rights.

Next, I turn to the book's main argument: how the bundle of issues long existent in the mass public became aligned in the party system. By transforming the composition of the parties' electoral coalitions on issues like abortion or gun control, the racial realignment fundamentally changed the parties' ability to position on these issues. A core theme is that mass-level forces are integral to understanding this transformation. Third, I discuss the role of interest groups in this changing environment. The racial realignment was crucial for structuring which party would be more receptive to interest groups related to specific culture war issues. The chapter concludes by developing a revised theory of party sorting that is driven by mass-level forces: politicians can and do shape public opinion, but the positions they take are informed by what they perceive to be popular among their potential constituencies (e.g., Zaller 2012; Key 1961).

The Parties Polarize on Civil Rights

Today the alliance of African Americans in the Democratic coalition and partisan fights over race and ethnicity are defining features of the party system. But this has not always been the case. This section outlines the shifting relationship between partisanship, race, and views toward racial equality over the twentieth century.

Going into the 1960s, the national parties actually held similar positions on civil rights, and partisan conflict largely centered on government intervention in the economy (Carmines and Stimson 1989; Schickler 2016). Factors dating to the Civil War shaped partisan racial conflict, or the lack thereof, in the mid-twentieth century. The legacy of Civil War sectionalism lingered over national partisan politics for decades: while the Democratic Party dominated the South in the decades after the Civil War, other parts of the country, particularly the Midwest, were nearly as heavily Republican (O'Brian 2019).

Between Reconstruction and the New Deal, Democrats held 93% of the South's congressional seats (O'Brian 2019), and in presidential elections, with the exception of the 1928 election, Democrats won nearly every single state in the Deep South between 1880 and 1932. Democratic dominance in the South was not simply because of the party's popularity. Democratic hegemony relied on suppressing black people, and any white people who sympathized with them, from voting in elections (Key 1949; Mickey 2015). In 1964, on the eve of the Voting Rights Act of 1965, just 7% of African Americans were registered to vote in Mississippi (US Commission on Civil Rights 1975).

The importance of civil rights to southern politics and white Democratic partisanship cannot be understated. The Democratic Party's opposition to black political and civil rights, and their commitment to the preservation of Jim Crow, locked white southerners into the Democratic Party from the Civil War until at least the 1950s. While southern Democrats fought over other issues between the 1870s and 1960s, these were secondary to first guaranteeing white political and civil hegemony (Caughey 2018; Fenno 1977).

The Great Depression and Democrat Franklin Roosevelt's New Deal upended this equilibrium and expanded the Democratic Party's geographic reach. The popularity of Roosevelt's New Deal thawed Democratic antipathy outside the South and ushered in an era of national Democratic dominance. Not only would Democrats win each presidential election between 1932 and 1948, but they also held large congressional majorities through 1946. So grim was the standing of the Republican Party in the 1930s that Gallup asked Americans if they thought the Republican Party was dead (Lange 2016).

The expansion of the Democratic Party into not just a national party, but the dominant national party, meant that new voters entered the Democrats' coalition. Some of these newly Democratic voters were African Americans who had gained voting rights when they migrated from the South and began supporting Democrats on the basis of New Deal programs. This broke from the pre-Roosevelt era in which African Americans, when they could vote, supported Republicans (which had been the party of Lincoln). By the 1930s, this meant that the Democrats' New Deal coalition included both the white South, which was still locked into the Democratic Party and enamored with Roosevelt, and an increasing number of African Americans. While the white South and African Americans were polarized by their views toward civil rights, they were bound together by the economic crisis and New Deal programs. This is important: African Americans did not enter the Democratic coalition because the party was making pro–civil rights appeals. National efforts to secure political and civil rights for African Americans after Reconstruction, by either party, were sparse (Jenkins, Peck, and Weaver 2010). Indeed, Democratic leaders, including Roosevelt, tried to downplay civil rights to avoid intraparty conflict throughout the mid-twentieth century. Early New Deal programs excluded explicit conversation around its effect on African Americans, and core programs, like the Social Security Act, excluded benefits to agricultural laborers and domestic workers, two professions populated by African Americans (Katznelson 2013).

However, as the political currents shifted, it became increasingly difficult for national Democratic leaders to avoid the growing African American constituency in their party. This is partially because New Deal economic policies, while supported by the white South in its early years, started to lose their popularity as the racial implications of these policies became clear. As the 1940s turned into the 1950s, white southerners began to shift their view of New Deal policies from one of economic self-interest to seeing "government activism in the economic sphere as threatening the region's system of racial hierarchy" (Caughey 2018, 85–86).

Although Democrats continued to dominate congressional and subnational elections in the South, Republicans were making inroads among white southerners. This concerned national Democrats. A fear that Democrats might also lose African American support in northern cities amplified these concerns. In the early twentieth century, the great migration of African Americans from the South to cities in the non-South meant that the African American vote could be pivotal to winning northern states (Jenkins, Peck, and Weaver 2010, 79). For example, in Detroit in 1910, African Americans composed 1.5% of the city's population. By 1940, that number grew to 9.2%, nearly doubled to 16.2% in 1950, and in 1960, almost 29% of Detroit's population was African American (Sugrue 1996, 23). Without black voters, northern cities—and thus states—might return to the Republican Party if African Americans, momentarily brought into the Democratic Party by the New Deal, returned to the GOP (Carmines and Stimson 1989, 33). The death of Roosevelt, a political giant whose personality undoubtedly attracted voters outside of his specific policies, further imperiled the Democrats' New Deal coalition.

Worried about dwindling support and in an effort to secure black voters in the 1948 election, Democratic President Harry Truman announced a civil rights program to a joint session of Congress in February 1948. That summer, the Democratic National Convention, for the party's first time, supported a civil rights plank.[1] Between 1948 and 1960, both national parties would tepidly support a pro–civil rights platform (Carmines and Stimson 1989, 35).

But even tepid support for civil rights proved to be an untenable position as the percentage of African Americans and racial liberals expanded in the Democratic Party. To continue to address civil rights in a haphazard way posed a risk for candidates pursuing the Democratic nomination. Fearing a primary challenge from the left, Democrat Lyndon Johnson in 1963 and 1964 saw embracing racial minorities as essential. Simply winning the South would be insufficient to gain the party's nomination (Schickler 2016, 232). The Democratic Party in 1963–64, once the party of the Confederacy and the Jim Crow South, came out in support of the strongest civil rights program since Reconstruction.

For Republicans, the shifting allegiances of African Americans toward the Democratic Party perhaps threatened the Republicans' old way of doing business, but also presented a new opportunity. Conservative operatives believed that (white) blue-collar and white-collar workers, despite holding divergent economic preferences, could be united by a cross-class opposition to the racial (and later cultural) liberalism of the 1960s (Scammon and Wattenberg 1970; Phillips [1969] 2014; Rusher 1975a). In other words, the GOP could pick off conservative southern Democrats by opposing the growing civil rights movement.

Some strategists believed that appealing to southern conservative Democrats was not just an opportunity, but essential for the Republican Party to survive: the GOP had become the de facto minority party in Congress since the 1930s, and in surveys of the mass public, few identified as Republicans. Campaigning on economic conservativism alone, or appealing to African Americans and white racial liberals, would maintain this status quo. Winning the South was essential. Without it, the Republican Party would fail, operatives believed.

In 1963, William Rusher wrote in *National Review* that Republicans had as much of a chance of winning California or New York from John

F. Kennedy as did Mao Tse-tung (Rusher 1963, 109). This was striking because California and New York were the geographic heart of the mid-century Republican Party and had been instrumental for Republicans seeking to win national elections in the 1940s and 1950s. Yet Rusher argued that Republicans could win the general election without those states. How? By peeling off voters from the South and its border states from the Democrats with anti–civil rights appeals. But not just any Republican could do this; only a conservative Republican, which in 1963 meant Barry Goldwater. Goldwater "can carry enough southern and border states to offset the inevitable Kennedy conquests in the big industrial states of the North and still stand a serious chance of winning the election," Rusher concluded (1963, 112).

The growing importance of the South and the declining power of the Northeast emerged not just in general elections, but also as a strategy in primary elections and conventions. Calculating that African Americans had become entrenched in the Democratic Party, Goldwater and his backers sought the Republican Party's nomination by winning delegates in the South and West with a message that civil rights was a state-level and not a national-level problem (Schickler 2016, 259).

This strategy and messaging diverged from the pre-1964 Republican Party, which had been controlled by the northeastern Republican establishment. Led by New York Governor Thomas Dewey in the 1940s and Nelson Rockefeller in the 1950s and 1960s (and which favored Dwight Eisenhower in the 1950s presidential contests), the Northeast establishment represented the party's liberal faction, which supported, although sometimes only modestly, civil rights (Hacker and Pierson 2010; Bowen 2010). More broadly, Republican critics accused the midcentury party of effectively being a copycat of the Democratic Party (Lowndes 2009).

Although Goldwater needed support outside the South, the South was crucial for securing the GOP's nomination, and contemporaneous observers dubbed Goldwater's strategy the "Southern Strategy" (Perlstein 2001, 188). Goldwater's victory at the 1964 convention—883 delegates for, 425 against—"demonstrated, with mathematical finality, that a Republican candidate did not need the support of [the Northeast] to nominate him" (Rusher 1975a, 49).

Maintaining a liberal civil rights platform, as the northeastern wing demanded, was not only unnecessary to win the GOP's nomination, but by the mid-1960s, it represented a political liability. Richard Nixon, who in 1960 went out of his way to accommodate a civil rights platform to win the Republican nomination, would mimic Goldwater's southern strategy in 1968 and embraced the racial backlash that had ascended within the party. In 1964, the national parties did not simply divide on civil rights, but race and civil rights became a core axis of national electoral coalitions (e.g., Carmines and Stimson 1989; Sundquist 1983; Scammon and Wattenburg 1970). Despite Goldwater losing in a landslide, it marked a new and promising way for the party to do business, and perhaps, given the electoral landscape and changing nature of the party's base, the only way to do business. While opposition to basic civil and voting rights for African Americans in Congress polarized the Deep South, segregation in housing and services polarized northern cities, too. National, state, and local politicians exploited these cleavages for political gain (Sugrue 1996; Edsall and Edsall 1992). Opposition to busing, affirmative action, fair housing laws, and other implicitly racial social policies, such as crime, developed as campaign issues used by Republican candidates to appeal to socially conservative Democrats and Independents in the outer South and across the country (Lowndes 2009, ch. 4; Maxwell and Shields 2019; Perlstein 2008).

As this section elucidates, the racial realignment was the eruption of slow-moving forces that had churned for decades. It was not a contingent choice made by party leaders, but determined by the structural forces shaped by the prior three decades (Chen 2007; Schickler 2016; Chen, Mickey, and Van Houweling 2008). Politicians like Lyndon Johnson or Barry Goldwater were reacting to broader forces.

At the same time, 1964 marked a rapid divergence from how business had been done, and it spurred politicians and activists to behave differently than they had prior to the national parties polarizing on civil rights. Richard Nixon exemplifies this: just moments before the 1960 Republican nominating convention, to forestall a challenge from Nelson Rockefeller and the left, Nixon, the Republican front-runner for the presidential nomination, added Rockefeller's preferred language in favor of "aggressive action" on civil rights to the Republicans' 1960 plank. When Nixon arrived at the 1960 convention, he told reporters, "I believe it is essential that the Republican convention adopt a strong civil rights platform" (Perlstein 2001, 86, 90). (Nixon won the GOP's nomination in 1960.) But Nixon read the tea leaves of 1964 and realized that to win the Republican nomination in 1968, he could not use the same strategy he had deployed in 1960. In 1968 Nixon moved toward Goldwater and the right and exploited the racial backlash brewing in the Republican Party.

The 1964 election also changed how voters saw the parties, and this mattered. In 1963–64, the parties' positions on civil rights became visible to the electorate *because* the major presidential candidates had staked divergent positions (Kuziemko and Washington 2018, 2839). In 1960, both southerners and non-southerners perceived that the Republican Party was slightly more likely to support school integration. This perception matched the political reality of the previous decades. By 1964, that flipped; people were 30 percentage points more likely to perceive that Democrats, rather than Republicans, supported school integration.

This perception sent a shock wave through the electorate and moved previously Democratic voters to support the Republican presidential candidate. This is most plainly illustrated by the swing of white southerners' vote intention before and after Kennedy came out in favor of an aggressive civil rights bill in June 1963. In February 1963, Kennedy had a 30 percentage-point lead over Goldwater (60% for Kennedy to 30% for Goldwater) among white southerners. In a survey at the end of June 1963, soon after Kennedy's televised endorsement of civil rights, Goldwater led Kennedy by 20 percentage points among white southerners; a *50 percentage-point* shift toward Goldwater in a manner of months (Kuziemko and Washington 2018, 2855).

A large swing occurred among black voters as well. About a third of African Americans voted for Nixon in 1960 (recall that Nixon and Kennedy held similar positions on civil rights in 1960). That number plummeted in 1964, and when Nixon ran again in 1968, he received almost 20 percentage points less of the black vote than eight years earlier (Bump 2015).

Thus, even while the processes of racial realignment started before 1964, 1963–64 mattered for what followed. Indeed, this is central to the book's argument: the 1964 election may have peeled off some parts of the South from the Democrats' coalition, but it left many others as uncomfortable Democrats or politically homeless. The South was up for grabs, and Republicans developed strategies to appeal to the region and other racially conservative voters who had become unmoored from the Democratic Party. As I lay out in the coming pages, the deployment of abortion and gun messaging were issue appeals that did exactly that.[2]

The Racial Realignment's Cascading Effect Across the Party System

The 1964 presidential election marked an astounding change in partisan voting patterns in parts of the South. In Barbour County, Alabama, Republican Dwight Eisenhower won just 23% of the vote in 1956. In 1960, Republican Richard Nixon won just 35%. In 1964, Barry Goldwater won nearly 80% of the county vote (Leip 2019). In total, Goldwater won five states in the Deep South in 1964, including Georgia, which for the first time ever voted for a Republican presidential candidate: "Goldwater rode a wave of states' rights protest votes to victory," the *Macon Telegraph* announced (Associated Press 1964a).

On the surface, it seemed that the parties' coalitions were changing with respect to civil rights. And they were; the Republicans absorbed regions of the country deeply opposed to civil rights. But underneath the surface, the racial realignment quietly redistributed the preferences of the parties' coalitions on issues other than civil rights, too; issues that would soon define partisan conflict. Underlying this transformation is the fact that people who hold more conservative racial views also hold more conservative views on a range of social issues including abortion, guns, and gay rights. I say "quietly," because in 1964 abortion and gun control were not nationally salient political issues. But this is the central point: when they became salient, the already-changing partisan allegiances of abortion and gun voters shaped how parties could respond.

To illustrate the importance of the racial cleavage and the mechanisms by which it facilitated partisan sorting on other issues, consider a political world with three policy issues: abortion, race, and economic issues. Consider two hypothetical scenarios. In scenario A, civil rights has not been activated as a partisan cleavage, and the parties divide perfectly along economic lines. Furthermore, assume economic attitudes are completely unrelated to abortion attitudes. This was both empirically true (see table 3.3; Layman and Carsey 2002) and, as this chapter discusses, perceived to be true by conservative activists and politicians in the 1970s. With respect to the Republicans' economic position, activists or party leaders could take the party in either direction on abortion and cross-pressure the same number of voters along the economic cleavage. That is, Republicans staking a liberal abortion position might both attract and repel a similar number of voters.

Now consider hypothetical scenario B, where a racial cleavage engenders a partisan realignment such that the parties in the electorate divide perfectly by attitudes toward civil rights. Furthermore, assume that those who are conservative on civil rights also hold more conservative abortion attitudes (as chapter 3 shows). Now what happens when abortion becomes politically activated? As public opinion toward racial policy and abortion overlap, when abortion becomes salient, anti-abortion voters are already inside the Republican Party, and pro-abortion voters are already inside the Democratic Party. Consequently, it becomes less costly for Republicans to oppose abortion rights, and easier for pro-life interest groups to work inside the GOP.

Hypothetical example A might describe the United States in the pre–racial realignment days; large constituencies within the Republican and Democratic parties both supported and opposed abortion. Republicans cast in the mold of New Deal conflict, like Nelson Rockefeller, pursued liberal abortion policy, thinking of constituencies that voted for Republicans in the pre–racial realignment days. But a growing intraparty schism over civil rights put stress on New Deal party allegiances; parts of the Democratic South and blue-collar areas in the Northeast defected to the Republican Party, and these voters happened to already hold quite conservative abortion views. Republicans who gained prominence in the post-1964 Republican Party saw that staking conservative positions on social issues like abortion presented a currency for appealing to this set of voters who had moved, or were in the process of moving, to the Republican Party. This represents hypothetical scenario B. The next section details how the racial realignment pushed the issue bundles, long present in the mass public, into the party system.

The Racial Realignment Changes the Parties' Primary Electorates

One mechanism enforcing party sorting was the shifting compositions of the parties' primary electorates. While the Republican Party had been dominated by the liberal northeastern establishment in the decades following the New Deal, by 1968 conservatives dominated Republican nominating conventions by a margin of "about 9 to 4" (Rusher 1975a, xx). Whether one could win the nomination without the South, the heartbeat of the conservative coalition, became increasingly difficult by the late 1960s.

As Republican candidates sought out new issues to appeal to this ascending conservative wing, they began to message conservative positions on issues like abortion and gun control. Many of the voters who supported Goldwater and other racially conservative candidates ascendant in the Republican Party already held comparatively conservative positions on these issues (see chapter 5). That is, the racial realignment increased the number of abortion or gun conservatives in the Republican Party, even without those issues initially being present on the political agenda. Politicians, seeking a leg up in the nominating process, converged around anti-abortion or pro-gun stances in the decades to come.

To illustrate this, compare the people who voted for Ronald Reagan during his first primary campaign for California governor in 1966 to those who voted for him in the 1976 Republican presidential primary a decade later. Reagan played the role of insurgent conservative in California, upsetting the state's liberal GOP establishment, just as Goldwater did in the 1964 presidential election and Reagan himself would do a decade later on the national stage. (Reagan was the figurehead of the California Republican Party's Goldwater faction.[3])

In the 1966 California Republican primary for governor, Reagan competed against the liberal Republican San Francisco mayor, George Christopher, a race that many expected Christopher to win (Perlstein 2008). In 1966, civil rights visibly divided Reagan from his liberal opponent in the Republican primary. Although race was not the only catalyst propelling Reagan's ascendancy in California, opposition to fair housing featured prominently during Reagan's first campaign for governor. In 1963, California had passed the Rumford Fair Housing Act, which was legislation to prevent housing discrimination on the basis of race. However, voters nullified the Rumford Act in a 1964 ballot proposition. The issue remained deeply divisive in 1966 and shaped that year's gubernatorial campaign. Historian Mark Brilliant (2010, 6) writes, "In 1964, [California] state voters resoundingly rejected a 1963 fair housing law, which, in turn, anticipated the 1966 eclipse of Pat Brown [the incumbent Democratic governor] by Ronald Reagan. . . . As gubernatorial candidate in 1966 and 1970 . . . Reagan patented a 'Southwestern strategy.' A complement to his party's much better known and infamous 'Southern strategy.'"

To appeal to the right wing of the Republican Party, Reagan publicly opposed the Rumford Act, which protected against racial discrimination in housing, while Christopher supported it (*Oakland Tribune* 1966; Perlstein 2008). The division between GOP candidates on fair housing was reflected in the Republican primary electorate. Figure 2.1 shows that in the 1966 Republican gubernatorial primary, 83% of Reagan supporters opposed the Fair Housing Act compared to 62% of Christopher supporters (and 71% of all Californians opposed it). However, Reagan supporters in the primary were also more conservative on abortion and guns than Christopher supporters. This was despite Christopher and Reagan lacking positions

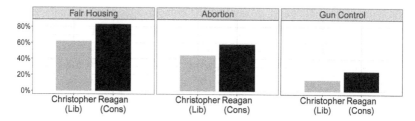

FIGURE 2.1. 1966 California Republican Gubernatorial Primary. Each panel shows public opinion among GOP primary voters in 1966 for the policy listed above the graph. The graph splits voters between whether they voted for liberal nominee George Christopher or the conservative nominee Ronald Reagan. Higher values are more conservative. Data from the January, June, and August 1966 Field Poll.

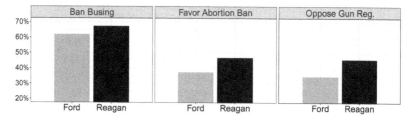

FIGURE 2.2. 1976 Republican Presidential Primary. Each panel shows public opinion among Republican voters who reported voting for either Ford or Reagan in the 1976 presidential primary for each policy listed above the graph. Higher values are more conservative. Data from Time Soundings #8530, *Time Magazine* (1976).

on guns or abortion. A cohesive package of issues followed Reagan and Christopher around, even when those candidates lacked policy positions on those issues.

Fast-forward to 1976, when Reagan attempted to unseat incumbent President Gerald Ford for the Republicans' presidential nomination. In 1976, as was the case in 1966, Reagan played the role of conservative insurgent against a more moderate establishment candidate. Reagan's 1976 primary supporters, just like a decade earlier in his campaign for the California Republican primary for governor, were more conservative on abortion and gun control than voters for his moderate opponent, Ford. Figure 2.2 shows that Reagan voters were about 9 percentage points more likely to favor an abortion ban, 6 percentage points more likely to favor a ban on school busing, and 11 percentage points more likely to oppose mandatory registration of handguns. The difference in 1976 was that Reagan and the political right recognized that these issues could be deployed to appeal to the party's right wing, just as civil rights and race had in the 1960s.

The 1976 Republican primary illustrates the pressures facing Republican nominees to appeal to cultural conservatives, and the potential perils of not doing so. Republican President Ford assumed the presidency after both Spiro Agnew, Richard Nixon's first vice president, and then Nixon himself, resigned from office. This becomes important because Ford, although not a liberal, was not part of the ascendant conservative wing that nominated Goldwater in 1964 or Nixon in 1972. Ford, a longtime representative from Michigan, stood in the ideological middle of the Republican Party in Congress (according to DW-NOMINATE, a measure of how liberal and conservative a member of Congress is; Lewis et al. 2023). As a member of the House of Representatives, Ford supported the 1964, 1966, and 1968 Civil Rights Acts, as well as the 1965 Voting Rights Act. Perhaps tellingly, Ford chose Nelson Rockefeller, the northeastern liberal Republican and the face of the fading liberal GOP establishment, as his vice president. This infuriated conservatives.

Ford was a fish out of water leading a national party whose base in many ways had moved to the right of Ford's politics. To win the Republican nomination in 1976, Reagan's team saw abortion, guns, and the Equal Rights Amendment as an opportunity to win over the old Goldwater voters and conservative wing of the Republican Party that was upset at the Ford-Rockefeller administration. In fact, Goldwater himself wrote President Ford in May 1976, "You are not going to get the Reagan vote [in the primary election]. These are the same people who got me the nomination and they will never swerve" (Goldwater 1976). Issues like abortion or gun control for the first time featured, although only marginally, as campaign issues in the national *Republican primary* (Nixon effectively ran uncontested in the 1972 primary, and issues like gun control, gay rights, and abortion were not meaningfully present in the 1968 primary).

When Reagan began publicly campaigning as an abortion conservative during the 1976 primaries, Ford's staff alleged that Reagan was doing so as "the result of calculated vote searching" (Hauser 1976). This is because as governor of California, Reagan had signed a bill liberalizing abortion in instances where the health of the mother was at risk or in cases of rape (although he quickly expressed regret doing so) (*New York Times* 1976). Reagan also flipped his position on the Equal Rights Amendment. As late as 1972, Reagan "was all for the Equal Rights Amendment" (Hager 1976).

But early in the 1976 primary election, Reagan's campaign manager worried the campaign was putting many conservatives to "sleep." As a remedy, he advocated that Reagan "sharpen certain basic issues . . . to reassert our appeal to the right as being different from Ford." One of the issues Reagan's campaign manager listed was the Equal Rights Amendment, which he believed Reagan could frame as taking away a mother's rights; presumably to highlight threats to traditional family structures valued by social conservatives (Sears 1976).

And while Ford generally opposed gun control, as a member of Congress he voted for the 1968 Gun Control Act and also supported a ban of "Saturday night specials," which were cheap guns that could be purchased through the mail (Lacombe 2021). This clashed with Reagan's more absolutist view in 1976, and Reagan used the sliver of difference as an opportunity to campaign in the rural South, charging that Ford was a supporter of gun control (Naughton 1976a).

The threat of Reagan campaigning from the right posed a significant challenge for Ford. In a trip to Iowa, Wisconsin, Illinois, and Kansas in the summer of 1975, just before Reagan announced his candidacy, conservative operative Paul Weyrich noted that support for Ford was sagging: "It appears the swing to conservatism is real, and that consequently, President Ford is in some trouble out here. . . . Reagan and George Wallace are the two names on everybody's lips in the mid-west" (Weyrich 1975a). The gripe, Weyrich reported, came from officeholders to rank-and-file voters.

While the grievances were broad, First Lady Betty Ford's nationally televised comments on social issues elicited particular angst among conservatives: "The reaction to Betty Ford's interview on '60 [M]inutes,' with her endorsement of abortion and pre-marital sex and marijuana and all, has been violent in these parts. . . . Mrs. Ford's views cost President Ford support, some of it permanently," Weyrich (1975a) reported.

Perhaps unfairly, the public linked President Ford with his family's positions on social issues, a fact that Ford's team sought to downplay (Naughton 1976b). Public opinion data illustrate some of Ford's predicament. In the states mentioned by Weyrich, just 16% of Republican primary voters supported legalizing marijuana, and 55% believed abortion should be illegal in most circumstances. The Equal Rights Amendment, which Ford supported, also polled poorly: 55% of Republican primary voters in these states opposed the ERA, even though it was quite popular nationally (nearly 80% of all voters, regardless of party identification, supported the ERA in 1976) (ANES 1976).

Gun control posed a similar threat to Ford's nomination. Neal Knox, then editor of *Rifle Magazine* and who would later become a leader in the National Rifle Association, wrote Ford that "the results [of supporting the ban of Saturday night specials] will be a wholesale loss of votes to 'conservative' GOP candidates in the primaries, and to George Wallace in the general" (Knox 1975). Public opinion polling commissioned by the Ford administration echoed this sentiment. Ford's pollster summarized that "the greatest opposition to gun control positions comes from the Deep South, the Outer South, the Mountain States, rural areas . . ." (Decision Making Information 1975). These are the very states that formed the base of Goldwater's nomination in 1964 and were the states that Reagan was successfully seeking delegates from in 1976. It is worth elaborating this point: these regions of the country, which opposed gun control the most, had become important for securing the 1976 GOP nomination *because* the racial realignment had already loosened them from the Democratic Party.

Fearing Reagan, Ford tried to move right, or at least emphasize conservative positions on guns and abortion. The *New York Times* editorial board remarked that Ford, once interested in appealing to "the moderate Republicanism" of the urban East, had by November 1975 resorted to "old Nixon strategies and campaign themes." "The new Ford strategy," the *Times* continued, "is based on the conviction that the President can successfully compete with Mr. Reagan for the votes of conservative Republicans in the South and Southwest" (*New York Times* 1975).

While Ford ultimately defeated Reagan, the threat Reagan posed to an incumbent president illustrated the precariousness of holding moderate-to-liberal social views and trying to run for the Republican Party's nomination by 1976. Indeed, Ford's presence as a serious contender was perhaps only because of his accidental ascendancy to the White House. Ford, the sitting president, won 53% of the vote to Reagan's 46% in the 1976 primary, and the two entered the convention without either nominee securing sufficient delegates. It would be an open convention, the last time a Republican convention began without a nominee, and it was nearly the first time since 1884 when the incumbent president (Chester Arthur) did not win their party's nomination (Rudin 2009).

Of course, what Reagan failed to do in 1976, he succeeded at in 1980: winning the Republican primary for president. By 1980, the socially liberal Republican wing had shrunk further, and conservative activist groups had become better organized (or organized at all). Socially liberal Republicans like John Anderson and George H. W. Bush struggled in the Republican primaries.[4]

While the Republican primary electorate moved rightward in the aftermath of the racial realignment, the Democratic electorate drifted leftward. A somewhat parallel dynamic played out in the Democratic primary: the racial realignment shrank the Democrats' southern wing and pushed conservative Catholics away from the party. This meant the types of issue appeals that could secure a path to the party's nomination had changed. To win the party's primary, candidates had to be increasingly attentive to the ascendant liberal wing that held more liberal positions not just on race, but on other emerging culture war issues like abortion and gay rights as well.

For example, in the 1972 Democratic primary, Senator Henry "Scoop" Jackson, although not a hard-core conservative, expressed hawkish positions on Vietnam and defense spending, opposed busing, emphasized law and order, and expressed disdain for the Democratic Party's growing liberal constituencies. One journalist wrote that Jackson's campaign treated the Democrats' liberal wing as a passing fad: "They could not see that a revolution had occurred" (Kaufman 2000, 312). Jackson's campaign for the nomination in 1972, which had started with optimism, fizzled out.

Compare Jackson's campaign with more strategic candidates, who shifted left. For example, Hubert Humphrey softened his pro-Vietnam stance in the 1972 primary. Ted Kennedy, who opposed abortion in 1970, moved leftward on the issue in the early 1970s, presumably forecasting the position's currency among liberals in the party's primary (Lader, undated memo A).

Jimmy Carter illustrated that even walking in the ideological middle was a risky primary strategy in a party increasingly dominated by liberals. Carter, the former governor of Georgia, had a southern base that the Carter campaign perceived to be essential to winning the primaries. But Carter also realized that the party's shifting landscape, and the shrinking power of the South in the post–racial realignment Democratic Party, required him to cater to the Democrats' growing liberal wing. He tried to position himself in the middle; a move to the left or to the right would alienate an essential part of the coalition. It was a "zero-sum game," a Carter adviser remembers (Eizenstat 2018). Carter took moderate positions across issues and used his initially low profile in the primaries to obfuscate. For example, Carter took pro-choice positions in New York but pro-life positions in the South (Kaufman 2000, 324).

While successful in 1976, it was not a sustainable political strategy. Carter's moderation—an attempt to evenly appeal to the party's two wings—represented the last gasp of a party system that had passed. Whether a more conservative candidate than Carter could secure the Democratic nomination by 1976 is doubtful; George Wallace's failed effort in 1976 is a good example. And had a more liberal candidate secured the Democratic nomination in 1976, which certainly was a possibility, this likely would have hastened the South's exodus to the Republican Party in the general election, which Carter's candidacy only momentarily slowed (and was helped by Ford's presence on the Republican ticket). Indeed, Carter's standing in the Democratic Party somewhat paralleled Ford's standing in the GOP: a nominee, and then president, who in many ways relied on a political coalition whose time had passed.

Carter's failure to move further left during his presidency threatened his ability to secure renomination in the party's 1980 primary. Constituencies that had become central to the ascendant liberal wing of the Democratic Party were upset that the Carter administration, while left of center, did not do enough. In 1980, as a sitting president, Carter faced a fierce challenge in the Democratic primary from liberal Ted Kennedy. The 1980 Democratic primary contest was not just about the culture wars, with the Iranian hostage situation and inflation featuring prominently, but Kennedy's formidable challenge to a sitting president revealed deep intraparty ideological fault lines (Ward 2019). Kennedy, who initially thought he would win the primary and set his sights on the general election, hammered Carter from the left when the primary campaign tightened to win over liberal voters who were upset with Carter's middle-ground politics. Kennedy, the *New York Times* wrote, repeatedly asserted himself as a "pure Democrat, whereas Mr. Carter is a closet Republican." On labor and health care, but also abortion and gun control, Kennedy positioned himself to the left of Carter (Ayres 1980a).

Whether Kennedy could have campaigned as far left as he did not just on race but other culture war issues, absent a racial realignment, and still had a chance to unseat Carter is doubtful. Indeed, in the early 1970s, Kennedy, already eyeing the presidency, worried that the South and conservative forces would thwart his chances to receive his party's nomination, a fear that lessened as the party's conservative wing declined (Gabler 2020, 706–13).

Parts of the Democratic primary contest, particularly moments of Kennedy's popularity, pushed Carter to the left just as Reagan's candidacy had

pushed Ford rightward in 1976. For example, Kennedy's candidacy and appeal to the LGBT community (particularly in California) pressured Carter,
and the party's platform, to the left on gay rights, an issue that Carter had
tiptoed around in 1976 (Stanley 2010, 106–7). On issues of women's rights,
too, Kennedy pushed Carter leftward. While Carter favored the ERA and
modest abortion liberalization, women's groups were upset that he did
not do enough given his power. Kennedy sought to exploit this, as well as
defend his own image of indifference to women's interests, and made early
efforts to win over support from women voters and delegates (half of the
1980 Democratic National Convention was pledged to women delegates)
(Roberts 1979).

A similar pattern played out with Mexican Americans and immigration. The Kennedy family's long-standing alliance with Mexican Americans
worried Carter, who faced criticisms of not doing enough for the Hispanic
community. This is despite Carter campaigning heavily for and receiving
82% of the Hispanic vote in 1976. Carter toured around the country to
shore up Hispanic support, promising to do more for undocumented immigrants and to fill key administration roles with more Hispanic people
(see chapter 7).

And although Kennedy lost the 1980 primary—perhaps due to idiosyn-
cratic world events or the stacking of southern states toward the beginning
of the primary cycle—the relative success of the Kennedy campaign against
a sitting president revealed the party had moved leftward and that failure to
go along posed risks (Ward 2019, 204). (Rarely do parties fail to renominate
the sitting president, and it has not happened since the McGovern-Fraser
Commission reforms, which introduced popularly elected primaries.) In future campaign cycles, candidates for the Democratic nomination converged
around liberal positions that even a couple cycles earlier were absent from
campaigns. A gay rights activist—in the midst of Jesse Jackson, Gary Hart,
and Walter Mondale courting gay constituencies in the 1984 Democratic
primary—said, "Eight years ago there was nobody. Four years ago, there
was only Kennedy. Now it's all three" (qtd. in Stanley 2010, 107).

Republicans Capture the Democrats' Conservative Wing

While the racial realignment changed the composition of the parties' primary electorates, it also changed the composition of the general election
electorates. Republicans, long seeking inroads into the Democratic coalition, saw civil rights as an opportunity to siphon off southern Democratic

voters who had been locked in the Democratic Party for nearly a century (Key 1949). While some racial conservatives left the party in 1964, another pool of voters, perhaps because of the stickiness of partisan attachments, became increasingly disaffected with the liberal direction of the national party but, lacking a better option, reluctantly still voted for Democrats.

The elections following 1964 generated efforts by the Republican Party to layer on other issue messages that could sweeten the GOP's appeal to racially conservative Democrats and finish the job started by the racial realignment. Nixon's 1968 campaign (and especially his 1972 campaign) was perhaps the first effort to deploy nonracial social issues to secure southern Democrats and conservative Catholics and build what operatives called the "New Majority" conservative coalition.

Nixon and his advisers, like other Republicans, realized the importance of growing the Republican coalition beyond its base of Republican identifiers, who at that time were a small proportion of the population. But what voters would they target? To broaden the party, Republicans could do one of two things. They could shift left and appeal to liberal constituencies that once had a greater foothold in the GOP. Nixon in 1960 tried to do this and failed. Alternatively, Republicans could move to the right and capture Wallace and Goldwater Democrats and Independents. (George Wallace ran as a third-party candidate in 1968 as effectively a one-issue candidate opposed to racial integration.) Nixon in 1972 tried this and succeeded.

The racial realignment, by changing which voters were up for grabs and those which were no longer, shaped Nixon's decision to go left or right in 1972. Recall that in 1960, Nixon worried about alienating African Americans and the northeastern establishment and as a consequence moved *leftward*. But the racial realignment took African Americans and white racial liberals, broadly speaking, out of reach for the Republican Party. Liberal constituencies that had previously straddled party lines, including African Americans, had become locked into the Democratic Party by the end of the 1960s (Frymer 2011). Republican politicians realized this constraint: "Stop concentrating on the 'media's minorities' (Blacks, Mexican Americans, Spanish-speaking) which are tough to crack, almost solid Democratic—and begin focusing on the larger ethnic minorities (Irish, Italians, Poles, Slovaks, etc.)," a Nixon aide advised before the 1972 election (Buchanan 1971). "From now on," Kevin Phillips told the *New York Times*, "the Republicans are never going to get more than 10 to 20 percent of the Negro vote and they don't need any more than that" (Boyd 1970).

While the racial realignment locked in white liberals and African Americans to the Democratic Party, it dislodged white conservative Democrats. Scholars often focus on the racial realignment's effect on southern white people, but racial politics roiled political alliances of northern cities, too (Sugrue 1996; Edsall and Edsall 1992). Nixon's 1972 campaign became focused on winning Catholic immigrants and children of immigrants living in urban areas in the Northeast or Midwest. Catholics "were Democratic from time immemorial," a Nixon aide wrote, but they were up for grabs because of the Democratic Party's liberalization on race (Buchanan 1971). One White House staffer remarked, "Blue collar urban Catholics are on the firing line of the racial problems that plague our city cores." Catholic voters, this staffer believed, wanted to retain control of parochial schools to maintain "racial separation" (Morey 1971).[5] This made conservative Catholics ripe for the picking: "Catholic Democrats are more numerous and easier to win over than black Democrats and Jewish Democrats," a Nixon aide remarked (Buchanan 1971).

But simply disliking the Democratic Party's new direction might not have been enough for Republicans to win over these voters. "Many of these voters," pollster Robert Teeter told Nixon's chief of staff H. R. Haldeman, "now feel strongly cross pressured politically because their philosophical beliefs tend to push them more towards voting Republican but they have grown up disliking Republicans and formed fairly strong Democratic voting patterns" (Teeter 1972a). Developing issues to appeal to these voters was essential, Nixon aide Pat Buchanan (1971) advised, "When [Nixon] comes out for aid to parochial schools, this will drive a wedge right down the Middle of the Democratic party. The same is true of abortion; the same is true of hard-line anti-pornography laws." The cost of staking a liberal position was equally clear: "If the President were to take anti-Catholic positions, i.e., pro-abortion, anti-Parochial aid, etc., no doubt he would lose this group" (Finkelstein 1971).

The Nixon team knew that the campaigns of Barry Goldwater in 1964 and George Wallace in 1968 had dislodged Catholic voters from the Democratic fold, and if targeted again, they would defect again (Buchanan 1971). Of the Catholic voters discussed above, "there was (in 1968) and is today some definite Wallace support among this group" (Teeter 1972a). This search for issues that would secure Wallace voters pervaded national Republican candidates for the next three elections. As chapter 5 shows, Wallace voters by 1968 already held quite conservative positions on abortion, gun control, and gay rights, *even though Wallace did not campaign on those issues.* If the best path to gaining national majorities was by incorporating Wallace Democrats, a strategy that Nixon, Reagan, and ultimately Ford embraced, then staking conservative positions on abortion and gun control was lucrative.

Ford's 1976 general election campaign was a stress test of whether the Republican Party could go left. As discussed above, in some ways Ford was an interlude to the southern strategy. Ford represented the Republicans' moderate establishment, and his advisers initially saw a southern strategy as either inadvisable or not suited to Ford's style. This is partially because Ford was running against Jimmy Carter, a former southern governor, who they believed would lock up the South's votes. Instead, an adviser wrote, in the president's reelection campaign, Ford should try to win the industrial states of the East and Midwest; "the New Majority strategy has almost never worked in these states" (Reichley 1976).

But if this was Ford's initial strategy, it changed as the general election wore on (Perlstein 2020). This shift in Ford's approach occurred because of the parties' changing platforms. Carter, although a southern Baptist and former governor of Georgia—two demographics that seemed well suited to win southern votes—was at odds with southern politics of the 1970s; he was more liberal on race and other ascendant social issues than white people in the region probably preferred, perhaps in part because Carter realized he needed support outside the declining southern base. In September 1976, Carter made an infamous campaign gaffe during an interview with *Playboy* magazine in which he said, among other things, that he had committed "adultery in my heart" (Perlstein 2020, 17–23). If nothing else, it illustrated for Carter's opponents that Carter was out of step with the once-Democratic region. Pollster Robert Teeter told the Ford team that evangelicals "could be the most powerful political force ever harvested." Ford deployed "a new sort of Southern strategy—with religion, not race, at its center" (Perlstein 2020, 23). Others in the Ford camp echoed Teeter's advice. One aide advised that First Lady Betty Ford, who expressed liberal positions on social issues, "should eliminate any references to 'new morality,' liberalized marajuana [*sic*] laws, etc." Doing so would alienate blue-collar workers, who, upset at Carter's liberalness, could go over to Ford (Cashen 1976). With this in mind, Ford swung through Texas and made a belated effort at the southern strategy (Perlstein 2020, 26–29).

It was not just "morality" issues. By the fall of 1976, Ford campaigned in the South, declaring his opposition to gun control. "The law-abiding citizens of this country should not be deprived of the right to have firearms," Ford asserted at a Mississippi rally. A White House aide privately admitted there was little to be gained, but potentially a lot to lose politically, by campaigning in favor of gun control (Naughton 1976c). Indeed, the Ford White House had been inundated with mail urging him to oppose gun control efforts, which Ford largely did (Higgins 1976).

Ford, like Nixon four years earlier, made a choice to move right in the general election (as he did in the primary), because the South and racial conservatives had already become loosened from the Democratic Party. They were, even against Carter in 1976, up for grabs. Tacking to the right on guns, abortion, and other "moral" issues were new messages to sweeten his appeal to the region.

Four years later, the Republican Party nominated Ronald Reagan, who by all accounts was more conservative than Ford. While Reagan's election and legacy as a social conservative loom large over the Republican Party today, it was not a foregone conclusion at the time that Reagan would move to the right on social issues. Many wondered if Reagan would build his coalition by moving the party leftward and regain the trust of the liberal establishment that had defined the midcentury GOP, or tack rightward (the same decision that Nixon and Ford had faced).

Conservative activists of the New Right lobbied Reagan to move rightward. Carter, although unpopular, was still a southern Democrat and by southern identity alone posed a threat to win southern votes. Conservative operatives believed that socially conservative voters such as white southerners or northeastern Catholics either would support Carter on the basis of economic issues, as they had throughout the New Deal era, or stay at home, if Reagan and Republicans down the ticket did not emphasize culture war issues. Howard Phillips, the leader of the New Right organization the Conservative Caucus, expressed this dismay: "In 1976 Jimmy Carter carried every Southern state except Virginia. . . . Ronald Reagan will not win those votes by reviving the spirit of [liberal Republican] Nelson Rockefeller" (Phillips 1980).

Conservative operatives believed that by moving rightward, Republicans could peel off Carter supporters and other Democrats and mobilize nonvoters into the Republican fold. While commonplace today, Paul Weyrich in the late 1970s first pushed the idea that nonvoters could be mobilized by conservative social issues like abortion (Chamberlain 1980; Wiese 1979). Weyrich commissioned polls of nonvoters to prove his point, and he and other New Right leaders—the label assigned to culturally conservative activists of the 1970s—brought voter mobilization explicitly to Reagan's attention:

[Social conservatives] do have a place to go if they become dis-enthralled with the Reagan campaign; back to their jobs, back to their Bibles, back to their families, and away from a political process which they have, only tentatively, entered, to fight for prayer in the schools, against ERA, for lower taxes, against abortion, for a strong national defense, against forced busing, for the punishment of crime and against drafting wives, mothers, sisters, and daughters. . . . [I]nstead of worrying about the votes which John Anderson might take away if Governor Reagan is "too conservative," concern should be focused on the voters who will stay away from the polls, if the differences between Reagan and Carter are unclear in 1980, as they were in 1976, between Carter and Ford. (Phillips 1980)

This theme—the need to emphasize social issues as a means to win general elections—persisted throughout Reagan's first term. Preparing for the 1983 State of the Union, Reagan White House aide Morton Blackwell noted, "We cannot outbid the liberal Democrats on economic issues. . . . [Reagan] should take the initiative and raise the visibility of issues which divide millions of conservative Democrats from their liberal party leadership." Blackwell detailed the consequences if this path was not taken: "Unless traditionally Democratic voters are broken away from the liberal Democratic leadership on these [social] issues, we cannot expect 1984 election results much different from 1982" (Blackwell 1982). (Democrats gained twenty-six seats in the House of Representatives in the 1982 midterms.)

Weyrich told Howard Baker, Reagan's chief of staff, that it was "becoming very, very difficult now to sell to the lower middle class folks who constitute the bulk of the pro-family movement, for example, the Administration's economic programs when the Administration is insensitive to them on things that they feel strongly about." Weyrich stressed that "the constituents that we have been reaching are largely Democrats, they are largely Independents, non-voters, people who have switched their allegiance in order to support Ronald Reagan and are embittered over some of the statements [on social issues] by the Administration" (Weyrich 1981b).

This is what made the racial realignment, and building the coalition first stitched together by Goldwater, so constraining in the decades to come. Republicans in the 1960s–1980s were campaigning from a losing position; they were the minority party and needed to expand their base. Tacking rightward on culture war issues offered a means to accomplish that. Economic issues alone, many conservative activists and politicos believed, would not be enough to lure New Deal Democrats into a Republican coalition.

This point is worth elaborating. A reader might wonder if the Democrats truly lost the South in the 1960s. Carter won much of the region in 1976 and 1980, and the Democrats nominated southern statewide officeholders in the 1992, 1996, and 2000 elections. Democrats remained, to varying degrees, a threat in the region. This pushed Republicans to double-down on social issues that could peel off economically populist Democrats. Conversely, it pushed Democrats to try to focus on economic appeals that could win over southern Democrats even as their social policies drifted leftward. But perhaps what pushed the region out of the Democrats' hands was not the appeals that could be made in the general election, but the types of candidates who could win the Democratic primary as the party drifted leftward and as culture war issues gained salience. Nominating a Democrat conservative enough to hold the South proved increasingly difficult. Even Bill Clinton in the 1990s and Al Gore in 2000, two Democratic nominees who held statewide offices in the South, largely ceded the region to the GOP in the general election. (George W. Bush swept the southern states in 2000.)

Opportunities and Constraints for Interest Group and Party Alignment

The previous sections details how politicians responded to a shifting electorate. But the racial realignment not only changed how politicians responded, but reshaped the partisan political environment in which interest groups worked, too. This section argues that the racial realignment shaped polarization on culture war issues like abortion or guns because it meaningfully closed off the opportunity for conservative activists and interest groups to enter, or at least find consistent support for their issues, in the Democratic Party. Likewise, it precluded liberal activist groups from entering or sustaining themselves in the Republican Party.

Despite an intense focus on the role of interest groups in shaping parties' positions, little work focuses on why interest groups align with one party over the other (McCarty and Schickler 2018). While the alignment of interest groups and activists in the party system is taken for granted today, such alignments did not characterize the partisan interest-group landscape of the 1960s.

First, as chapter 1 details, many candidates in the 1960s and early 1970s did not have any or at least not a firm position on now-salient culture war issues. Second, the interest groups that now dominate our political landscape were either nonexistent or, at most, nascent groups that lacked the power to shape politics as they might today. The Sierra Club, a major player in the late twentieth-century environmental movement, was founded in 1892. But on the eve of renewed environmental consciousness in 1960, it had only about 15,000 members (Mitchell, Mertig, and Dunlap 1991). Likewise, while the National Rifle Association (NRA) had existed for over a century by the 1970s, its membership through the mid-twentieth century was a fraction of the 5 million members the NRA boasts today (Karol 2009; Lacombe 2021). In the early 1970s, the pro-life movement was fairly small, and the Religious Right, to the extent it existed, was a backroom operation. And the National Abortion Rights Action League (NARAL) had just 627 individual members in November 1971 (Gidding 1971).

The leaders of the then-fledgling interest-group movements were searching for political support and were willing to take it from whomever gave it to them. Katherine Krimmel's work on special interest partisanship outlines a series of reasons why groups, at least when firm alliances do not already exist, might want to ally with both parties. The simplest explanation is that allying with both parties means groups will have influence regardless of who is in power. Thus, rather than interest groups offering an explanation for why the parties took the positions they did on abortion or guns, how groups entered one coalition over another is "another side of the puzzle" (Krimmel 2017, 150).

I argue that the racial realignment created an opportunity structure for interest group–party alliances that would have not existed had the parties maintained overlapping positions on civil rights. In fact, many conservative activists and thinkers who made up the New Right were indifferent to party, supported the formation of a conservative third party, or actually preferred the Democratic Party. Many conservatives viewed GOP leadership (e.g., national party chairs, high-ranking officeholders) as inept and almost nearly as committed to liberalism as the Democrats. "The established leadership of both the Democratic and Republican Parties in this country is in the hands of more or less liberal leaders who quibble only over details," Weyrich lamented (Hartman 1975). Indeed, one of the most prominent leaders of the pre–racial realignment GOP, Nelson Rockefeller, who served as Ford's vice president in the 1970s, was a leading voice in favor of abortion rights and gun control.

Weyrich and other conservative organizers were willing to, and did in fact, support members of both parties. To them, commitment to ideological principles (in this case, conservatism), not party, was what mattered. Richard Viguerie, the so-called godfather of the New Right, articulated this sentiment of ideological commitment, rather than party fealty: "I've been saying for years that it should make absolutely no difference whether a candidate is a Republican or a Democrat—only whether he is liberal or conservative . . ." (Rusher 1977). In the late 1970s, Weyrich and other New Right leaders worked to unite conservative Democrats and conservative Republicans in order to elect the Speaker of the House. Conservatives, William Rusher declared, must go "for candidates who deserve it, whichever party they may belong to" (1977).

Rather than activists choosing to enter the Republican rather than the Democratic Party (or perhaps starting a third party), structural forces pushed social conservatives to the GOP. The eventual alignment of these New Right activists with the GOP was less out of desire than the lack of other options. Weyrich (1977) acknowledged that the Republican Party, rather than the Democratic Party, was just better for conservatives. Rusher, too, despite his at times outward belief that Democrats would support the conservative cause, remarked, "The Democrats, dominated by their liberal majority, are not an inviting prospect" for conservatives (1975b).

An analysis of the types of Democrats Weyrich's organization donated to in 1976 illustrates why this group found themselves squarely in the Republican camp: nearly all the Democrats they supported were conservative Democrats in the South (Weyrich 1976). While the reddening of southern politics took time, viable conservative Democrats became rarer, and conservatives found that most of their ideologically sympathetic candidates ran as Republicans. Running conservative Democrats in primaries was difficult in a party increasingly dominated by African Americans and white racial liberals. Weyrich, although looking for ways to support Democrats, admitted his organization "is not very credible in a Democrat primary" (1975b).

Issue-specific groups also wanted to avoid picking a party but felt similar constraints that made them more viable in one party over the other. As chapter 6 explores, the cordoning of the pro-life movement into the GOP was an alliance that came reluctantly to the leading figures of the early pro-life movement—an ideologically diverse group of people, many of whom might have preferred the Democratic Party. In 1976, pro-life groups surveyed the primary field and supported two Democrats—George Wallace and Ellen McCormack, a single-issue anti-abortion candidate—and one Republican, Ronald Reagan. All of these candidates lost in the primaries. In the general election, anti-abortion forces, perhaps reluctantly, lined up behind Ford because he was more conservative than Carter on abortion.

A similar process played out among the earliest gay and lesbian activists. Andrew Proctor (2022) argues that the earliest national activists at the National Gay Task Force and the Gay Rights National Lobby hoped to enter and gain influence in both parties. In the 1980 primary campaign, they surveyed the field of both Democrats and Republicans, looking for candidates amenable to their cause. They ultimately endorsed Kennedy in the Democratic primary and John Anderson in the Republican primary (Anderson, a liberal Republican, would run as a third-party candidate in the general election) (Proctor 2022, 781, 783). Gay and lesbian activists turned to explicitly targeting the Democratic Party only after Reagan's election in 1980, which relied heavily on the Religious Right and culturally conservative voters. Proctor argues that "the gay-Democratic alliance was neither natural nor preformed but, rather, an outcome of dynamics in the two-party system" (2022, 784).

Likewise, prior to the 1970s, leaders of the National Rifle Association worried about taking partisan sides. Matt Lacombe's (2021) analysis of the NRA finds that they only started making explicit connections to partisan politics in the late 1960s and early 1970s, and then only rarely. This alignment of the NRA with Republican politics arose, according to Lacombe, "as the NRA's ideological commitments started to intersect with changes in the ideological commitments of the parties" (159).

The racial realignment also constrained the ability of which party pro- and anti-immigrant groups could align with. While Latino groups in the 1960s did not organize around immigration from Central and South America—as they would by the 1970s—many Latino groups were demanding civil rights. The racial realignment predisposed these groups toward the Democratic Party because of the Democrats' position on civil rights. Likewise, Republican appeals to these groups, while successful at times, ran up against the wall of growing ethnocentrism in Republican ranks in the post–racial realignment era. These Latino groups would play a crucial role in pushing the Democratic Party to the left on undocumented immigration from Central America when the issue gained political salience in the 1970s and 1980s.

In this view, activists reinforced and locked in the equilibrium set in motion by the realignment. The counterfactual, where a racial realignment did not occur, was that conservative thinkers and activists would have been quite happy to work in the Democratic Party with candidates who aligned with their views. And they did for a while, but as the decades wore on, the space for conservative Democrats and liberal Republicans became smaller.

Voters, Interest Groups, and Politicians: A Dynamic Process of Party Sorting

This final section revisits a core debate that consumes the existing literature on parties: How much room do political leaders have to establish their party's position? Much of the existing scholarship on party sorting on issues like abortion and gun control argues that the process started with politicians and flowed down to the mass public (e.g., Levendusky 2009). But this chapter has detailed a more dynamic process in the 1960s and 1970s. Strategic politicians, especially on the right, were looking for voters to build a winning coalition, and the political landscape offered opportunities and constraints. Nixon, for example, could have gone to the left on abortion; there was nothing locking his hands. But Nixon perceived that messaging conservative abortion appeals would reinforce the Republican Party's appeal to racially conservative Democrats already moving toward the Republican Party.

When Nixon, Ford, Reagan, and other Republican presidents adopted conservative abortion stands, this undoubtedly shaped public opinion on the ground (e.g., Lenz 2012). But the reasons those politicians sent conservative messages were shaped by electoral forces in the first place. In other words, elites can influence public opinion consistent with top-down accounts, but I argue that elite cues are often endogenous to what elites perceive will be popular among their supporters (Zaller 2012, 571; Arnold 1992; Key 1961). Elite cues are not random to public opinion.

Elite actors may follow latent public opinion by (1) measuring support and testing the waters before taking new positions, (2) taking policy positions they believe will get nonvoters to turn out for them, (3) abandoning old positions if activated opinion deems them unpopular, or (4) being replaced if they continually embrace unpopular stands on crystallized issues. The prior sections' vignettes are replete with such examples. In such a view, politicians strengthen preexisting cleavages by sending signals that are informed by latent opinion among their (potential) constituencies.

To be sure, politicians strategically or otherwise take politically risky positions. This is perhaps especially pronounced in periods of political change when politicians aligned with the party's descendant wing take positions that are, or eventually become, politically unviable. For example, Nelson Rockefeller, a leader of the once-strong northeastern liberal Republican establishment, expressed liberal positions on civil rights, abortion, and gun control—a suite of positions that were no longer winning issues in the GOP by the 1980s. Rockefeller, unlike Nixon or Reagan, was either unwilling to change his position or did not see that the GOP had changed.

A similar process plays out among activists and movement leaders, too. Interest-group leaders hold sway among their members and are important for communicating campaign messages. But like politicians, interest groups and social movement leaders are sensitive to the appeals that can generate attention and increase membership. Messaging does not come out of nowhere. Indeed, the fact that most people have little interest in politics propelled organizers of mass-based movements to find issues and frames that *would* engage the public. Conservative organizer Paul Weyrich (1981a) outlined this dilemma and solution:

> The average person is less interested in politics than other things in his life. Sports, for example, command more attention than other issues for many people. Through the use of survey research, we can identify those issues of importance to people and relate our ideas to them.

Sometimes groups used survey research to tailor messages in order to build membership lists and raise money (Kelly 1975). Other times, activists stumbled on issues. For example, scholars attribute the failure to ratify the Equal Rights Amendment to conservative activist Phyllis Schlafly's efforts. Yet Schlafly only began organizing against the ERA when she accidentally realized the tremendous support it generated; Schlafly had not taken much interest in feminism prior to the early 1970s (Critchlow 2018, 217–18). In other words, although Schlafly's involvement shaped the political outcomes of the Equal Rights Amendment, her very involvement was a response to mass-level forces.

More broadly, interest groups organizing in the 1960s and 1970s, perhaps because they were organizing around then-fledgling issues, realized they needed mass support, or at least the perception of mass support, to gain influence. Interest groups are important, but without the perception that groups have votes, their organizational capacity means little. The book's opening vignette of the Catholic Bishops lobbying Ted Kennedy exemplifies this; without public support, the Catholic Bishops knew they could not change Kennedy's position.

The other side of the coin is that public opinion by itself is not enough, either. Activist leaders are needed to sharpen and propel sentiment on the ground. In 1979, Weyrich articulated interest groups' role in organizing alliances once the New Deal coalition fell apart:

> The new deal [*sic*] coalition was really broken in 1968 with the Nixon/Wallace vote. But nothing happened until recently to effectively make inroads into the opposition camp precisely because in 1968 conservatives did not have the institutions capable of making use of what was happening. . . . It must be remembered that such operations as Gun Owners did not exist then and Right to Work had but 25,000 members compared with 1.3 million today and there was no Right to Life groups. (Weyrich 1979)

Conclusion

This chapter laid out how the racial realignment not only polarized the parties on civil rights, but how it also created an opportunity structure for the parties to divide as they did on a host of other culture war issues as well. While polarization on these issues did not occur only because of the racial realignment, the 1964 racial realignment generated path dependence that pushed the parties to sort as they did. A distinguishing feature of path dependence is that the initial shock or outcome of a critical juncture creates institutions or forces that then maintain or build on the initial outcome (Page 2006, 88). The 1964 racial realignment transformed how people and groups that acted within the US party system and fundamentally altered how politicians pursued voters.

In some ways, the transformations occurring within the Democratic and Republican primary electorates mirrored each other. In the Republican Party, the once-powerful liberal wing was shrinking while the conservative wing grew. In the Democratic Party, the reverse happened. However, change did not occur at the same pace in both parties. The Democratic Party's dominance in the South is a partial explanation; the region did not shed a century of partisan loyalties to the Democratic Party overnight. Conservative Democrats continued to win primary (and then general) elections in the region because a large chunk of the party's primary voters were still conservative on race and other social issues. Conversely, as racial conservatives entered the previously empty southern GOP primary electorate, they brought with them conservative attitudes on a range of other issues as well; there was no liberal southern Republican wing to counteract the ascendant conservatives' power.

CHAPTER THREE

Issue Connections in the Mass Public

In January 1940, Gallup for the first time asked about government regulation of guns on a public opinion survey. An overwhelming majority,
nearly 80% of those with an opinion, supported the statement that gun
owners should be required to register firearms with the government. The
same poll also asked whether respondents supported a federal law to make
lynching a crime.[1] An interesting pattern emerged. The poll shows that respondents who *opposed* anti-lynching legislation were also 10 percentage
points more likely to oppose firearm registration (compared to those who
supported the anti-lynching legislation).

To a contemporary observer of politics, these issue connections might
make sense: the Republican (Democratic) Party is the more conservative
(liberal) party on both civil rights and gun control. Yet in 1940, the Republican Party, if anything, was slightly more liberal on civil rights. And gun
control, to the extent it was a political issue, was nonpartisan. Congress
passed the 1938 Federal Firearms Act, one of the first federal pieces of gun
control legislation, by voice vote—a procedure used for noncontroversial
legislation.[2]

Nor was gun control a major issue in ideological media outlets. By my
search, in the entire decade of the 1930s, *The Nation*, a magazine known
for its liberal outlook, published no articles about gun control and the liberal *New Republic* (1936) published just two sentences, in a single article,
and they were not in favor. And although it existed in the late 1930s, the
National Rifle Association was not aligned with a party, was less politically
prominent than they are today, and had a membership roll of just 50,000
(this is 100 times less than current NRA membership of about 5 million;
Lacombe 2021, 11–12). When the parties divided on civil rights in the

1960s and gun control by 1980, the positions clustered in the party system matched public opinion that had been present since the earliest public opinion polls in the 1940s.

This chapter investigates the long-run correlates of racial attitudes before and during polarization's formative years in the 1970s. The chapter starts by using historical public opinion data (described in the next section) to document the long-run relationship between attitudes toward civil rights and racial equality with gun control and four other issues that have defined the culture wars: abortion, women's equality, gay rights, and environmentalism. (Chapter 7 provides a similar analysis of immigration.) More liberal voters on civil rights (defined in multiple ways) are also more liberal on each of these other culture war issues dating to the earliest public opinion polls. I use "more liberal" to refer to what is today considered the leftward policy alternative. As the above account of gun control shows, these issue connections existed long before issues like guns or abortion divided the national parties. While, for example, the fact that racial and gun control attitudes fit together is well known today, the fact that a similar pattern extends back to 1940 has not been documented by public opinion research. The persistence of these trends has implications for our understanding of the relationship between public opinion and parties.

After exploring these long-run trends, this chapter uses data from the American National Election Study (ANES) in 1972, 1976, and 1980 to systematically explore the relationship between racial attitudes and effectively every other policy issue surveyed in the 1970s ANES. I find that racial conservatism correlates with more conservative views on effectively every issue asked on the 1970s ANES. I focus on these years for both practical and substantive reasons. Logistically, the ANES first asked questions in 1972 on many issues that now define party conflict. Substantively, I am interested in the 1970s because issues such as abortion and gun control were becoming salient, yet the national parties had yet to take distinct positions. This enables analysis of issue attitudes prior to their political crystallization. Also, unlike data from multiple polling firms, the ANES has often identical language between years.

The next section argues that pre-political values, not signals from political elites, underpin the enduring nature of these long-term connections between civil rights and other culture war issues. The existence of these issue bundles, both among activists and ordinary people, was underpinned by a varying commitment to preserve traditional order and hierarchies (e.g.,

Hetherington and Weiler 2009, Stenner 2005; Adorno et al. 1950; Kinder and Sears 1981; Bobo 1983).

I then explore a prominent alternative explanation for these issue bundles: that people packaged racial views with other policy stances because they learn what issues "go together" from political elites. I first analyze whether these issue bundles exist simply because people have learned that issues go together from *partisan* political elites. The literature on party positioning, and especially elite-mass interactions, largely focuses on national *party* leaders' ability to shape public opinion (e.g., Zaller 1992; Carmines and Stimson 1989; Lenz 2012; Barber and Pope 2019). People learn where their candidate or preferred party stands on an issue and develop similar attitudes, this scholarship argues. However, I find that the issue bundles discussed above predate the national and state parties' dividing on these issues. Furthermore, people who do not know where the parties stand on issues in the 1970s, or perceive the parties to stand at the same position, still bundled these issues together. Partisan cues cannot wholly explain the persistence of these issue bundles.

I then explore whether these issue bundles emerge from people learning what goes with what from cues outside the national party system. For example, the Supreme Court can provide cues on issues (Franklin and Kosaki 1989), or ideological journalists and media sources can message positions on newly salient issues (Noel 2013). I find that people who know little about politics, or lack knowledge of where media outlets stand on issues, still packaged these bundles together in polarization's formative years. Moreover, knowledge of where liberals and conservatives stood on issues, even the most prominent ones, was strikingly low in the 1970s, suggesting that ideological learning was not a prominent substitute for partisan learning.

These findings have clear stakes for an existing literature in political science arguing that party platforms are contingent choices made by elites or bargained by interest groups. This evidence pushes back against the textbook view that voters do not cluster issues together like elites, or that they do so only after learning policy positions from elite sources (Fiorina et al. 2004, 137). If this textbook view of public opinion is true, then when the parties moved on civil rights in the 1960s, it would leave party positioning on other issues, like abortion or gun control, open-ended. Alternatively, if the mass public clustered attitudes before the parties sorted on various policy dimensions, this would potentially mean that the positions that parties take on one issue limits their ability to take positions on other issues. As chapter 2 argues, political elites' messaging on abortion or guns did not come out of nowhere. Rather, elite messaging has reinforced and strengthened this preexisting cluster of public opinion.

The Long Run: Correlates of Racial Attitudes

This section explores the long-run relationship between attitudes toward civil rights and five other issues that defined the culture wars. To explore these historical trends, I searched for all relevant questions archived at the Roper Center for Public Opinion Research at Cornell University (most of which are Gallup polls during the early time frame) and the Louis Harris Data Center at UNC at Chapel Hill, which has archived old Harris polls. I use Gallup and Harris because these surveys stretch to the 1930s and the early 1960s, respectively. For these questions, I use all polling data available prior to 1972 held in either of these two polling archives, which to my knowledge are the primary warehouses for public opinion data before the 1970s. For data after 1972, I primarily rely on the American National Election Study and General Social Survey, which did not begin asking questions about many culture war issues until the 1970s.

Since these survey companies sometimes ask multiple questions in each year, and rarely do the same questions span the years before the 1970s, I standardize each variable to have a mean of 0 and standard deviation of 1, and then average across items in each survey. I then re-standardize the indexed variable.[3] Averaging across issue areas reduces measurement error (Ansolabehere, Rodden, and Snyder 2008) and circumvents arbitrary decisions as to which variables to include.

These data have the advantage of analyzing views over a longer time period, in some cases for decades, but have the drawback of inconsistent wordings between years. Furthermore, the political context of issues change over time.[4] Despite these drawbacks, they illuminate patterns of public opinion before survey companies asked more consistent questions.

Each panel in figure 3.1 graphs the long-run relationship between racial attitudes and five different issues that have defined the culture wars (I use the earliest data available for each issue). Each point can be interpreted as a correlation coefficient between racial attitudes and attitudes toward the other variable of interest. For readers unfamiliar with correlations, they are a statistical measure that tell us how much two variables vary together.

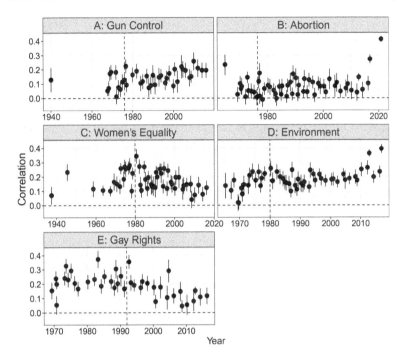

FIGURE 3.1. Correlation between Racial Attitudes and Culture War Issues. Each point represents the regression coefficient from regressing issue-specific questions (as noted by the title of each panel) on questions related to civil rights or racial inequality in a given survey. I code each variable such that higher values represent more conservative attitudes. In each year, I standardize each variable to have a mean of 0 and a standard deviation of 1. In years with more than one question, I average across questions and then re-standardize the variable. Consequently, each point can be interpreted as a correlation coefficient. The vertical dashed line approximates when the national parties took differentiated stands on the issue.

In this case, positive coefficients mean more conservative racial attitudes correspond to more conservative positions on gun control, abortion, and so on. The historical data suggest that (1) the observed linkages have persisted for decades, and (2) they clearly predate the national parties staking a position on the respective issue.

Panel A shows that conservative positions on race correspond with opposition to gun control dating back to at least 1940. This is despite the national parties not diverging on gun control until the 1970s. (See chapter 1 for a timeline of party positions.)

Panel B explores the relationship between racial attitudes and views on abortion. Gallup first polled on abortion in 1962 in response to a woman

flying to Sweden to receive an abortion after inadvertently ingesting tha-
lidomide, a drug that could potentially hurt (deform) the fetus. While the
survey does not ask direct questions about people's racial views, they do
ask white respondents a question that echoes more contemporary questions designed by political scientists to measure resentment toward racial
minorities. Gallup asked, "[African Americans], of course, wish to gain
equality with white people in all departments of life. If you were asked
to advise them on how to accomplish this, what would you say?" Most
of the answers provided (as well as the question itself) are either racially
resentful or racist. Most white respondents (the question was not asked of
black survey takers) said African Americans should either "raise their standards," should not be so insistent, should "improve themselves physically
and morally," or "raise their level through education" in order to achieve
equality. Of the eleven possible categories of answers, just 2% of respondents stated that the United States needed more anti-discrimination laws
or that existing anti-discrimination laws should be enforced as a means to
achieve equality.

Even at this early date, racial liberals already held the most liberal
abortion attitudes among the mass public. For example, of the 2% who
identified that government should protect minority rights as a means to
achieve equality, 77% said that abortion should be legal if the baby was at
risk of birth defects. Among those who said African Americans could gain
equality by "raising their standards" and working harder, just 52% said
abortion should be legal if the baby had birth defects (and this is compared
to 66% of all white respondents who said abortion should be permitted).

While the 1962 data are only suggestive, they fit a pattern consistently
observed in opinion research since. The next time a polling firm surveyed
about abortion in 1965, they directly asked about racial attitudes; the suggestive patterns observed in 1962 persist (first point, fig. 3.1, panel B). This
survey, which was only among college students, showed that students in
the 1965 survey who opposed affirmative action were 9 percentage points
more likely to believe abortion access should be restricted compared to
respondents who supported affirmative action. This is eight years before
Roe v. Wade and fifteen years before the parties meaningfully polarized on
abortion in the 1980 election. Furthermore, these bundles existed before
even the earliest endorsements of abortion rights by women's rights groups
(Greenhouse and Siegel 2012, 38–39).

On broader questions of women's rights (panel C), belief in equality for
women correlated with support for civil rights and racial equality dating

to the 1930s. In a 1945 survey of white men, those men who opposed equal rights for African Americans were about 20 percentage points more likely to say women's role was in the home (as opposed to having jobs outside the home). And in a nationally representative survey in 1958, those opposed to racial integration were 14 percentage points more likely to say they would not support a female presidential candidate. These trends existed before the 1960s women's rights movement and before the parties diverged on the Equal Rights Amendment in 1980. (Both parties supported the ERA between 1944 and 1976.)

Similar linkages exist on environmental questions dating to the earliest polls in the mid-1960s. In a 1965 survey, racial liberals were 13 percentage points more likely to say they felt bad about environmental pollution. By the mid-1970s, 41% of respondents who believed the civil rights movement was moving too quickly opposed regulating car emissions compared to just 31% who believed it moved not quickly enough. This is despite both parties supporting environmental reform in the 1960s and early 1970s. The Republicans' rightward shift on environmentalism came after these bundles existed among ordinary voters.

On gay rights (panel E), the first public opinion data show that racial liberals generally had more liberal attitudes toward gay rights or tolerance of gay and lesbian people as a group than did racial conservatives. For example, in August 1970, those who supported school segregation (by race) were 27 percentage points more likely to express that homosexuals are "harmful to the country" compared to those who opposed school segregation.

Systematic Analysis: Correlates of Racial Attitudes

Racial attitudes and five other culture war issues have moved together since the earliest public opinion polls, some of which date to the 1930s. While I focus on these issues for the reasons discussed in the prior chapters, they represent only a portion of the political agenda. This section systematically analyzes the linkage between racial attitudes and effectively every issue asked on the American National Election Studies in the 1970s. I focus on the 1970s because the ANES begins to consistently ask relevant questions on culture war issues and it captures opinions before these issues emerged (or crystallized) in the party system.

Figure 3.2 presents a nearly exhaustive analysis of issue bundles asked on the ANES with respect to three racial questions: Attitudes toward gov-

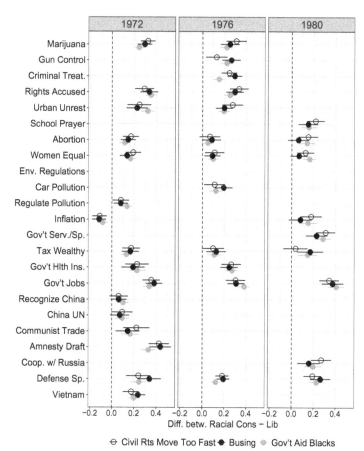

FIGURE 3.2. Relationship between Racial Attitudes and Other Political Beliefs. Each point represents the difference in the proportion of racial liberals and racial conservatives who also take a conservative position on the secondary variable. Positive coefficients mean that racial conservatives hold more conservative attitudes on the secondary position, too. With the exception of inflation in 1972, conservative racial attitudes predict conservative attitudes on every other issue. Lines represent 95% confidence intervals.

ernment aid to minorities, support for busing to integrate schools, and whether the civil rights movement was moving too quickly or not quickly enough. To differentiate between racial "liberals" and racial "conservatives," I code all respondents who are left of center on each racial question as liberal (o) and those right of center as conservative (1).[5] To interpret the results, I then recode each secondary variable where 1 is a conservative position (reflects right-of-center position) and all other values are coded

0. I then regress secondary-issue attitudes (such as abortion, gun control) on the indicator variable of racial attitudes.[6]

For readers unfamiliar with statistics, regression analysis is a method of finding the average of one variable (in this case attitudes toward abortion, gun control, etc.), conditional on the value of another variable (in this case, a respondent's views toward race). The regression coefficient, indicated by the points in figure 3.2, simply represents the difference in the proportion of racial conservatives and racial liberals who hold conservative attitudes on each of the issues listed down the left-hand column. For example, the top set of points on the top-left panel (in 1972) shows that those holding a right-of-center position on busing are approximately 29 percentage points more likely to hold a right-of-center position on marijuana legalization, when compared to busing liberals. (The lines going through each point are 95% confidence intervals, which present the amount of certainty of the regression coefficient.)

The differences vary by question and over years, but substantive differences persist: on every issue, with the exception of controlling inflation, conservative racial attitudes predict conservative attitudes on other issues. In 1972, the most polarizing of the three elections, the biggest divides between racial liberals (as measured by their attitudes toward busing) and conservatives involve amnesty for draft dodgers (44% difference), whether government should provide jobs (38%), and defense spending (33%).[7] These linkages remain after controlling for multiple demographic variables including race, region, religious affiliation, income, education, and party identification.[8]

It is worth highlighting that white voters are primarily driving these issue bundles, especially in the earlier years. African Americans represented 11% of the population in 1970, and other non-white populations that would grow in the latter part of the twentieth century were still relatively small, even in the 1960s and 1970s (the 1970 Census identified about 5% of the population as of Hispanic origin and less than 1% as Asian American and Pacific Islander[9]). Furthermore, on some questions of civil rights in the earlier years, there is not much variation in black respondents' attitudes (e.g., African Americans overwhelmingly favored anti-lynching laws and supported civil rights legislation). However, figure A.3 in the appendix uses an over-sample of black voters in the General Social Survey in 1982 and 1987 (which is necessary because only a couple hundred respondents are included in nationally representative polls) and finds a similar cluster of attitudes generally persist among African Americans by the 1980s.

Why the Issue Bundles?

This book builds around a long-standing, but underappreciated, feature of public opinion in the United States. People who are more conservative on race, as the previous sections show, have long held more conservative views on a host of other culture war issues. This section outlines how racial views and attitudes on these other issues become linked together among the mass public.

As chapter 1 discusses, while many of these culture war issues were not "new," their focus in partisan conflict in the United States significantly heightened during the 1970s. The rise of so-called "post-material" social issues swept across advanced industrial Western publics in the mid- to late twentieth century, not just the United States. Rising levels of economic security in the United States and other Western democracies, scholars argue, enabled the rise of post-material goals such as environmental protection and minority rights (Inglehart 1977, 27). A burgeoning middle class, raised in economic comfort, might direct their attention not to achieving economic security, but to other concerns.

If post-materialism allowed people to focus on advancing women's rights or environmental causes, it also created a backlash among those who believed that society was changing from what it should be. In the United States, a growing political movement known broadly as the New Right represented the conservative side of post-material political conflict. Paul Weyrich, a leading organizer of the New Right, articulated what many academics expressed more formally: society and norms were changing and many people did not like it. "Millions of largely apolitical Americans have grown suspicious of 'new moralities' and other instant causes. They may not be connoisseurs of high culture, but they understand the advantages of the culture we already have" (Lind and Weyrich 1987).

The kinds of people that post-materialism conservatism spoke to were not necessarily the wealthy economic conservatives who resisted the New Deal programs of the 1930s, but blue-collar and middle-class people, many of whom had grown up as Democrats and who, perhaps because they had moved to the middle class, shifted their focus from demanding government intervention in the economy to seeing politics as a means to address social change. "Culturally destructive government policies—quotas and busing come to mind as examples—are to the New Right more immediately important [than economic issues] in the realm of action," Weyrich surmised (undated memo).

Rather than government standing on the sidelines, culturally conservative activists viewed government as necessary to restore social order. Connie Marshner, an activist who worked alongside Weyrich in founding the Religious Right, defined the New Right's movement as "grounded in moral convictions, and they [the New Right activists] are seeking a public order which respects those convictions" (Marshner, n.d.). The New Right, Weyrich (undated interview) argued, advocated for nothing other "than what has been our historical tradition."

The language of activists used to describe the culturally conservative movement mirrors scholarship on the underlying values that drive people's positions on many social issues. A literature in political psychology shows that desire for order or preserving existing hierarchies predicts and underpins politically conservative attitudes on social issues (Hetherington and Weiler 2009, Stenner 2005; Adorno et al. 1950; Kinder and Sears 1981; Bobo 1983). For example, Kinder and Sears (1981) argue that white racial prejudice is rooted in a feeling that black people violate "whites' moral codes about how society should be organized"—norms such as hard work, individualism, and self-reliance (Sears et al. 1997, 22). Theories of hierarchy and traditionalism extend to attitude development beyond the racial context. For example, Oxley et al. (2008) show that sensitivity to threatening stimuli predicts support for policies that protect the existing social structure. Threats take the forms of "norm violations" such as expanding gay rights or liberalizing abortion access.

Many of these themes emerged in conservative activists' writings and communications. For example, on gay rights, Marshner (1981) told Congressman Jack Kemp, "Legislation extending the protection of the Civil Rights Act to 'sexual preference' would send a message that social order can be tampered with . . . which is precisely the opposite of the message necessary to rebuild the foundations of society."

The need for order and safety comes not just from symbolic threats, but also from physical threats (Hetherington and Weiler 2009; Filindra and Kaplan 2016, 258). For example, Bill Richardson, founder of Gun Owners of America (the more radical version of the National Rifle Association), saw gun regulations as leaving people "rendered defenseless" in their own homes against the threats of socialism and crime (Tangner 1975).

From this lens, the relationship between opposition to black civil rights and women's equality, abortion access, gay rights, and gun control are about each of these issues tapping into a broader values system or psychological schema. Fights over civil rights and racial equality, while not always at the center of partisan conflict, have been ubiquitous in the United States and represent a core cleavage of social change. When women's rights or gay rights emerged on the agenda, they mapped on to this dimension of social change.

Part of this resistance to change is regional, Maxwell and Shields (2019) argue. Like civil rights, other shifting norms threatened the white South's traditional way of life. For example, the South played a prominent role in blocking the enfranchisement of women in the nineteenth and twentieth centuries (Keyssar 2000; Maxwell and Shields 2019, 12), and later became a geographic center of gravity for opposing the Equal Rights Amendments and legalizing abortion. "White resentment toward a more level racial playing field was easily transferred to, or simply intensified by, the goal of a level gender playing field," Maxwell and Shields (2019, 9) argue. Maxwell and Shields contend that the Republican Party became increasingly southern by adopting a suite of conservative cultural issues, like opposition to gender equality or abortion rights, that had ties to traditional and biblical worldviews; worldviews that were southern in their nature (14).

While the South is central to this transformation, similar resistance to change extends beyond the region. As chapter 2 details, white blue-collar workers in the Midwest and Northeast, fueled by the racial change of the 1960s, also served as core constituencies of the conservative social movements of the 1970s.

Of course, the relationship is not one-to-one. For example, prominent activists who favored women's suffrage in the nineteenth century framed their movement in specifically racial terms, and many people who were committed to securing black political civil rights were indifferent to women's suffrage (Keyssar 2000). Likewise, chapter 6 details prominent antiabortion activists who held otherwise liberal views on other social justice issues. And while these are examples of activists, many ordinary people fit such a description as well (chapter 4 discusses what happens to these cross-pressured voters).

But, as this chapter shows, all available public opinion data point in the same direction: people who opposed civil rights or exhibited higher levels of black racial prejudice, on average, are more likely to express conservative views on issues of women's rights, gay rights, and abortion *from the earliest available data*. These bundles existed before the national parties polarized and had a tremendous consequence for elite partisan conflict.

An equally important part of these micro-foundations is that an overarching view that government should be hands-off—one that underpins classical views of economic conservatism—did not explain conservatism toward noneconomic cultural issues. Indeed, some outside commentators view the alignment of anti-abortion or anti–gay rights conservatives in the Republican Party as puzzling because of conservatism's popular connotations with less government. But this was not the case for many cultural conservatives. As chapter 1 shows with respect to issues of women's rights, and as this chapter will show across other issues, economic views were largely uncorrelated with nonracial cultural issues until the 1980s or 1990s. While economic conservatism and cultural conservatism would later become interlinked among the mass public because of the political coalitions that formed in the 1970s, these linkages were not consistently observed in the mass public prior to the 1970s.

This presented both opportunity and constraint for the GOP. It was a constraint for the Republican Party because economic appeals would be insufficient to expand the party's appeal to the South or to white blue-collar voters in the Northeast. Conservatives, Weyrich reportedly declared, had been hamstrung by "the Chamber of Commerce candidate with the Mobil Oil ads draped around his neck . . . that doesn't make it in the middle [working]-class neighborhoods" (Denier 1980). But it was an opportunity because it allowed Republican politicians to exploit the racial cleavage and seek out culturally conservative voters without pushing away the economic conservatives who still sat in their party (on average).

This is not to say that economic issues were absent from the culturally conservative right-wing social movements of the 1960s and 1970s. But as work by scholars of race and political development has shown, the South's turn against economic intervention in the economy was shaped by the perception that economic redistribution went to a racial out-group (Caughey 2018; Schickler 2016). The emerging conservatism on economic issues could not be abstracted from race or the broader classification of the undeserving poor (e.g., Mendelberg 2001; Gilens 1996; Elder and O'Brian 2022).

Finally, while much of the conservative political movement in the 1960s and 1970s was white, African Americans in the 1960s and 1970s generally held conservative attitudes regarding abortion, gay rights, and other social issues (Tate 1993). Underlying values that predict conservatism on these issues, such as authoritarianism, also predict social conservatism on abortion, gay rights, and other social issues among black voters as well. Furthermore, authoritarianism predicts more punitive racial attitudes and racial conservatism among African Americans in the contemporary era (Jefferson

2023, 10). Yet in the midcentury United States, African American public opinion toward contemporaneous issues of civil rights and racial equality was quite liberal. For example, the 1964 ANES shows that 96% of black survey takers supported the civil rights bill. This complicates understanding the attitudinal linkages between racial and culture war issues among African Americans in the mid-twentieth century.

Alternative Explanations: Why the Issue Bundles

This next section explores a set of alternative explanations for the existence of these issue bundles that undermine the bottom-up nature of party sorting laid out in chapter 2: that political elites, particularly partisan elites, created the ideological structure along the racial axis. As I will show, this set of explanations cannot account for the persistence of these issue bundles before and during polarization's formative years.

Do Voters Just Follow Partisan Elites?

An established literature argues that elites construct issue bundles and then pass them down to ordinary voters (Levendusky 2009; Achen and Bartels 2017). Elite cues may come from different sources, but an influential literature on parties and public opinion focuses on cues from partisan leaders, especially major party presidential candidates (e.g., Zaller 1992; Lenz 2012). This focus is well-grounded: research shows that higher-level party leaders' cues (e.g., presidential nominees) matter more for shaping public opinion than lower-level party cues (e.g., members of Congress) (Agadjanian 2021). The stakes for these theories are high: if politicians simply construct issue bundles and the mass public follows the leader, not only is the mass public not placing pressure on the party system, but the process works in reverse.

The over-time data in the prior section casts doubt on entirely elite-party-driven explanations given that the issue bundles existed prior to the parties adopting distinct positions. That is, the parties lacked positions on gun control in the 1940s, and thus diverging elite partisan messages cannot explain why attitudes toward gun control and civil rights are already bundled in the mass public. However, it is possible that by the 1970s, even though the parties lacked formal policy positions, knowledgeable respondents had become aware of emerging partisan differences. For example, although the parties did not have formal positions on marijuana policy in

1972, McGovern was associated with decriminalizing marijuana and Nixon supported harsher penalties.

This section analyzes whether voters who do not know or perceive differences between the parties still bundled issues together in the 1970s. To do this, I compare issue bundles between respondents who perceive or know the parties' relative policy positions with those who do not. On some questions, and in some years, the ANES asks respondents to place the Democratic and Republican Party's position on a given issue on a 1–7 scale where 1 is the most liberal and 7 is the most conservative.[10] I code those who place the Republican Party to the right of the Democratic Party on the respective issue as "knowers" and all other respondents as "don't know." This analysis separates respondents who have received or perceive distinct partisan cues from those who have not. For example, those who place the Republican Party to the right of the Democratic Party on both marijuana policy and on government aid to minorities have received partisan cues and are labeled as "knowers." On some policy questions, knowing the parties' positions would reasonably mean placing both parties at the same point. However, I label these respondents as "don't know" because, consistent with the theory, they have not received distinct partisan cues.[11]

If partisan elites construct issue bundles, there should be no consistent relationship among those who have not received partisan signals or do not perceive the parties to differ on an issue. Figure 3.3 shows that respondents who lack knowledge of the parties' positions still consistently package issues together, especially in the polarizing 1972 election. For example, among "knowers" in 1972, racial conservatives are 53 percentage points more likely to oppose marijuana legalization than racial liberals. However, among those who do not know the parties' relative positions on either issue, racial conservatives are still 17 percentage points more likely to oppose marijuana legalization than racial liberals.

This pattern is consistent with a more circular theory of public opinion laid out in the previous chapter. Those who do not perceive partisan differences package issues together, but those who have received partisan cues have tighter issue bundles because their preexisting views have been reinforced by partisan messaging.

What about Non-Party Elite Cues?

The above section shows that people who do not perceive the parties to differ on issues still package race and other policy attitudes together. How-

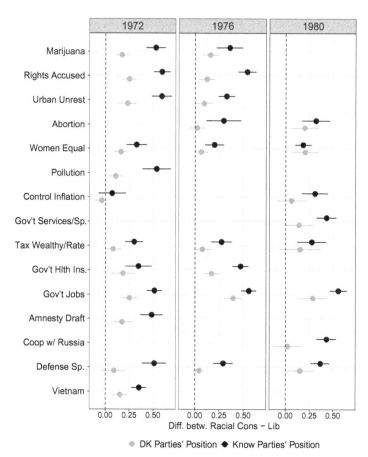

FIGURE 3.3. Know vs. Don't Know Party Positions. Panels break down issue bundles between respondents who know (black dots) and don't know (gray dots) the parties' positions. I code respondents that place the Republicans to the right of Democrats (and thus have received some partisan cue) on the given policy position as "knowers." The gray points show that even respondents who lack knowledge of the parties' relative positions still bundle racial positions with other attitudes. Lines represent 95% confidence intervals. (Note: Wording on inflation and taxes differs in 1972 and 1980.)

ever, elite cues come from a variety of sources, not just national party leaders.

One alternative explanation is that people might not receive partisan communication flows, but they may receive ideological communication flows. Even if the parties' positions on issues were not known or unclear, people might know where liberals and conservatives stood on issues. The process for ideological learning follows that of partisan socialization. People who are otherwise liberal (conservative) receive cues on a new issue from liberal (conservative) elites, and then align their position with their preferred ideological leader (Converse [1964] 2006; Noel 2013).

While data availability makes directly testing this hypothesis difficult, limited evidence casts doubt that ideological cues are the primary source for these issue bundles in the era discussed here. This is because people did not know where liberals and conservatives stood on major issues in the 1970s! In 1976, the American National Election Study asked voters where they believed liberals and conservatives stood on whether government should guarantee jobs and income for Americans and whether the rights of the criminally accused should be protected. While these are the only two questions asked in 1976—and the ANES only rarely asks about ideological placement—they paint a suggestive picture. In 1976, only 46% of respondents knew that liberals were to the left of conservatives on the government guaranteeing jobs and income (Elder and O'Brian 2022, 7). Unsurprisingly, nearly 70% of the people who did not know where the parties stood on economic redistribution also did not know where liberals and conservatives stood on the issue. On whether the government should guarantee rights for the criminally accused, a major issue in the 1960s and 1970s, people were again confused. Only 42% perceived that liberals were more likely to want to protect the rights of the accused compared to conservatives. And again, over 70% of the people who did not know where the parties stood on the issue also did not know where liberals and conservatives stood.

In 1982, the ANES again asked where liberals and conservatives stood on government jobs, and this time also where they believe liberals and conservatives stood on aid to minorities (a question that has been used to measure issue bundles above). This was during the first years of the conservative Reagan White House, an extremely polarizing administration along both racial and economic lines; however, only 52% of people knew that liberals were more favorable of economic redistribution (a 6 percentage-point increase since 1976), and only 56% knew liberals were more favorable to helping minority groups than conservatives. These data cast doubt on whether people, unaware of where the parties stood on issues, were packaging issues together because of ideological cues; knowledge of where ideological groups stood on issues was low even for economic redistribution, an issue that had been central to ideological conflict for decades. Whether much newer issues, like abortion or gun control, were clearly linked in the public's mind with liberals and conservatives seems unlikely. The 1982 data allows, in a limited way, an additional test of the racial issue bundles: Do racial liberals and conservatives, even if they do not know where liberals and conservatives stand on race or economic redistribution, still package issues together? Among people who do not know where liberals and conservatives stand on these issues or perceive conservatives and liberals to hold the same position, racial conservatives are about 45 percentage points more likely to oppose government guarantee of jobs compared to racial liberals. That is, people who do not know where liberals and conservatives stand on these issues still bundle these issues together. Furthermore, among people who know *neither* where the parties stand or where liberals and conservatives stand, racial conservatives are still 40 percentage points more likely to hold conservative economic views compared to racial liberals.

An alternative explanation is that even if people lack knowledge of where liberals and conservatives stand, they may receive their news from a liberal or conservative source, and thus bundle issues together as a result, perhaps without knowing the ideological label of the media source.

While the media are fragmented and quite polarizing today, and people reasonably know where Fox News and MSNBC stand on issues, such a media landscape did not characterize even the 1970s United States. Televised news sources, for example, were restricted to the few major networks; Fox News did not emerge until the 1990s. And while media outlets like Fox reach millions of people and shape mass opinion, circulation at magazines that promoted specific ideological views in the 1960s and 1970s was small. In 1972, *The New Republic* had 135,000 subscribers, *National Review* had just 110,000 readers (and was in debt), and *The Nation* had even fewer subscribers (Buckley 1972). Moreover, thinkers at these ideological outlets stayed largely quiet on culture war issues in the decades prior to the 1970s, and when they did write about them, the earliest messages were mixed. An examination of *The Nation*, a liberal magazine founded by abolitionists in the 1860s, illustrates both the relative absence and mixed messaging of thought leaders on culture war issues before the 1970s. In an analysis of articles published between 1950 and 1969—the eve of the culture wars— *The Nation* published just six pieces on gun control. The first, published in 1959, was quite conservative: "With every respect for the legislators' honorable intentions," *The Nation* wrote with regards to state laws that curbed gun ownership, "it must be noted that similar regulations were decreed by Hitler, Mussolini, Franco and, of course, the Communists everywhere" (Cort 1959, 475). Not until June 1964 did *The Nation* publish a piece supportive of gun control.

The Nation was also fairly quiet on gay rights and prejudice toward gay people, publishing only six pieces on the issue in the time period studied. Of these six pieces, three were liberal, two conservative, and one expressed both support and condemnation of gay people. All of these pieces were published in the 1950s. For the entire decade of the 1960s, *The Nation* remained silent on the issue. Abortion followed a similar path. In the twenty years before 1970, *The Nation* published just seven pieces expressing some sort of stand on abortion. The first, a 1952 piece by Margaret Sanger about population control in Japan, struck a conservative tone toward abortion. (Sanger, the founder of Planned Parenthood, opposed abortion.) "I rejoice that [Japan's Organization for Research on Population Health] has taken the correct strong stand against induced abortion," Sanger (1952) wrote.[12] And even though *The Nation* had shifted left by the 1960s, abortion was not a central concern. When *Roe v. Wade* was handed down in 1973, liberal thinkers at *The New Republic* and *The Nation* were almost completely silent (see chapter 6 for further discussion).

With this historical context in mind, the question still remains: Do the issue bundles presented above persist among people who did not know where media outlets stood in polarization's formative years? The lack of data availability in this time period makes it difficult to evaluate this hypothesis. However, a 1985 survey of national households conducted by the *Los Angeles Times* asked respondents what newspaper they read the most frequently and what policy positions that paper's editorial page or news stories endorsed across a range of questions including affirmative action, abortion, and gun control. The survey posed the same questions to editors and journalists of those same papers as well (*Los Angeles Times* 1985). This dataset enables an analysis of how readers and employees perceived their paper's position on major culture war issues at three of the nation's largest newspapers: the *New York Times*, the *Los Angeles Times*, and the *Washington Post*.[13]

While journalists and editors at the major papers viewed their publication as quite ideological, this perception (or knowledge) was much weaker among readers. For example, when asked where the *New York Times* stood on major political issues of the 1980s, journalists and editors for the paper, citing the editorial page's position, declared the paper was quite liberal. Eighty-six percent of editors and journalists for the *NYT* said that the paper favored liberalizing abortion laws, 84% saw the paper as favoring gun control, 79% saw the paper as favoring affirmative action, and 69% viewed the paper as supporting gay rights.

Everyday people who said they read the *New York Times* frequently, though, were markedly less aware of the paper's positions. Only 41% of *readers* viewed the *New York Times* as favoring liberalized abortion laws, only 55% perceived the paper as favoring gun control, 38% saw the paper as favoring gay rights, and around 38% saw the newspaper as favoring affirmative action. Most people said they were unaware of their paper's position or that they perceived no position. A similar pattern exists among *Los Angeles Times* and *Washington Post* readers. To put it plainly, even in 1985, people lacked widespread knowledge of where the newspaper they read, even the most prominent ones, stood on issues like abortion or gun control. This might be surprising to readers interested in political science or politics more generally (myself included) because we are so tuned into political conversations that we forget, for most people, politics is a sideshow.

This dataset allows analysis of whether people who were unaware of where their newspaper stood on major issues still packaged attitudes together. That is, are racial liberals more liberal on other issues, even if they lacked knowledge of where their newspaper stands on issues? Table 3.1 splits respondents between those who know and do not know where their paper, defined as the paper they read most frequently, stands on affirmative action and each of the social issues listed across the top of the tables. (These are readers to the three major newspapers, listed above, because the papers' positions can be discerned.) A similar pattern exists among those who know and do not know their paper's position: people who hold more racially liberal views are more liberal on gay rights, school prayer, abortion, and gun control irrespective of their knowledge of the newspaper's positions.

General Political Knowledge

The prior sections explore prominent explanations for the persistence of issue bundles in the mass public prior to party polarization. While these tests address prominent sources of political cues, there are many potential opportunities for elite learning that are not captured by the prior tests. For example, people may bundle issues together after hearing partisan messaging from subnational politicians, despite not having knowledge of (or perceiving) differences between the national parties.

TABLE 3.1. Issue Bundles by Knowledge of Where Most Read Newspaper Stands on Issue, 1985

People who know where their newspaper stands on issues				
	% taking conservative position on . . .			
	Gay Rights	School Prayer	Abortion	Gun Control
Favor Affirmative Action	13%	21%	16%	15%
Oppose Affirmative Action	26%	25%	33%	50%

People who don't know where their newspaper stands on issues				
	% taking conservative position on . . .			
	Gay Rights	School Prayer	Abortion	Gun Control
Favor Affirmative Action	12%	58%	18%	27%
Oppose Affirmative Action	26%	63%	28%	44%

Note: Table shows the percentage of people who hold a conservative position on each listed across the columns. As in the other analyses, I divide the sample between those who are racial liberals and racial conservatives (defined here by affirmative action). The top panel shows respondents who know where their own newspaper, which they report reading frequently, stands on the issues listed across the top. The bottom panel shows respondents who do not know where their paper stands on the respective pairing of issues. For example, the bottom left set of points shows that 12% people who favor affirmative action oppose gay rights and 26% of people who oppose affirmative action oppose gay rights. This is among people who do not know where their newspaper stands on affirmative action and gay rights (these are self-reported readers of the *Washington Post*, the *New York Times*, or the *Los Angeles Times*).

It is difficult to directly test each of these possibilities, but there are general measures of political knowledge (e.g., knowing which party controls Congress) that correlate with people's proclivity to receive elite cues from a range of sources. People who are generally politically knowledgeable are more likely to know where the parties stand, but are also more likely to know Congress members' positions on issues or recognize prominent Supreme Court rulings (Zaller 1992, 17; Hitt, Saunders, and Scott 2019). To investigate this possibility, I compare issue bundles among respondents by general political knowledge. ANES interviewers rate the respondents' general political knowledge on a 1–5 scale, where 1 represents respondents with the highest levels of knowledge, 3 represents average knowledge, and 5 represents the lowest levels. (The interviewers rate respondents based on their broader awareness of politics, not just their knowledge of where parties stand.) People who rank as having low awareness by the ANES interviewer are, in fact, not well aware of politics. For example, in 1972, 74% of respondents knew a president's term is four years. Among the lowest-knowledge respondents, only 50% knew that fact. And just 11% of low-information respondents knew that a senator's term lasts six years.

Unsurprisingly, people who are ranked as generally low knowledge also lack information about where the parties stand on issues. For example, in 1980 just 36% of the low-knowledge respondents perceived Democrats as more favorable than Republicans toward aid to minorities, despite the issue being central in the 1980 election. These numbers fall further when asked about subnational figures. In 1980, for example, 92% of the lowest-knowledge respondents said they saw no difference between the Democratic and Republican candidate for Congress in their district on aid to minorities. And with regards to ideological groups, in 1976 just 18% of the lowest-knowledge respondents perceived liberals to be more demanding of economic redistribution than conservatives.

To investigate the relationship between issue attitudes by general political knowledge, I divide respondents between those the interviewer rates as above average (1 or 2), average (3), and below average (4 or 5). I regress attitudes of nonracial policies on racial attitudes for each issue question asked in the 1972, 1976, and 1980 ANES (the same issue questions plotted in figure 3.2). In this analysis, I measure racial attitudes by whether people support or oppose government aid for African Americans or other minorities.

Each point in figure 3.4 represents the average difference between racial liberals and conservatives, as defined in the previous section, who take a conservative position on each of the nonracial policies laid out in figure 3.2. These are a (weighted) average of results; so each point is an aggregate. Higher values mean more racially conservative voters are more likely to take conservative views on other issues. (The lines going through each point are the weighted 95% confidence intervals, which measure certainty of the measurement.) Figure 3.4 shows that respondents ranked as having above-average knowledge by the interviewer generally express tighter linkages between the issues. However, the bundles persist even for the low-knowledge respondents, too. That is, people who have the lowest amounts of political information, and are the least likely to have received cues from political figures, still package these issues together.

These data fit the same pattern as observed before. While the most knowledgeable bundle issues together at the highest levels, perhaps because their preexisting attitudes have been reinforced by political messaging, people who know little about politics, and are the least likely to have received political messaging, still package these issues together.

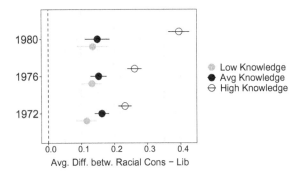

FIGURE 3.4. ANES Interviewer Knowledge (Precision Weighted Average). Graph divides the
sample between those who the ANES interviewer judges to have above-average knowledge
(open points), medium knowledge (black points), and below-average knowledge (gray points).
Each point is the precision weighted average (across all issues) in each year. High-, average-,
and low-knowledge respondents package issues together. Lines represent 95% confidence
intervals. Higher values mean that people who hold racially conservative views, on average,
also hold more conservative views on other nonracial issues when compared to racial liberals.

Issue Bundles Along the Economic Axis

This book's core argument is that the racial realignment dislodged abortion
and gun conservatives from the Democratic Party because racial conservatism correlated with conservative views on a host of other culture war
issues. But how did economic conservatism correlate with other issues?

To see public opinion along the economic axis, table 3.2 shows the relationship between whether respondents believe the government should
guarantee jobs and income and each issue listed down the left-hand column. This parallels the analysis above, but rather than using racial attitudes,
I use attitudes toward economic redistribution. Positive values mean people who are economically conservative also hold more conservative values
on the other issues, compared to economic liberals. Standard errors, which
indicate the certainty of the relationship, are in parentheses.

Column 1 shows that among all respondents, people who are more economically conservative generally express more conservative views on other
issues. For example, the top point of column 1 shows that people who hold
more economically conservative attitudes are about 4.5 percentage points
more likely to hold conservative attitudes toward legalization of marijuana compared to economic liberals. This parallels the racial issue bundles
shown above. But columns 2 and 3 show which respondents drive this
relationship. People who know where the parties stand on economic issues

TABLE 3.2. **Issue Bundles by Government Guarantee of Jobs, 1972**

	(1) Full Sample	(2) Know	(3) Don't Know
Marijuana	0.045 (0.024)	0.353 (0.053)	–0.046 (0.035)
Rights of Accused	0.191 (0.027)	0.479 (0.049)	0.049 (0.046)
Urban Unrest	0.193 (0.033)	0.277 (0.061)	0.173 (0.051)
Abortion	–0.012 (0.025)	—	—
Women Equal	0.008 (0.024)	0.169 (0.051)	–0.016 (0.038)
Pollution	0.051 (0.026)	0.222 (0.07)	0.048 (0.042)
Recognize China	–0.033 (0.027)	—	—
China in UN	–0.08 (0.034)	—	—
Trade w/ Communists	0.001 (0.042)	—	—
Amnesty Draft	0.276 (0.034)	0.53 (0.053)	0.037 (0.062)
Defense Spending	0.162 (0.037)	0.524 (0.059)	–0.085 (0.068)
Vietnam	0.143 (0.025)	0.312 (0.04)	0.049 (0.05)

Note: Each cell is the bivariate relationship from regressing the secondary variable on attitudes toward whether the government can guarantee jobs. This can be modeled by the following regression equation:

$$\text{Abortion}_i = \alpha_1 + \beta_1 \text{GovtJobs}_i + \varepsilon_i.$$

Standard errors in parentheses.

and the policies listed down the left-hand column tend to know which issues go together. Among those respondents who *do not* know where the parties stand, they do not bundle the issues together, or at least do so inconsistently. This differs from the relationship observed above where more racially conservative people who, regardless of whether they knew where the parties stood, still bundled issues together.

Among people who do not know where the parties stand, the relationship between economic attitudes and other policy attitudes does not statistically differ from zero on most issues. For readers unfamiliar with statistics, social scientists generally say a relationship is statistically different from zero if the regression coefficient is about twice as large as the standard error (standard errors measure the certainty of a relationship). For example, column 3 of the second row shows that economic conservatives are about 4.9 percentage points more likely to say the rights of the accused should be protected (this is the regression coefficient). But a standard error of 4.6 means that this number is not statistically different from zero because the standard error is not twice the size of the coefficient. This means the difference between economic liberals and conservatives on rights of the accused cannot be said to be statistically different from zero. Column 3 shows this is quite common. The relationship between economic attitudes and views toward marijuana, rights of the criminally accused, women's equality, pollution control, amnesty for Vietnam draft dodgers, defense spending, and hawkishness on Vietnam are statistically unrelated in the mass public among people who do not know where the parties stand.

The bundling of economic issues with other policy views aligns more with top-down theories arguing that voters package issues together after learning what goes with what from political elites. It also fits with a literature that shows opinion leading is more prevalent on less emotional issues. "Easy issues," like abortion or race, which people hold strong preferences on, are less malleable (Lenz 2012, 213).

Conclusion

This chapter shows that an important bundle of the issue positions, now absorbed into the party system, existed in the mass public prior to the parties taking positions on those issues and persist among people who pay little attention to politics. These data push back against a prominent explanation of parties arguing that party platforms are first bargained by political elites and then the cluster of issue positions are passed down to voters. The persistence of these issue bundles over time and levels of political knowledge (and as chapter 8 shows, across countries as well) are much more consistent with literature on opinion formation that point to pre-political sources for attitude formation that are then adopted by the parties.

A skeptical reader may wonder whether the issue bundles, even if they precede elite conflict, are large enough that politicians would heed them. An existing literature on public opinion points to weak correlations between various issue attitudes as evidence that the public cannot exert pressure on the party system (Converse [1964] 2006; Kinder and Kalmoe 2017). However, even small correlations represent substantive divides. In 1972, the difference between racial liberals and racial conservatives on other policy positions[14] ranged from 9 percentage points to 35 percentage points with an average difference of 21 percentage points. Among those who lack knowledge of either party's positions, this difference ranges from 8 to 25 percentage points with an average difference of 17 percentage points. In elections decided by a few percentage points, or voter persuasion efforts focused on a fraction of a percent, even 8 percentage points represents a substantial divide. Furthermore, these cleavages are sizable by social science standards. Phillip Converse has remarked: "Survey researchers are often forced to 'prove' arguments with 5–8% differences and are thrilled to work with 20% differences" (2000, 345).

More importantly, qualitative accounts of politician decision-making typically characterize politicians as risk averse, and even small differences between groups of voters motivate policy positions on visible issues (Arnold 1992; Kingdon 1989; Key 1961). Furthermore, politicians often act based on how the public would respond should the issue become salient or opinion should solidify (Arnold 1992; Zaller 2012). In other words, issue linkages do not need to be massive and voters do not need to carefully monitor the actions of public officials for public opinion to exert pressure on the party system.

CHAPTER FOUR

Cross-Pressured Voters

Chapter 3 shows that racially liberal voters have long held liberal positions on effectively every other major policy issue. However, this is not a one-to-one relationship. A sizable number of voters held cross-pressured views: they expressed conservative positions on one issue and liberal positions on another. What happens to these cross-pressured voters?

In his classic essay, Phillip Converse ([1964] 2006, 4) argues that different idea elements vary in their centrality to a belief system, and when two elements are in conflict, people change the less central issue. Scholarship addresses this question primarily with respect to issues and party. When voters realize their party identification and issue preferences are incongruent, do voters change their party or change their policy position? Less research explores what happens when two issue attitudes are in "conflict" with one another. If a voter holds liberal abortion positions and conservative racial positions, do voters update their abortion views to align with their racial views or vice versa?

This chapter explores these cross-pressured voters in the 1970s as the parties began to polarize. Using panel data from the 1970s, I show that voters consistently update their views on nonracial attitudes to align with their preexisting racial attitudes, but do not consistently shift racial attitudes to align with other views. This finding is robust across issue attitudes in this era and persists even after controlling for a host of alternative explanations.

I argue that racial predispositions created pressure for voters to align their attitudes across disparate issues (in this era) for two primary reasons. First, many policies such as crime and economic redistribution, if not explicitly, are implicitly about race (e.g., Gilens 1996; Mendelberg

2001). Voters who perceive or learn that ostensibly nonracialized policies have an underlying racial element, bring their views on these policies in line with their racial views. Underlying this mechanism is that attitudes toward racial equality are a core predisposition: they are a durable value that structure the types of information that people accept or reject (Zaller 1992, 23–24). Just as racial predispositions might affect how one evaluates apolitical outcomes (e.g., whether to hire someone; stereotyping), associating a policy with a racial group creates similar pressure. Second, race had been reshaping what it meant to be liberal or conservative well before partisan allegiances shifted. While some issues are not racialized, conflict over racial equality represented a core division between liberal and conservative by the 1960s (e.g., Carmines and Stimson 1982). I argue that as a consequence, people sympathetic (or opposed) to the civil rights movement updated their attitudes on issues of women's rights, for example, because they became viewed to be on the same side of the ideological divide.

These findings contextualize a principal argument of this book: race is central to understanding contemporary party sorting in this time period. If voters moved their racial attitudes to align with their views on tax policy or abortion attitudes, one might wonder whether abortion or tax policy, not race, is central to contemporary polarization.

These findings also emphasize that race, not partisanship, was the primary lens through which people organized their beliefs in the years following the 1960s racial realignment. While political behavior generally views party identification as the "unmoved mover" and the lens through which people evaluate other political objects (e.g., Campbell et al. 1960), partisanship in the 1960s and 1970s was at a low point because the electorate was realigning along the racial axis. Indeed, after accounting for racial views, partisanship lacks or has secondary predictive power for understanding how people change their attitudes in this era.

This chapter is organized as follows: First, I explain why racial views serve as a core predisposition that shapes and organizes how voters view the political world and why voters might update their nonracial views to align with their racial views. Second, I present empirical evidence that voters in this era consistently updated their nonracial attitudes to match their prior racial attitudes, but did not consistently do so in reverse. Third, I explore five potential mechanisms for *why* voters sort along the racial axis. In addition to isolating why this sorting occurred (discussed above), the analysis rules out several prominent explanations associated with party sorting: partisanship, religiosity, and urban-rural divides.

Theory: Why Sort by Racial Attitudes?

This chapter asks a simple question: When people's racial attitudes are out of step with their other policy views (e.g., a racial liberal but abortion conservative), how, if at all, do they reconcile these differences? Why might there be pressure to align views, and why does race serve as the organizing force?

Attitudes toward racial equality are a core predisposition: they are a long-lasting value that structures the types of information that people accept or reject (Zaller 1992, 23–24). First, public opinion between black and white respondents on race-targeted policies has historically been polarized (Hutchings and Valentino 2004, 389). Second, unlike more abstract policies, scholars characterize race as an "easy issue" about which people are easily able to form and then express an opinion (e.g., Carmines and Stimson 1989). Third, while the mass public expresses unstable preferences on many issues over time, racial attitudes, like party identification, are durable (Converse [1964] 2006; Freeder, Lenz, and Turney 2019; Kinder and Kalmoe 2017). Fourth, racial prejudice is socialized at an early age, and even if opinion on specific policies change, anti-black or pro-black affect is stable (Kinder and Sears 1981). In short, racial attitudes are stable, widely held, deeply felt, and often learned from an early age.

Consequently, I argue that racial prejudice is a psychological attachment, like party identification or ideological identification, that shapes views of the political world and pushes voters to align their attitudes on other issues to match the group norm (Campbell et al. 1960; Jacoby 1991, 180; Conover and Feldman 1981). For issues that are implicitly seen as racial, such as crime and welfare, voters may bring their attitudes on these issues into line with their views on race because they perceive what racial groups support or benefit from certain policies. Elder and O'Brian (2022) show that while many voters in the 1970s did not know where the parties or ideological groups stood on issues, they did know what policies racial groups preferred (e.g., black people are more likely than white people to support economic redistribution). Those who place African Americans to the left of whites on economic issues, for example, aligned their views on economic issues to match their racial predispositions. However, there is no correlation between economic views and racial predispositions among those who do not know where racial groups stand on economic issues. Consequently, and in the context of this chapter, "learning" which side of an issue a group stands, may lead voters to align their economic and racial attitudes. This closely corresponds with experimental evidence which shows that telling people policies are implicitly racial shifts those attitudes (e.g., Gilens 1996; Mendelberg 2001).

On other issues, racial attitudes proxy broader ideological identification. While some issues do not cleave on black-white lines, they divide along lines of those who are fighting and opposing racial equality. Race redefined what it meant to be a liberal or conservative (Carmines and Stimson 1982; Sears and Funk 1999). As people began to identify as liberal because of issues beyond economic regulation, this created new attachments to broader labels of liberalism and conservatism. Thus, racial predispositions were a core benchmark for a broader group belonging. This does not require that voters understand what it means to be liberal or conservative, but that they recognize a salient cultural divide—such as the fight for racial equality—and update their attitudes accordingly on issues that are in a similar bundle.

An important element of this theory is political context. First, for racial attitudes to serve as a group identity, racial conflict needs to be salient (e.g., Conover 1984). This varies both across time and between communities. In the 1960s and 1970s, fights over race were particularly salient across the political spectrum and represented a core political cleavage. Not only was race salient, but party identification was historically weak in this period. Throughout the 1970s, the number of voters identifying as Independents swelled, and split-ticket voting spiked among white voters (e.g., Converse 1976; Aldrich 2011, 262). Still further, the parties lacked clear positions on now-salient issues such as abortion, pollution, women's rights, and gun control. Given the weakness of parties in the electorate, and the salience of race, this created an environment ripe for racial predispositions to be the driving force.

This aligns with Engelhardt (2021), who finds a shifting effect of racial attitudes on other policy positions over time. In the 1990s, when the parties in the electorate were relatively weak (compared to the 2010s), racial views affected party identification, and sometimes party identification affected respondents' racial views. Once party polarization hardened partisanship in the electorate, party drove racial attitudes, but the reverse did not occur.

Data

To explore what happens to people who hold "conflicting" policy views, I use data primarily from the 1972–76 panel portion of the American National Election Studies. I focus on the 1970s because I am interested in what drove the connections observed in chapter 3. That is, how did voters behave *before* issues like abortion or the environment had become crystallized in the party system. Studying the 1970s differs from studying the 2010s, for example, when attitudes toward abortion or gun control had been cemented into the electorate by a generation of voters socialized into the post-1970s party system (e.g., Carmines and Stimson 1989; Stoker and Jennings 2008).

To understand change over time, I analyze respondent attitudes in both 1972 and 1976 using a cross-lagged dependent-variable model expressed by the following form:

(4.1) $\text{Marijuana}_{1976} = \alpha_1 + \beta_1 \text{Aidblack}_{1972} + \gamma_1 \text{Marijuana}_{1972}$

(4.2) $\text{Aidblack}_{1976} = \alpha_2 + \beta_2 \text{Marijuana}_{1972} + \gamma_2 \text{Aidblack}_{1972}$

Unlike cross-sectional data, this model helps understand whether racial views shape other policy views, if the reverse is true, or if the relationship is reciprocal. In equation 4.1, β_1 shows whether attitudes regarding aid to minorities in 1972 can explain marijuana attitudes in 1976, holding 1972 marijuana attitudes constant. Algebraically, this is equivalent to the change in marijuana attitudes between 1972 and 1976, holding 1972 marijuana attitudes constant. In equation 4.2, β_2 shows the reverse: Can changes in attitudes on aid to minorities be attributed to prior attitudes on marijuana?

I repeat these models for each policy question asked on both the 1972 and 1976 ANES. If race is the more central element, respondents should change their attitudes on marijuana to match their racial attitudes (equation 4.1), but not change their racial attitudes to match their prior attitudes toward marijuana (equation 4.2). These tests examine whether voters are sorting along this racial axis, much like other studies ask whether voters sort based on party.[1]

Lagged dependent-variable models show how variables respond to each other between given points in time, but it is also theoretically and substantively important to consider how given attitudes were formed before time

1 (in this case, 1972). A core theoretical point is that racial attitudes form at an early age and are "pre-political" in ways that other attitudes, such as economic redistribution or marijuana use, are not.

Empirical Evidence

Figure 4.1 presents the coefficients from the cross-lagged dependent-variable models outlined in the previous section. For this analysis, I recode all variables on a 0 (the most liberal) to 1 (the most conservative) scale. The black points represent change between 1972 and 1976 with respect to racial attitudes. That is, do racial attitudes in 1972 predict change in nonracial attitudes between 1972 and 1976? The answer is consistently yes. The positive coefficients mean that voters are aligning their nonracial views with their 1972 racial attitudes. For example, the first black dot on the bottom of figure 4.1 shows that between 1972 and 1976, the most racially conservative voters move approximately 0.12 points (on a 0–1 scale) to the right on the rights of the accused when compared to racial liberals. To illustrate the magnitude of this shift, consider the marginal effect of a racial liberal and racial conservative who in 1972 have identical attitudes toward the rights of the accused. By 1976, the racial conservative had moved a full scale point to the right of the racial liberal on their attitudes toward rights of the accused (most of the ANES questions in 1972 were asked on a 1–7 scale that I have recoded to range from 0 to 1. A movement of one point on a seven-point scale is 0.14 on the 0–1 scale).

To test for a reciprocal relationship, I repeat the process but use the "aid to minorities" question as the dependent variable. That is, do people update their racial attitudes between 1972 and 1976 to match their prior views on other nonracial attitudes? The gray dots in figure 4.1 show that this happens less consistently, and when it does, it is of a lesser magnitude. Only on the rights of the accused, government-provided health insurance, and government guarantee of jobs does the relationship work in the opposite direction (at the conventional level of statistical significance).

The fact that voters update other attitudes to match their prior racial attitudes, but do not do so in reverse, suggests that racial attitudes are the more central predisposition when pitting race against other issues. But are voters sorting with respect to other issues, too? For example, fights over abortion rights gained increasing political salience in the 1960s and 1970s and remain a core feature of the culture wars today. Perhaps voters update

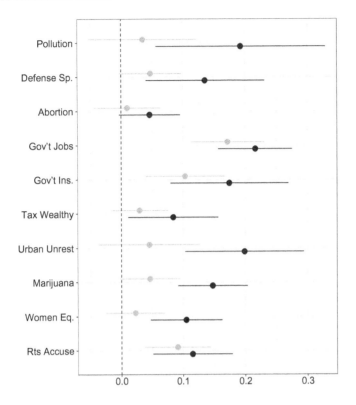

Pollution
Defense Sp.
Abortion
Gov't Jobs
Gov't Ins.
Tax Wealthy
Urban Unrest
Marijuana
Women Eq.
Rts Accuse

0.0   0.1   0.2   0.3

○ Nonracial Attitudes Predict Change in Racial Attitudes
● Racial Attitudes Predict Change in Nonracial Attitudes

FIGURE 4.1. Attitude Change over Time, Aid to Minorities. Black points represent results from models of the following form: $\text{Marijuana}_{1976} = \alpha_1 + \beta_1 \times \text{Aidblack}_{1972} + \gamma_1 \times \text{Marijuana}_{1972}$. That is, are people updating their attitudes on marijuana, for example, to match their racial attitudes? Gray points are results from models of the following form: $\text{Aidblack}_{1976} = \alpha_2 + \beta_2 \times \text{Marijuana}_{1972} + \gamma_1 \times \text{Aidblack}_{1972}$. Lines represent 95% confidence intervals.

their views on other policy issues to align with their preexisting abortion attitudes. I repeat the same process as before, but this time using attitudes on abortion and tax policy: two central issues to contemporary politics. Do voters update their policy views to align with their prior views on abortion or tax policy? Figure 4.2 presents evidence that voters do not. On the issue of taxation, a central theme in US politics, voters do not bring their other policy views into line with their views on taxation. The only issue with some sorting was the question of whether the government should provide jobs and a good standard of living, a closely related issue.

On abortion, voters do not consistently update their non-abortion views to align with their prior views on abortion, either. The strongest sorting occurs on the issue of equality for women, a closely linked issue. The only two other issues with some sorting appear to be marijuana legalization and pollution control. Even though people had stable abortion attitudes by the 1970s, this evidence suggests that abortion did not hold as central a position in people's political belief systems in the 1970s.

Mechanisms

The previous section established that voters align their attitudes on non-racial policies with their prior racial attitudes. Why does this happen? This section explores two possible explanations—group-based policy learning and ideology—while the next section explores three alternate explanations: partisanship identification, religiosity, and urbanicity. While effects differ across issue areas, I argue that this sorting primarily works through (1) voters learning that certain policies benefit or are supported by different

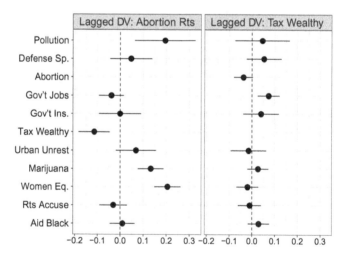

FIGURE 4.2. Attitude Change over Time, Abortion and Tax Wealthy. These figures repeat the process in figure 4.1, this time with lagged abortion attitudes (left panel) and lagged tax attitudes (right panel) as the predictive variable of interest: $Y_{1976} = \alpha_1 + \beta_1 \times \text{Abortion}_{1972} + \gamma_1 \times Y_{1972}$. People do not consistently update their views to match their prior views on abortion or tax policy. Lines represent 95% confidence intervals.

racial groups and (2) an ideological identification that has been shaped by racial views.

Group-Based Policy Learning

One explanation for sorting along the racial dimension is that people are learning that ostensibly nonracial policies are, in fact, quite racial. Political efforts of the 1960s and 1970s used "dog-whistles" that crime, drugs, and economic welfare programs are racial (e.g., Mendelberg 2001; Hillygus and Shields 2009). As racial conservatives (liberals) learn that policies have become associated with a racial out-group (in-group), this might affect their perceptions of the policy.[2]

To test this, I use a series of questions asked by the American National Election Study in the 1970s. The ANES asked where voters thought "most whites" and "most blacks" stood on certain policy issues. For example, in addition to asking respondents where they place themselves on a policy scale (e.g., government guarantee of jobs from 1 to 7), the ANES also asked where respondents believe most white/black people fall on the scale (on a select number of questions, see figure 4.3). On each policy view, voters (correctly) perceived black people to hold more liberal views than white people (Elder and O'Brian 2022).

I split the sample between voters who perceive that "most blacks" are more supportive of the various policies when compared to "most whites" and people who do not perceive this difference. If people perceive that certain economic policies benefit or are supported by African Americans, those voters might reasonably change their attitudes on economic policies to align with their racial attitudes. If people do not know that certain policies benefit or are supported by various racial groups, they should not update their attitudes.

I repeat the same lagged dependent-variable model as before ($\text{Jobs}_{1976} = \alpha_1 + \beta_1\text{Aidblack}_{1972} + \gamma_1\text{Jobs}_{1972}$), where I am interested (to use an example) if people are bringing their attitudes on government guarantee of jobs into line with their prior attitudes on aid to minorities. However, I compare those who have linked government guarantee of jobs with racial minorities with those who have not. The black points in the left panel of figure 4.3 shows that among those who perceive differences between racial groups, voters are bringing their attitudes on secondary policy questions into line with their attitudes on aid to minorities. Among those who perceive no difference between racial groups—graphed by the gray points

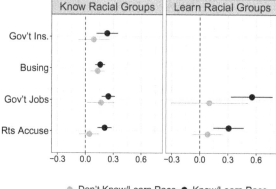

FIGURE 4.3. Sorting by Knowledge of Racial Groups. The left-hand panel is the lagged dependent-variable model of the following form: $Jobs_{1976} = \alpha_1 + \beta_1 \times Aidblack_{1972} + \gamma_1 \times Jobs_{1972}$. A positive value means people are aligning their nonracial view between 1972 and 1976 with their 1972 racial view. In the left-hand panel, I subset respondents to those who know (black points)/don't know (gray points) that African Americans are more liberal than white people on each issue listed down the left-hand column. In the right-hand panel, I subset responses to those who do not know that the policies are associated with racial groups in 1972, but learn they are in 1976 (black points) and those that that do not learn of this association by 1976 (gray points). Racial group positions are asked on only two issues, rights of the criminally accused and government guarantee of jobs, in both years.

in the left-hand panel—voters change their attitudes to a lesser degree or not at all.

In this case, when voters know where racial groups stand on issues, they bring their attitudes in line with their broader racial predispositions. What about those respondents who did not know policies were racialized in 1972, but learn they are racialized in 1976? This process occurred on many issues throughout the mid- to late twentieth century. For example, the white South advocated for the income tax in the early twentieth century and supported key tenets of the New Deal. It was not until economic policies became perceived as going to minorities that the white South moved to the right (Kuziemko and Washington 2018).

Unfortunately, the availability of data limits the issues that can be examined. Voters are asked about their racial knowledge only on the question of rights of the accused and government-provided jobs in both 1972 and 1976. I subset respondents who did not know the racial group positions in 1972 but learned them by 1976. That is, people who learned about linkages between policies and racial groups between survey waves might adjust their attitudes on the given policy to match their prior racial views. The right-hand panel of figure 4.3 shows clear results: learning racial group positions induces sorting by racial attitudes. The black points show that those who learned between 1972 and 1976 that black people are more supportive of white people on questions of rights of the accused and government-provided jobs brought their attitudes on these two issues into line with their previous attitudes on government aid to minorities. The gray points show that those who did not learn where racial groups stood on issues did not update their attitudes.

Ideology

While some issues are racialized (e.g., economic redistribution, rights of the accused), other issues are not or are less explicitly so. For example, women's rights, abortion policy, and the environment were not heavily racialized issues in 1970s political discourse. Why might voters update their abortion views to align with their racial views? One explanation is that African Americans as a group became increasingly aligned with liberalism after the New Deal. While parties in the 1970s were at a low point, ideological identification had already begun to align with the now-familiar left-right pattern on race and other social issues.

Sorting along the racial axis may be tied up with the fact that by the 1970s people who favored civil rights saw the civil rights movement as part of a broader liberal coalition. If racial views feed into changing ideological identification in the years prior to the 1970s (Sears and Funk 1999; Carmines and Stimson 1982), ideological identification and racial views may be picking up the same underlying construct that pushes people to update their nonracial views to align with their racial views.[3]

While the availability of data limits investigation into the extent that racial liberalism drives ideological identification, the 1970s panel data offer suggestive evidence. In 1972, more than half of respondents rated themselves as moderate, or that they had not thought much about their ideological identification. Yet by 1976, some of these respondents *did* call themselves liberal or conservative. What underlying attitudes predict eventual liberal or conservative self-placement? To investigate this, I subset respondents who reported that they "haven't thought much about" whether they were liberal or conservative in 1972, but then did place themselves on the left-right scale in 1976. I then regress 1976 ideological placement on 1972 policy attitudes. Figure 4.4 plots the coefficients from this test. Higher

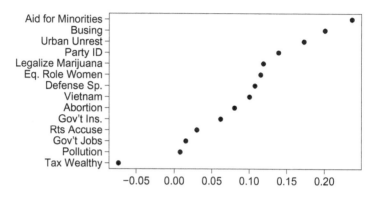

FIGURE 4.4. Predictors of Ideological Self-Placement. Each coefficient predicts how well the given issue attitude in 1972 predicts ideological self-placement in 1976. Results are restricted to respondents who indicate "they haven't thought much about" their ideological self-placement.

values mean that being conservative on the issue listed down the y-axis in 1972 predicts respondents identifying as a conservative on a liberal-conservative identification scale in 1976. Of the various issues asked in 1972, racial attitudes (aid for minorities and busing) best predict ideological self-placement four years later.

To place this in perspective, each variable ranges from 0 to 1 (a recode from the original 1–7 scale). Thus, moving 1 point on the seven-point scale is about 0.14 on the recoded 0–1 scale. The top point on the graph—associated with aid to minorities—has a coefficient of 0.24. This means that going from the most liberal to conservative on the aid to minorities scale in 1972 predicts that someone will be about 1.7 points more conservative on a liberal-conservative self-identification scale in 1976. This is a substantive divide: for example, during the 1972 presidential election, which many consider a polarizing election, the difference between Nixon and McGovern voters was about 1.3 points on the ideological self-placement scale.

If racial liberalism drives people to identify as liberal and advocating for women's rights, abortion access, or the environment is part of the liberal coalition, then sorting along this racial axis may be tied up with a broader ideological self-identification. Furthermore, ideological identification, like party, serves as a psychological attachment through which people filter outside political knowledge (Jacoby 1991, 180).

To test the effect of ideology for sorting along the racial axis, I run the same lagged dependent-variable models as above, but control for ideological self-placement in 1972. Table 4.1 shows that controlling for ideology

TABLE 4.1. Controlling for Ideology, 1972 and 1976

	(1) Accuse '76	(2) Women '76	(3) Marijuana '76	(4) Unrest '76	(5) Tax '76	(6) Ins '76	(7) Jobs '76	(8) Abortion '76	(9) Defense '76	(10) Pollution '76
Aid Black '72	0.110***	0.058*	0.115***	0.133**	0.093**	0.167***	0.189***	0.020	0.127**	0.108
	(0.038)	(0.034)	(0.034)	(0.056)	(0.043)	(0.054)	(0.034)	(0.031)	(0.059)	(0.084)
Ideology '72	−0.070	0.171***	0.156***	0.159**	0.054	0.260***	0.170***	0.101**	0.196**	0.235**
	(0.053)	(0.049)	(0.051)	(0.076)	(0.061)	(0.079)	(0.046)	(0.045)	(0.085)	(0.119)
Lagged DV	0.423***	0.462***	0.530***	0.265***	0.298***	0.407***	0.330***	0.654***	0.265***	0.271***
	(0.033)	(0.028)	(0.028)	(0.048)	(0.033)	(0.042)	(0.032)	(0.028)	(0.036)	(0.083)
Constant	0.315***	0.051*	0.139***	0.159***	0.313***	0.093**	0.231***	0.109***	0.476***	0.122*
	(0.029)	(0.026)	(0.027)	(0.038)	(0.035)	(0.044)	(0.026)	(0.026)	(0.048)	(0.063)
N	832	834	791	375	775	383	811	831	459	403

Note: Standard errors in parentheses. Asterisks represent statistical significance at the 0.01 (***), 0.05 (**), and 0.1 (*) levels.

mediates the relationship between racial attitudes and changing attitudes on other policies and is itself predictive of changing attitudes. People who identify as conservative become more conservative on most policy issues between 1972 and 1976.

Alternative Explanations

The previous set of analyses explored two mechanisms that drive sorting along the racial axis. The following sections explore three alternative mechanisms that do not consistently drive the effect in this time period: partisan identification, religiosity, and urbanicity.

Partisan Identification

A large literature in political behavior research argues that party identification is the "unmoved mover" and lens through which people evaluate other political objects (e.g., Campbell et al. 1960). Consequently, party identification may drive sorting along the racial axis. As new issues gain salience, voters bring their policy views into line with their party, and racial views are a proxy measure for party.

To examine whether the observed effect is reducible to party, I use the same lagged dependent-variable model used in the sections above, but this time control for 1972 partisan identification. If partisan identification explains sorting, the predictive power of the racial axis should dissipate. Alternatively, if the racial axis is dominant, racial views should continue to predict sorting. The left-most panel of figure 4.5 shows the results of the lagged dependent-variable model. On only three of ten issues does prior party identification (represented by the gray points) predict over-time change in nonracial attitudes at the conventional level of statistical significance (lines represent 95% confidence intervals).That is, voters do not update their beliefs to bring them in line with their party. However, the black points show that voters are consistently aligning their nonracial views to match their prior racial attitudes, *even after controlling for party identification.*

These findings underscore a core thesis of this book: Race, not partisanship, was the core predisposition through which people viewed the political world in this era. Why? Partisanship in this era was weak; the number of voters identifying as Independents swelled, and split-ticket voting

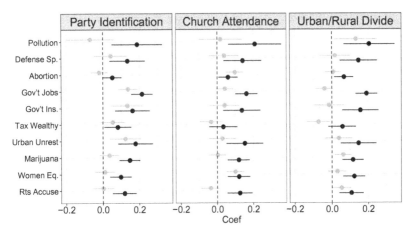

FIGURE 4.5. Alternative Explanations. Each of the above panels uses the lagged dependent-variable model outlined earlier in the chapter, controlling for 1972 partisan identification (left panel), frequency of 1972 church attendance (middle panel), and the urbanicity of the respondent's 1972 place of living (right panel). The model takes the general form: $Jobs_{1976} = \alpha_1 + \beta_1 \times Aidblack_{1972} + \beta_2 \times PID_{1972} + \gamma_1 \times Jobs_{1972}$. For the urban/rural divide, I also control for the respondent's race. The black points represent the regression coefficient for the respondent's 1972 attitudes toward racial minorities; the gray points represent the regression coefficient for 1972 partisan identification, church attendance, and urbanicity, respectively. Lines represent 95% confidence intervals.

spiked among white people (e.g., Converse 1976; Aldrich 2011, 262). Consequently, partisan identification—the very lens through which political science believes voters so often interpret the political world—is weakened (Aldrich 2011, 263). Alternatively, civil rights, which played a large role in declining partisanship, was strengthened.

Religiosity

Religion presents another alternative explanation for sorting along the racial axis. It could be that culturally conservative voters are updating their attitudes because of religious predispositions. The alignment of party, policy positions, and religiosity coincides with the racial realignment and emerging culture wars (e.g., Layman 2001; Hunter 1991; Mason 2018). The contemporary intersection of religiosity and contemporary politics, scholars have argued, is not about traditional fights between Catholics and Protestants, for example, but rooted between the poles of religious orthodoxy on one side and religious progressivism on the other (Hunter 1991). The Religious Right, for example, is an ecumenical alliance of conservative Catholics, Protestants, and Jewish people with a worldview distinct from liberal Catholics, Protestants, or Jewish people. These worldviews, Hunter (1991) argues, predate and shape views on cultural issues such as abortion or affirmative action. Not only do these religious divides represent an important schism, but scholars also argue that religious actors shape the laity's opinion on relevant cultural dimensions (Layman 2001).

Unfortunately, in the 1970s panel, the ANES does not ask respondents whether they view themselves as Orthodox, conservative, liberal (and so on). Consequently, I use the frequency of church attendance in 1972 as a proxy for the religious divide. Although a different aspect of religiosity, the cultural sorting between those who attend church and those who do not is a visible cleavage that divides Republicans and Democrats (Layman 1997; Margolis 2017).

The middle panel of figure 4.5 uses the same lagged dependent-variable model as before, but controls for church attendance. The gray points are the regression coefficient measuring frequency of 1972 church attendance, and the black points are the regression coefficients measuring 1972 racial attitudes. Figure 4.5 shows that the electorate is not sorting along this religious divide in the early 1970s, except for on issues of abortion and women's equality. That is, people who attend church more regularly are becoming more conservative on women's equality and abortion rights than people who do not regularly attend church. However, it does not appear that religiosity supplants racial views; they reinforce one another.

Urbanicity

Another set of explanations suggests that the urban-rural divide drives polarization (e.g., Cramer 2012; Rodden 2019). The geographic divide represents a long-standing schism in US politics. Consequently, initial issue cleavages that fall along urban and rural lines may polarize the political environment.

The right-most panel of figure 4.5 repeats the lagged dependent-variable model, controlling for urbanicity in 1972 (represented by the gray points). Urbanicity has an inconsistent relationship to shifting attitudes across policy dimensions and does not attenuate the effect of racial attitudes.

Empirical and theoretical evidence contextualize this null finding. For example, Cramer (2012) argues that rural resentment generates economi-

cally conservative attitudes in rural areas. Cramer's theory of rural resentment relies not simply on rural-ness, but a group consciousness around
living in a rural place, which then in turn influences political attitudes.
Perceived class and racial differences between urban and rural areas are
two mechanisms that activate this consciousness. From this perspective,
racial resentment (or class resentment) is necessary to activate this regional
divide.

Likewise, in a longitudinal study of internal migration in Switzerland,
Maxwell (2019) finds that sorting largely drives the urban-rural divide:
people who are already more liberal are more likely to migrate from rural to urban areas. If this partially explains trends in the United States, it
would contextualize why geographic location is not predictive of changing
political views.

Conclusion

This chapter shows that racial attitudes serve as a central political predisposition around which people organized their attitudes in the 1970s. I find
that racial conservatives are more likely to become conservative on other
political issues over time, but that the effect does not consistently work in
reverse. However, these findings are constrained to political context. In the
1960s and 1970s, political parties were weak, and civil rights was a salient
force realigning the electorate. Once partisanship crystallized, it became
the driving force for other issue attitudes (e.g., Engelhardt 2021; Elder
and O'Brian 2022). These findings also highlight the limitations of elite
leadership. Leaders cannot simply change opinions on any set of issues,
but are limited to frames and linkages that already exist in the mass public
and, even then, have less flexibility in changing some attitudes rather than
others.

CHAPTER FIVE

Vote Choice and Shifting Coalitions

Civil rights, which had long internally divided the Democratic Party, broke the New Deal coalition in the 1960s. The racial liberalism of the national Democratic Party drove white southern Democrats and conservative blue-collar Catholics in the Northeast away from the party they had, in some cases, identified with for generations. Conservative Democrats defected to Barry Goldwater in 1964, and then many of the same voters supported George Wallace's third-party candidacy in 1968.

In the lead-up to the 1972 election, Nixon's team focused on ways to win over white southerners, blue-collar Catholics, and other conservative Democrats who had shown a willingness to break from their party. However, because blue-collar Catholics, like white southern Protestants, had been heavily Democratic constituencies, many of these voters found themselves cross-pressured in the 1960s. They did not like the racial liberalism of the Democratic Party, but they also grew up disdaining Republicans and were not attracted by the economic message of the GOP. Charles Colson, director of the White House Office of Public Liaison, wrote to President Nixon of this dilemma: "Ideologically [alienated Democrats are] pulled towards us on the law and order issue and away from us on the economic issue" (Colson 1970). The Nixon campaign needed non-economic messages to reinforce the GOP's appeal to these voters. And as Nixon aide Pat Buchanan explained, they could not appeal on only one issue. Outreach should be "multi-faceted; it has to be" (Buchanan 1971).

And as has been detailed in the previous chapters, Nixon and other Republicans deployed a multipronged appeal to racially conservative members of the Democrats' New Deal coalition. This chapter provides context for why Nixon and other Republicans pursued Goldwater and Wallace Democrats using conservative messaging on abortion and other social issues: people who defected from the Democratic to the Republican Party in 1964—or voted for Wallace in 1968—on account of civil rights, were already *very* conservative on abortion, gun control, and gay rights. This is crucial for understanding the appeals made by Republicans in the 1970s: when Nixon, Reagan, and, perhaps to a lesser degree, Ford sought to win over Goldwater and Wallace Democrats—which was the key Republican strategy of the 1970s—they deployed issue appeals that spoke to these voters' preexisting sentiments.

This has important implications for understanding partisan sorting as bottom-up rather than top-down. If Goldwater Democrats already had conservative preferences on these issues, and politicians in the following elections were responding to preexisting preferences, partisan sorting would be understood as an issue that starts with voters and works its way up to politicians. Rather, if Goldwater and Wallace Democrats looked like everyone else on culture war issues, and later became more conservative because of elite appeals on these issues, then partisan sorting would be better understood as driven by politicians or other political elites.

The purpose of this chapter is to show that Democrats who abandoned the party in 1964 and 1968 because of civil rights brought their conserva- tive positions on other issues with them, even without campaigns making appeals on these issues. To do this, the first two sections focus on the issue preferences of split-ticket voters (i.e., people who vote for the Democrat in one race but Republican in another) in the South in the 1960s. I specifically focus on split-ticket voters who supported racially conservative Democrats in one race but defected to the Republicans when a racial liberal was on the ticket. The third section focuses on the issue preferences of Wallace voters in 1968.

Subnational Elections in the US South

This section explores state and substate-level elections in the South where a year's general elections feature one contest where the candidates have sorted on civil rights and one contest where candidates overlap on civil rights. That is, finding elections where voters may split their ticket be- cause there is a segregationist Democrat in one race and a racially liberal- moderate Democrat in another race. I expect that the election with candi- dates who have polarized on race also develop voter coalitions that have polarized on other nonracial dimensions like abortion, guns, and school prayer, *even without those candidates having taken explicit positions on those issues.*

Case Study: 1964 Split-Ticket Voters

The first test focuses on white southern voters in the 1964 election. In congressional races, many southern districts had a segregationist Democrat running for Congress (91% of southern Democrats in Congress opposed the 1964 Civil Rights Act). However, in the presidential race, for the first time, voters had a Democratic presidential candidate who embraced civil rights (Lyndon Johnson) and a Republican presidential candidate who opposed civil rights (Barry Goldwater). Some white southern voters, despite voting for the Democratic member of Congress, turned to Goldwater because they did not support Johnson's pro–civil rights stance.

While a detailed treatment of split-ticket voting extends beyond the purpose of this chapter, civil rights drove the white South's abandonment of John F. Kennedy, and then Johnson, for Goldwater in 1964 (Kuziemko and Washington 2018). Recall that in 1960, like the several elections prior, the major presidential candidates differed little on civil rights; Kennedy, in an effort to placate the southern wing, initially endorsed only modest civil rights legislation. This changed in the spring of 1963 when Kennedy gave a nationally televised speech and threw support behind an aggressive civil rights bill. As discussed in chapter 2, this caused a seismic shift in vote choice (a swing of 50 percentage points) from Kennedy to Goldwater in the white South.

While Kennedy was assassinated just months after he endorsed civil rights, the perception that Democrats had embraced civil rights stuck.[1] Johnson quickly picked up Kennedy's push for civil rights: in an address to Congress on November 27, 1963 (days after the JFK assassination), Johnson declared that he would pursue Kennedy's civil rights legislation. The next day, the front page of the *New York Times* read, "Johnson bids Congress enact civil rights bill with speed; asks end of hate and violence."[2] The candidates' messaging on civil rights influenced public perceptions of the parties' positions on the issue. During the 1960 election, voters saw no difference between the parties on the question of school integration. In fact, white southerners still perceived Republicans as a touch more liberal on racial integration in 1960. By the 1964 election, Southerners were about 25 percentage points more likely to perceive Democrats as favoring racial integration; a swing of over 30 percentage points (Kuziemko and Washington 2018, 2839).

While civil rights drove a bloc of white southerners to vote for Goldwater, it was also the leading policy issue that gave congressional Democrats
nearly complete control over the US South through the mid-twentieth
century (Key 1949). Out of the 105 congressional seats in the South in
1964, Democrats opposed to civil rights were on the ballot in 84. Seventeen
districts had a congressional Democrat who favored civil rights, and the
remaining four either lacked a record or their position was not discernible.
Thus, opposition to civil rights motivated many white southerners to support
a Democrat in congressional races, where old Democratic incumbents continued to dominate, but to defect to Goldwater in the presidential election.

These split-ticket voters, unsurprisingly, are quite conservative on race. I
want to investigate whether those who voted for a Democrat for Congress
but supported the Republican Goldwater for president also held different
views on nonracial culture war issues. There are two culture war policy questions available on surveys with both 1964 presidential and congressional
vote choice. First, a 1965 survey asks whether abortion should be legal under
different circumstances.[3] Another survey, in December 1963, asked respondents whether they "favor or oppose a law which would require a person
to obtain a police permit before he or she could buy a gun" (Gallup #681).
(By December 1963, Johnson had openly embraced the Civil Rights Act.)

Recall that abortion and gun control were not campaign issues nor were
they part of the national conversation in the manner they are today (see
chapter 1). In a search of digitized southern newspapers in the five states
that Goldwater won in the South, not a single paper links abortion or gun
control to the political stances of congressional or presidential candidates.
And in a search of the New York Times, in the month before and after the
1964 election, there were no mentions of gun control or abortion linked
to positions to either party (or presidential candidate). While difficult to
imagine in today's era, where these issues feature so prominently in political discourse, they were largely absent from the political arena in 1964.
Gun control briefly emerged after the Kennedy assassination, which is
likely why Gallup asked about it, but the issue crosscut partisan lines. And
while an abortion case caught public interest in 1962, it, too, crosscut partisan lines and remained, compared to even a decade later, largely out of
the political realm.

Figure 5.1 compares the attitudes of white southern split-ticket and
straight-ticket voters. To measure presidential vote choice, I use answers
to a question about who the respondent will/did vote for president in 1964:
Lyndon Johnson (Democrat) or Barry Goldwater (Republican). While

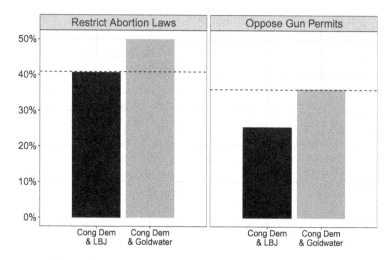

FIGURE 5.1. Ticket-Splitting, Southern Whites, 1964. Graph shows abortion and gun control attitudes among southern whites who voted for the congressional Democrat and Democratic presidential candidate Lyndon Johnson (black) and those who voted for the congressional Democrat and Republican presidential candidate Barry Goldwater (gray). Dashed line represents the average attitude among all southern Goldwater voters.

Gallup did not ask about specific candidates in a given congressional race, they did ask, "Which party would you like to see win this congressional district?" Because of the overwhelming opposition to civil rights among southern congressional Democrats in 1964, the generic ballot roughly captures Democratic positioning on civil rights in congressional races. This enables a comparison of voters who supported an anti–civil rights congressional Democrat, but defected to Goldwater in the presidential election, with those who supported Democrats in both the congressional and presidential election.

The gray bar in figure 5.1 shows the white southerners who voted for the congressional Democrat but defected to Goldwater (these are the split-ticket voters). The black bar shows those who supported the congressional Democrat and then also voted for Johnson (these are the straight-ticket voters).

On abortion, 41% of the straight-ticket Democratic voters expressed a conservative abortion position. Among split-ticket voters, 50% expressed a conservative position on abortion; a nearly 10 percentage-point difference. The dashed line, which benchmarks *all* white southern Goldwater voters, shows just how different the Goldwater Democrats were on abortion. Goldwater voters who voted Republican up and down the ticket (or didn't vote in congressional races) look similar to the Democratic stayers. This is crucial: the racial realignment not only brought more abortion conservatives into the Republican coalition, but brought in people who were uniquely conservative on the issue. It also reduced the presence of abortion conservatives in the Democrats' coalition. When Republican candidates targeted Goldwater Democrats in future elections, this graph makes clear why conservative abortion messaging was effective: these voters were already a sympathetic audience.

A somewhat similar pattern emerges on gun control. Twenty-five percent of voters who supported congressional Democrats and then voted for Johnson opposed registering firearms. Compare this to the 36% of split-ticket voters who opposed registering firearms. Again, the dashed line benchmarks these split-ticket voters with all-white southern Goldwater voters. The Goldwater Democrats, who would fuel the rise of the conservative GOP by expanding the size of the party's voter coalition, held comparatively conservative attitudes toward guns, creating an incentive for Republican politicians to pursue these voters on conservative gun appeals. Imagine a counterfactual scenario where racial conservatives tended to be more liberal on guns than the average voter: the entrance of racial conservatives into the GOP would dilute the demand for conservative gun positions, and the electoral incentives for polarization on gun control in the years that followed might be lessened.

Of course, it could be that even before the Goldwater-Johnson race, split-ticket voters were conservative on abortion and guns. It could be that southern Democrats started to vote for Republican presidential candidates because of economic issues (Shafer and Johnston 2009) and brought their conservative attitudes on guns and abortion with them. Ruling out this alternative explanation is crucial. This book argues that by polarizing on civil rights, the parties' bases changed differently than if the parties polarized along economic lines.

To investigate this alternative explanation, I conduct a placebo test using presidential elections before the 1964 racial realignment when the presidential candidates held overlapping positions on civil rights. In 1962 Gallup asked an identical set of questions on abortion and in 1959 an identical question on obtaining a police permit to buy a gun (these are the only pre-1964 questions on surveys that also ask about vote choice in congressional and presidential elections; questions which are needed to look at split-ticket voting).

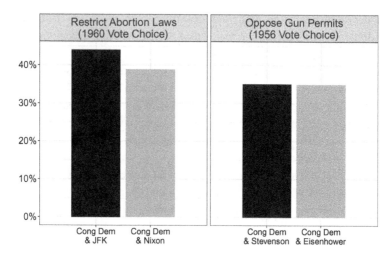

FIGURE 5.2. Placebo Test: Ticket-Splitting, Southern Whites, pre-1964. Graph shows abortion and gun control attitudes (see text for specific wording) among southern whites who voted for the congressional Democrat and Democratic presidential (black) and those who voted for the congressional Democrat and Republican presidential candidate (gray) in the respective year.

As before, I analyze the presidential vote choices of white southerners who supported the congressional Democrat in their district. The left panel of figure 5.2 shows abortion attitudes measured in 1962, by 1960 presidential vote choice; a contest that featured the Democrat Kennedy against the Republican Nixon. Those who supported a Democrat in the congressional race but defected to Nixon in the presidential contest actually held more liberal abortion views than straight Democratic voters (left-hand panel). This differs from patterns seen with regard to the 1964 presidential election when Democrats who defected to the Republican presidential candidate held much more conservative abortion attitudes than Democratic loyalists.[4]

The right-hand panel shows gun control attitudes by 1956 vote choice. Southern Democrats who defected to Eisenhower in the general election hold similar gun control attitudes to the Democratic stayers. Again, this differs from the patterns seen with regards to split-ticket voting in the 1964 election.

This highlights a crucial point: the Republican Party did grow in the South in the 1950s (albeit modestly), but a Republican Party built only on the back of economic conservatism did not generate sorting on other nonracial culture war issues among the Democratic defectors (recall that in 1956 and 1960 the presidential candidates held similar positions on civil

rights). This is because economic cleavages in the 1950s and 1960s crosscut
cleavages on the culture war issues that became salient in the decades to
come. When the national presidential candidates diverged on civil rights in
1964, it created a new type of split-ticket voter who brought conservative
views on other social issues with them.

Case Study: Texas, 1964

This next section turns to subnational political figures in Texas. The Republican Party, once nearly nonexistent in the South, began contesting
state-level and substate-level races in the mid-twentieth century (Schickler
2016). As the South realigned, subnational general election contests sometimes featured one race where the Democratic and Republican candidates
had polarized on civil rights and one race where the Democratic and Republican candidates overlapped on civil rights.

This characterized Texas politics in the 1960s. Consider the ideological
and partisan variation among three statewide officeholders in Texas in the
mid-1960s: (1) Senator John Tower, the first Republican to be elected to
statewide office in the South since Reconstruction, was a racial conservative who vehemently opposed the 1960s civil rights acts; (2) Texas governor Democrat John Connally, who although an ally of Lyndon Johnson,
opposed the integration of public spaces in the 1964 Civil Rights Act and
made antagonistic statements toward the civil rights movement (Associated Press 1964b); and (3) the liberal Democratic Senator Ralph Yarborough, leader of the Texas Democrats' progressive wing and the only
southern senator to support the 1964 Civil Rights Act.

Yarborough and Connally, although both Democrats, held diverging
positions on civil rights. Thus, Tower (the Republican) and Yarborough (the
liberal Democrat) were a Republican-Democratic pairing with divergent
civil rights positions, but Tower and Connally (the conservative Democrat)
were a Republican-Democratic pairing that somewhat overlapped on civil
rights. Although vote choice data are unavailable for these politicians, a
May 1964 Texas Poll (Belden Associates) asked respondents if they approved or disapproved of these three officials. The poll also asked about
racial integration and allowing prayer in public schools—an issue that became central to the culture wars in the 1970s and 1980s, but in 1964 was
not yet a partisan campaign issue. In fact, a majority of people perceived
no difference between the parties on school prayer, and among those who
did, they perceived Democrats to be the more conservative party. Further-

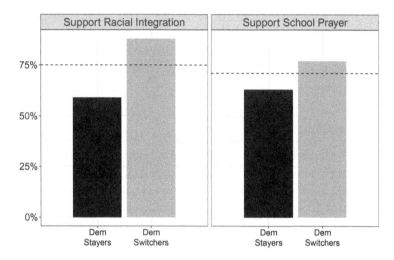

FIGURE 5.3. Candidate Favorability and Issue Attitudes, Texas, 1964. The question on integration asks respondents whether they think the present administration in Washington, DC, is pushing integration "too fast, about right, or not fast enough." The question on school prayer asks respondents whether they approve or disapprove of the Supreme Court ruling that "no state or local government may require the reading of the Lord's prayer or Bible verses in public schools." Dashed line indicates the average attitudes of all John Tower supporters.

more, a search of local Texas newspapers show no indication that Tower, Connally, or Yarborough campaigned or associated themselves with the issue of school prayer in 1964. Any voter movement between candidates cannot be attributed to the candidates' positions on school prayer because they lacked distinct (or any) position in 1964.[5]

Figure 5.3 compares the (1) "Democratic stayers"—those respondents who preferred both Yarborough (the liberal Democrat) and Connally (the conservative Democrat) to Tower (the conservative Republican) with the (2) "Democratic switchers." The switchers are those who preferred the conservative Democrat Connally to the Republican Tower, but would prefer the Republican Tower to the liberal Democrat Yarborough, or were indifferent between the two. This mirrors the comparison from the prior section: which white southerners abandoned the Democratic candidate when they were liberal on civil rights?

The Democratic switchers were considerably more conservative on both integration and school prayer. That they were polarized on integration is unsurprising given the candidates' public position on the issue. But that the bases diverged on school prayer, as previously mentioned, cannot be explained by the candidates offering diverging positions on school prayer. Note that the switchers' preferences on school prayer were more conservative than Tower's broader base of support (marked by the dashed line). The entrance of these social conservatives into the GOP fundamentally changed the composition of the party on this issue and, as chapter 2 argued, created an incentive for Republican politicians to pursue these voters on issues like school prayer to increase the party's appeal to Democrats alienated by the racial liberalism of their party.

However, unlike the national cases discussed in the prior section, it is difficult to attribute this Texas switch wholly to race. Connally and Yarborough represented warring factions of liberal and conservative Democrats on labor before they fought over civil rights (Viguerie 1980, 48). But in 1964, when this survey was conducted, Yarborough had just announced his support of the Civil Rights Act (the only southern senator to do so). Given the primacy of civil rights to the white South, a substantial portion of discontent with Yarborough is almost certainly about civil rights.

Case Study: Texas, 1968

This next case study compares voting patterns in "trial heats" of the 1968 Texas gubernatorial general election contest. Trial heats are where pollsters ask voters who they would vote for in different pairings of candidates. The contours of the gubernatorial race meant that Paul Eggers, the Republican nominee, would either face a civil rights liberal, Democrat Don Yarborough (no relation to Ralph Yarborough, discussed above), or a more traditional southern conservative Democrat, Preston Smith (Byers 1970; Tolson 2009). An April 1968 poll of Texas voters ran trial heats asking who voters would choose in a race between Eggers (the Republican) and either Yarborough or Smith. Fortunately, this 1968 survey also includes a question about racial integration and laws to require the federal registration of handguns. As before, I am interested in the preferences of voters who were comfortable voting for an old-school conservative southern Democrat but who abandoned the Democrats if a racially liberal Democrat ran on the ticket (the Democratic switchers).

Unsurprisingly, the Democratic switchers held considerably more conservative attitudes on racial integration. Of more interest are the switchers' preferences toward gun control. In a search of Texas newspapers, none of the three gubernatorial candidates had publicly expressed a position on gun control by April 1968 (when the survey was fielded), and the issue

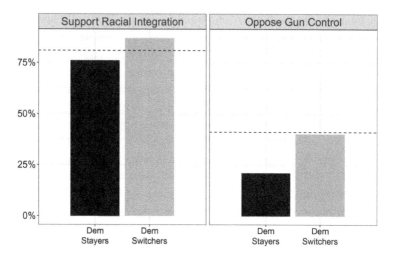

FIGURE 5.4. Gubernatorial Vote Choice and Issue Attitudes. The question on integration asks respondents whether they think the Johnson administration is pushing integration "too fast, about right, or not fast enough." The question on gun control asks, "Do you favor or oppose Federal laws which would control the sales of guns, such as making all persons register all gun purchases, no matter where they buy them." Dashed line indicates the average attitudes of all Paul Eggers supporters.

never gained salience in the gubernatorial race, although Eggers would eventually oppose gun control later in his campaign (Kinch 1968). Despite the absence of gun control as an issue in this campaign, voters who abandoned the Democrats when the racially liberal Yarborough was running had considerably more conservative views on gun control. Figure 5.4 shows that Democratic switchers are *twice* as likely to oppose gun control than the Democratic stayers. The exodus of gun conservatives decreased the presence of a conservative gun faction within the Democratic Party. It also doubled the size of Eggers's electoral coalition with people who held conservative gun views. This mirrors the patterns seen in the previous sections: party sorting on account of civil rights was accompanied by quiet sorting on other issues as well.

George Wallace's 1968 Presidential Campaign

This final section analyzes the 1968 presidential race, which featured a three-way race between Democrat Hubert Humphrey, Republican Richard

Nixon, and third-party candidate George Wallace. Wallace rose to national prominence in the 1960s as a staunch opponent of civil rights and infamously stood in the doorway of the University of Alabama to block black students from entering the school. While Wallace's campaign was not a true single-issue campaign, his candidacy in 1968 was fundamentally about opposition to civil rights and appealing to white segregationists. Wallace was the last third-party candidate to win electoral votes (five states), all of which were in the Deep South. Thus, the Wallace campaign offers a test of this theory: Did Wallace voters, attracted to his conservative position on civil rights, bring conservative views on other culture war issues with them?

This is especially important because contemporary and historical analysts view Wallace's 1968 campaign as a rest stop for disaffected southern Democrats making their way to the Republican coalition. As previously discussed, Nixon, Ford, and Reagan each targeted Wallace voters by making conservative appeals on issues like abortion, gun control, and gay rights. This section shows that Wallace voters, by 1968, already had conservative positions on these issues. The Republican Party's messaging to Wallace voters was a reaction to the issue positions these voters already held.

To analyze Wallace voters, I find surveys as close as possible to the 1968 election that ask questions relevant to the culture wars. I use a Louis Harris and Associates survey (#1933) from May 1969 that includes questions on feelings toward adults who "engage in homosexual acts" and whether the respondent favors or opposes a "federal law which would require the registration of rifles and pistols." I also use a Gallup poll from November 1969 that asks respondents whether they favor or oppose a law "which would permit a woman to go to a doctor to end pregnancy at any time during the first three months."

Figure 5.5 shows the stark difference of Wallace voters compared to Nixon and Humphrey voters on each of these issues in the months after the 1968 election. When asked whether abortion should be allowed for any reason in the first three months of pregnancy, 63% of Wallace voters said no compared to a little over 50% of Nixon and Humphrey voters. Wallace, as well as the other two candidates, did not campaign on abortion in 1968. In fact, Wallace and his vice-presidential pick, Curtis LeMay, each supported (albeit offhandedly) liberalizing abortion restrictions in 1968 (Flint 1968; Green 2016), although these positions effectively received no coverage.

On the question of gun control, respondents were asked whether they supported or opposed a federal law requiring the registration of rifles and handguns. Twenty-eight percent of Humphrey voters and 48% of Nixon

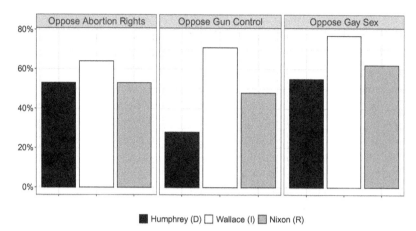

FIGURE 5.5. 1968 Vote Choice and Issue Attitudes. Each bar represents the percentage support-ing the conservative position. The question on abortion asks whether the respondent supports a law "which would permit a women to go to a doctor to end pregnancy at any time during the first three months." The question on gun control asks: "Do you favor or oppose Federal laws which would control the sales of guns, such as making all persons register all gun purchases, no matter where they buy them." The third panel asks if "adults want to engage in homosexual acts with each other they should be perfectly free to do so."

voters opposed registration. Yet 71% of Wallace voters opposed registra-tion. While Wallace did publicly oppose gun control, news coverage of Wallace's position during the campaign is hard to find; it was not a central issue. Indeed, of the *New York Times*' coverage throughout 1968, only one article covered Wallace's opposition to gun control: After Robert Kennedy was assassinated, a reporter asked Wallace if he would support gun control. Wallace responded that he would not (United Press International 1968).[6]

Finally, when asked if "adults want to engage in homosexual acts with each other they should be perfectly free to do so," 54% of Humphrey vot-ers disagreed, 62% of Nixon voters disagreed, and 77% of Wallace voters disagreed. This is despite gay rights not being a campaign issue. In a search of major newspapers in 1968, not a single article mentions both George Wallace and key words related to gay rights.

This underscores a core point: conservatives on abortion, gun control, and gay rights were not moving to Wallace because of his position on those specific issues. Wallace appealed primarily on conservative racial positions, and as a by-product of this, amassed a base who held very con-servative positions on other social issues well, *even without Wallace taking visible positions on that issue.* Not only are Wallace voters conservative (and thus increase the size of conservative support in the GOP when they arrive), but they are noticeably more conservative than people already voting for Nixon in 1968. In the ensuing elections, as Nixon, Ford, and Reagan sought to lure Wallace Democrats into the GOP, they used conservative messaging on culture war issues, I argue, because these voters already held conservative preferences.

Conclusion

This chapter shows that Goldwater and Wallace Democrats held very conservative positions on abortion, gun control, and gay rights, even without Goldwater or Wallace staking clear or any positions on these issues. I argue that this had a tremendous consequence for what came next. First, as these voters entered the Republican Party, Republican politicians realized that staking conservative positions on culture war issues was a path to win the nomination in an increasingly conservative party. Chapter 2's discussion of the 1976 primary, in which Ford and Reagan pursued voters on these issues, is a formative example of that process. Second, in general elections, Republican presidential candidates including Nixon, Ford, and Reagan appealed to Goldwater and Wallace Democratic voters on guns, abortion, and gay rights because, as this chapter shows, these voters already held conservative positions on abortion and gun control by the early 1960s. This was a process of politicians reacting to the preexisting preferences of these voters. Using abortion as a case study, the next chapter explores what happens when politicians try to disrupt these issue bundles.

CHAPTER SIX

An Alternative Outcome

The Development of Abortion's Partisan Divide

This book argues that the alignment of party and ideology that defined the party system in the 1980s–1990s matched a prominent constellation of attitudes first observed in the mass public. This raises the question: What was the possibility for an alternative outcome? I explore this in context of the emerging partisan divide on abortion in the 1960s and 1970s. Could elite and midlevel forces have disrupted the preexisting linkages and aligned the pro-life movement in the Democratic Party?[1]

Existing theories of parties argue that when polarization rested at its low point, either party could have been the pro- or anti-abortion party; the parties in the mass public held similar positions on abortion in the 1960s and 1970s. In fact, by partisan identification, Democrats were slightly *more conservative* than Republicans. In what has become one of the most cited pieces on partisan abortion politics, Adams (1997, 734) writes, "If the members of Congress were truly following the lead of the masses on abortion, Democrats in Congress should have become less pro-choice, not more. Thus, members of Congress could not have been driven by party masses." Adams (1997) and other scholars (Bawn et al. 2012; Karol 2009) argue that rather than responding to voters, interest groups propelled the parties to take the positions they did. Republicans emerged as the conservative abortion party because abortion interest groups and activists drove Republican politicians rightward.

This book argues, and this chapter details, that politicians were very much following voters on abortion policy in polarization's formative years. Partisan realignment triggered by civil rights in the 1960s meant Republicans sought and relied on voters who perhaps did not identify as Republican, but who voted for Republicans or were up for grabs because they had been alienated from the Democratic Party on civil rights. As the previous chapter shows, these disaffected Democrats were quite conservative on abortion. And because this realignment started before abortion became salient by 1972, even though Republican identifiers held more liberal views than Democratic identifiers, people voting for Richard Nixon held more conservative abortion views than people voting for the Democratic presidential nominee, George McGovern.

As this chapter lays out, abortion groups did not simply work their way into a party and force politicians' and parties' hands. Rather Republicans, trying to build a conservative "New Majority" voter coalition, realized that anti-abortion groups communicated with the very voters they sought to mobilize in general and primary elections. This propelled anti-abortion groups to work on behalf of Republican politicians despite many leaders of the early pro-life movement's reluctance to align with the GOP. In fact, many leaders of the early pro-life movement tried to enter the Democratic Party but failed. Rather than anti-abortion groups forcing the parties' hands, emerging partisan battle lines predisposed them to the GOP.

This chapter first explores abortion activists and interest groups, then prominent politicians, and finally public intellectuals involved in the early debate over abortion in the 1960s and 1970s. To develop this argument, this chapter relies on original archival research discussed in chapter 1, especially Paul Weyrich's papers at the American Heritage Center in Laramie, Wyoming; the papers of the US Conference of Catholic Bishops; Howard Phillips's correspondence in the Conservative Caucus Papers at Liberty University; the Southern Baptist Historical Library and Archives in Nashville, Tennessee; and the American Citizens Concerned for Life (ACCL) collection at the Gerald R. Ford Presidential Library and Museum in Ann Arbor, Michigan.

Interest Groups

Ideological Diversity in the Early Pro-Life Movement

The earliest anti-abortion activists were not the Christian Right, which only emerged in the late 1970s (Balmer 2006; Schlozman 2015). Rather, the pro-life movement was founded by an ideologically diverse group of activists, many of whom were otherwise liberal and tried to connect their movement

to other progressive causes (Williams 2016; Ziegler 2015). Part of the pro-
life movement's initial liberal dynamic resulted from the early national
pro-life movement being fairly small. First, prior to *Roe*, national pro-life
activism rested largely within the United States Catholic Conference and
the National Conference of Catholic Bishops (USCC/NCCB) under the
leadership of James McHugh.[2] Although heterogeneity exists throughout
US Catholic leadership, many leaders at the USCC/NCCB, and certainly
McHugh, took liberal positions on social welfare programs, civil rights, and
vocally supported nuclear détente (Williams 2016; *National Review* 1982).
In the 1976 election, one Ford staffer noted that the "platform statement
of the USCC reads like a laundry list for a Democratic Congress, except
for abortion" (Memo on "Religion," n.d.).

   Second, the Minnesota Citizens Concerned for Life (MCCL), one of
the earliest and most successful state-level right-to-life groups, provided
key leadership to the early national pro-life movement (this is partially
because they had successfully organized at the state level). The MCCL
was led by Marjory and Fred Mecklenburg, both political progressives
who strongly believed in social welfare programs and women's rights and
supported contraception (Williams 2016, 158). How can you oppose killing
in Vietnam while you support it at the abortionist's clinic, members of the
MCCL argued (Williams 2016, 164). "Contrary to pro-abortion jibes," a
MCCL leader wrote, most people in the Minnesota pro-life movement "are
'liberals' in the 1930's and 1960's sense. We expect to right the wrongs of
the world, to alleviate human suffering, to overturn social injustices . . ."
(St. Martin 1973).

   Marjory Mecklenburg served as the first chair of the board of the National Right to Life Committee (NRLC), which today boasts itself as the
largest and oldest pro-life group. Other liberals joined her, too. Warren
Schaller, the first executive director of the NRLC, favored the Equal Rights
Amendment and supported social welfare programs to dissuade abortion
for financial reasons (Hunt 1984; Ziegler 2015, 187). Indeed, early anti-
abortion efforts incorporated key tenets of economic liberalism. In tes-
timony to the US Senate in 1974, Schaller stated that American Citizens
Concerned for Life, the national successor to the Minnesota organization,
favored "mandatory maternity insurance benefits for all women" and that
"needy mothers should be eligible for AFDC payments for their unborn
child as soon as pregnancy is diagnosed and those benefits to continue for
the full duration of pregnancy" (Hunt 1984).

   Mildred Jefferson, the first black woman to graduate from Harvard

Medical School, served as both the chair of the NRLC's board and as the organization's president in the mid-1970s. Although conservative in many respects, Jefferson linked the pro-life movement with tenets of liberalism. Without securing the "right to life," other "great social issues" such as food stamps, electricity rates, and redistribution of wealth "will have no meaning," Jefferson (1976) argued. More generally, Jefferson viewed abortion as "class war against the poor," and like other pro-life activists, she painted the pro-choice movement as an assault on African Americans and likened the *Roe* decision to the *Dred Scott* Supreme Court ruling (qtd. in Klemesrud 1976; Williams 2016, 170).

However, as the national pro-life movement expanded, and although more politically diverse than stereotypes might imply, it increasingly included more right-wing members (Granberg 1981). In democratic organizations such as the NRLC, this meant new members supported more conservative leaders and that pro-life pragmatists lost their influence or were forced to accommodate conservative forces. Conservative members were upset at the Mecklenburgs and other NRLC leaders for making decisions that they viewed as out of step with the broader movement. They believed that the Mecklenburgs' liberal outlook, opposition to conservative Catholics, and general support for contraception hurt the movement (Engel 1974). Jefferson, then serving as chair of the NRLC's board of directors, felt as though "some people were after her scalp"; "If [Jefferson] would only wake up and fly right, she would gain credibility in many eyes," a pro-life activist surmised (Fink 1974b).[3]

In 1974, Marjory Mecklenburg lost her bid to become the NRLC's president and a couple months later left the NRLC to start an anti-abortion group that appealed to more moderate constituencies. In one planning session, she scribbled down that "peace activists" might serve as a core constituency (Mecklenburg, undated notes A). Despite Mecklenburg's political skill, her moderate abortion group never got off the ground, perhaps because rank-and-file pro-lifers took a range of conservative positions that did not fit Mecklenburg's vision. Other liberal leaders also left the NRLC. Thea Rossi Barron, a liberal Democrat who served as the NRLC's legislative director from 1976 to 1978, left the organization when the NRLC opposed the Equal Rights Amendment (Rossi 2018). Other liberals, like Warren Schaller, eventually left the organized abortion movement altogether (Ziegler 2015, 217).

Discomfort with the increasing alliance of the pro-life movement with the conservative right discomforted some Catholic leadership as well.

While the New Right was friendly to their abortion position, they clashed with Catholic leaders on other core issues. It is a "problem," Russell Shaw of the US Catholic Conference noted. "As long as the Democratic party and organized labor continue to hold the right-to-life movement at arm's length (or worse), Democrats and labor people have little reason to be surprised when right-to-lifers indicate responsiveness to overtures from the new right," he warned (Shaw 1980).

Rise of the Christian Right

Contrast early pro-life efforts to those of the Christian Right in the late 1970s. The very appeals made by Christian Right and New Right leaders— linking anti-abortion with other conservative causes—matched many of the preexisting opinion bundles among the mass public. In fact, many evangelical leaders stayed quiet or even supported moderate-to-liberal abortion policies in the early 1970s. (Initial aversion was partially because evangelicals viewed abortion as being an issue that belonged to Catholics, an out-group, and thus undesirable.) This is despite the Protestant evangelical laity expressing just as conservative positions on abortion as Catholics by the late 1960s (O'Brian 2020, 2022).

Figure 6.1 shows public opinion toward whether abortion should be legal during the first three months of pregnancy, by religious denomination. This poll, conducted by Gallup in 1969, occurred four years before *Roe* and before evangelical leaders mobilized. While Catholics expressed more conservative positions than mainline Protestants, they held nearly identical positions as Baptists. This is of interest because in the 1960s and 1970s, the Southern Baptist Convention (SBC) was the largest Protestant denomination and center of Protestant evangelism. But not all Baptists are Southern Baptist: the SBC is predominantly white and, as its name implies, concentrated in the South (O'Brian 2022). Analyzing white Baptists in the South offers a rough estimate for white evangelical thought in this era. (When evangelicals are discussed in political terms, it almost always refers to white evangelicals, despite many African Americans identifying as evangelical.) Breaking down Baptist opinion by region and race reveals a surprising pattern: 78% of white Baptists in the South opposed legal abortion in the first three months, which is 11 percentage points more conservative than Catholics, who were then thought to be uniquely conservative on the issue.

Despite public opinion, in 1971 the Southern Baptist Convention passed

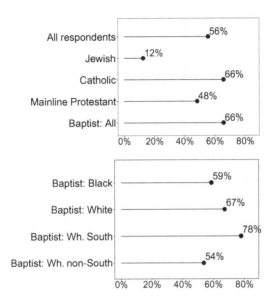

FIGURE 6.1. Percentage Opposed to Legal Abortion in the First Three Months (from Gallup Poll #793, November 1969).

a resolution that endorsed moderate abortion policies. The SBC's 1971 resolution both affirmed "the sanctity of human life, including fetal life" and expressed support for legislation that allowed abortion "under such conditions as rape, incest, clear evidence of severe fetal deformity, and carefully ascertained evidence of the likelihood of damage to the emotional, mental, and physical health of the mother."[4] This seeming disconnect between public opinion and SBC policy is largely because the organization's annual conventions, during which the SBC chose leaders and policy planks, were well attended by moderates while sparsely populated by conservatives and fundamentalists. Less-educated and lower-class evangelicals held more conservative abortion views (among other things) than the seminary-trained ministers and well-educated leaders of the Southern Baptist institutions that held sway over conventions.

Foy Valentine, the head of the SBC's Christian Life Commission (CLC), which at the time was the public policy wing of the SBC, took a moderate and at times almost liberal position on abortion. In 1977, Valentine signed "A Call to Concern" by religious ethicists that endorsed *Roe v. Wade*, and in 1978 he joined the advisory board of the Religious Coalition for Abortion Rights, whose goal was "to promote the pro-choice religious point of view"

(Valentine 1978).[5] Pro-life activists accused the CLC of outright supporting *Roe* in the months and years following the decision (Fink 1974a).

Valentine had company at the SBC. In February 1973, W. A. Criswell, a former SBC president whom the *Baptist Press* called "the patriarch of conservatism," endorsed a woman's right to choose (Schlozman 2015, 103; Briggs 1989).[6] Adrian Rogers, whose election as the SBC's president marked an initial victory for the conservative insurgency within the Southern Baptist Convention, told Valentine that his abortion position "[is] one that I basically agree with" (Rogers 1977). And Billy Graham in 1970 reportedly remarked that abortion was permissible in some cases and that "nowhere in the Bible was it indicated that abortion is wrong" (Weyrich 1971).

Other leaders simply stayed quiet. Jerry Falwell, who would later form the influential activist organization the Moral Majority, did not preach about abortion until 1978 (Schlozman 2015, 103). Francis Schaeffer, an evangelical theologian who many credit for raising the anti-abortion movement's salience among evangelical leaders, publicly opposed abortion only with prodding from his son. Schaeffer initially argued he did not want to risk his reputation on a "Catholic issue" (Schaeffer 2007, 266).[7] However, by 1980 the SBC had endorsed very conservative abortion positions, and white evangelicals had become the face of the anti-abortion movement. If national evangelical leadership expressed initial indifference to abortion, how did it become such a force within the evangelical community?

One part of this story rests inside the Southern Baptist Convention. As the public opinion above shows, when abortion gained salience, SBC leadership found themselves out of step with many in the rank and file. Rising conservative activists inside the SBC believed that despite the laity's conservatism on abortion, they may simply have been unaware that the church's formal positions differed from their own. Bob Holbrook, a leader of Baptists for Life, argued: "There may be any number of problems that have more of their attention at the moment [besides the SBC's abortion policy]. This is why time, money and effort should be directed toward motivating and enlisting this vast body of support we already have" (Holbrook 1975). A new wave of activist leaders did just that. The growing rift between establishment moderates and the more conservative laity, on both abortion and broader theological views, mobilized a new set of activists and leaders focused on taking over the SBC's institutions.

At the SBC's 1985 convention, which marked a watershed moment of the fight between the moderate establishment and insurgent conservatives,

45,000 convention delegates cast votes for the president of the SBC. Prior to that year, the next highest attendance at a national convention had been 22,000 (Ammerman 1990, 3). The rightward shift within the Southern Baptist Convention, including on abortion, is a story of ordinary churchgoers getting up from the pews and becoming activists to push their agenda rather than a shift in the existing establishment's position.

Outside the SBC, the Christian Right originally mobilized in national politics to protect tax-exempt status for racially segregated Christian schools, not abortion. Indeed, Christian Right leaders did not initially get involved in national politics over abortion and were generally absent from the Washington scene before 1978 (Balmer 2006). Ed Dobson, an early founder of the Moral Majority, recalls, "I frankly do not remember abortion ever being mentioned as a reason why we ought to do something" (qtd. in Balmer 2006, 16).

"Christian schools' battle with the IRS over tax exemptions, not abortion" prompted the Moral Majority's activism in the 1980 election, Paul Weyrich remembered (Babcock 1982). While Weyrich had been pushing the religious leaders of what would become the Religious Right to pick up the abortion issue for years, it initially fell on deaf ears (Balmer 2006, 15–16). The pivot to abortion politics in the Religious Right finally came when religious leaders began looking to build a broader political movement beyond fighting the tax-exempt status of Christian schools. On a conference call to brainstorm other issues they might mobilize around, Weyrich remembers, a voice on the call chimed in, "How about abortion?" And according to historian Randall Balmer, that "that is how abortion was cobbled into . . . the Religious Right" (2006, 16).[8]

The pivot from school integration to abortion politics was not because activist leaders linked these issues together in the public's mind, but because leaders realized that white southern evangelicals, who were conservative on civil rights, also already held conservative views on abortion. The American National Election Study shows that by 1972, well before the Christian Right mobilized, white non-evangelicals in 1972 were twice as likely as white evangelicals to say abortion should be allowed in any circumstance. White evangelicals also held significantly more conservative attitudes on questions related to school busing, aid to minorities, and the pace of the civil rights movement.

This suggests that preexisting public opinion created an environment enabling Christian Right leaders to enter the political arena and build a powerful social movement that reinforced issue connections already held by ordinary voters. And as has been told from many perspectives, midlevel actors played a crucial role in building the anti-abortion movement. New Right political operatives recruited evangelical leaders such as Jerry Falwell to become politically active (Layman 2001, 44). Evangelical leaders also provided crucial resources and an organizational infrastructure to mobilize latent constituencies and raise issue salience (e.g., Wilcox 1992; Layman 2001; Ziegler 2015, 201; Schlozman 2015). Still further, Religious Right and New Right leaders built ecumenical alliances and raised awareness that it was not only Catholics who opposed abortion (Schlozman 2015).

Pro-Life Activists to the Republican Party

Prominent theories of parties place activists at the center of party positioning on abortion (Adams 1997; Karol 2009; Bawn et al. 2012). These theories raise a hypothetical scenario: Could interest groups have pushed the Democrats to the right of Republicans? The historical contours of the early anti-abortion movement provide a test for this hypothesis. Both the earliest anti-abortion activists, as well as many leaders of the Christian Right, initially sought to ally themselves with the Democratic Party or were agnostic about which party aligned with their cause.

As chapter 2 discusses, interest groups might want to ally with both parties because it maximizes influence regardless of which party holds power (Krimmel 2017; McCarty and Schickler 2018). This is especially pronounced when group-party alignments have yet to be institutionalized. This characterized the landscape of conservative abortion activists in the 1970s. Anti-abortion activists talked to prominent politicians on both sides of the aisle and monitored which politicians favored their position. Mildred Jefferson, then the president of the National Right to Life Committee, wrote in 1976 that "the right-to-life is not a partisan issue and the movement must vote for the man or woman who will support our political objectives" (Jefferson 1976). In the 1976 presidential primaries, the National Right to Life Committee supported two Democrats (George Wallace and Ellen McCormack) and one Republican (Ronald Reagan). Each of these candidates lost their primary. The NRLC's eventual support of Ford over Carter in the general election was less a choice than the outcome handed to them by the relative positions taken by the major presidential candidates. The Democratic Party's opposition to a constitutional amendment banning abortions in 1976, Jefferson wrote, "makes it necessary for us to support the principle in the platform that was accepted by the Republican National Party" (1976).

Marjory Mecklenburg worked hard to build the pro-life movement within the national Democratic Party and worked with leading Democratic politicians and operatives to support her cause. Mecklenburg believed Democrats would support the pro-life movement as they had historically been an advocate for the "rights of the oppressed," a label often assigned by pro-lifers to the fetus (Mecklenburg 1976). If the NRLC could "be of assistance in some way to build a populist Democratic Party, we would welcome the opportunity," Mecklenburg wrote to Ben Wattenberg, an adviser to multiple Democratic presidential candidates and a former speechwriter for Lyndon Johnson (Mecklenburg 1974a, 1974b; Roberts 2015).

In fact, in 1976 Mecklenburg initially joined Sargent Shriver's campaign for the Democratic presidential nomination, a pro-life Democrat, because she admired his commitment to "strong family life," the less fortunate, and other liberal initiatives including Head Start and the Peace Corps (Mecklenburg 1975a, 1975b). However, the Shriver campaign failed, and any ambiguity about Carter's position or that the Democratic National Convention (DNC) would support a pro-life plank dissipated. In a letter to the DNC, Mecklenburg (1976) writes that their abortion plank will "alienate millions of Americans from the Democratic party."[9] Perhaps reluctantly, Mecklenburg notes that "Republicans have chosen to make abortion their issue," and without a Democratic alternative, she went to work for the Ford campaign (Mecklenburg, undated notes B).

Catholic leaders at the USCC/NCCB, although careful to stay out of explicitly partisan politics, expressed private disappointment that Democrats opposed their abortion stance. (Catholic leadership at the USCC/NCCB, like the Catholic laity, had been historically aligned with the Democratic Party.) "Unfortunately . . . our strongest support for a human life amendment seems to almost innately rest among conservative and moderate Republicans [in Congress] . . ." (Lynch 1974b). Other liberals encountered similar luck. Nellie Gray, who founded the March for Life, a pro-life rally that prominent politicians still attend today, was a self-identified feminist and held otherwise liberal political views. Alarmed at *Roe v. Wade*, she sought out Ted Kennedy and other liberal Democrats, assuming they, like her, saw overturning *Roe* as an extension of the civil rights movement. One by one, they turned Gray down before Senator James Buckley, a member of the Conservative Party from New York, agreed to help. One activist remembered that Gray's "jaw dropped" because Gray could not believe that a Republican would help her cause (Marshner 2018). When Ted Kennedy sought the Democratic nomination in 1980, Gray refused to endorse him because he supported a pro-choice plank, "regardless of his other votes [on non-abortion issues], no matter how good they are" (McCarthy 1980).

New Right abortion activists also did not envy the GOP: "No one wanted the pro-life issue to be wedded to the Republican Party," Connie Marshner (2018), a conservative "pro-family" activist, remembers. Even leaders who later served as the face of the Religious Right only turned to Republicans after it became clear that Jimmy Carter endorsed more liberal views. Televangelist Pat Robertson, a modern-day fixture of the Christian Right, stated that he had "done everything this side of breaking FCC regulations" to get Carter, a born-again Christian, in the White House in 1976 (Martin 1996, 166).[10]

In short, abortion groups did not simply work their way into a party and force politicians' and parties' hands. Rather, anti-abortion interest groups worked with Republicans because Republican politicians, in an effort to build a New Majority coalition, took stances that were more closely aligned with these interest groups' demands.

Feminism and the Pro-Choice Movement

The alignment of the pro-choice movement and feminism also followed a circuitous path. Prior to 1973, only a patchwork of organizations undertook efforts to repeal abortion laws, and the national movement's small size meant that the pro-choice coalition crosscut ideological lines (Staggenborg 1991, 27). This is because some of the earliest and loudest pro-abortion voices advocated for abortion reform not as a woman's right, but as a means for population control or to legally protect doctors (e.g., Friedan 1976; Staggenborg 1991). At the time of *Roe*, Zero Population Growth (ZPG) was the only pro-choice group with a lobbying operation in Washington, DC (Staggenborg 1991, 63). ZPG focused on abortion as a means of population control, not as a woman's right.

Organized pro-choice activists had yet to emerge as national power players by the early 1970s. Planned Parenthood did not endorse abortion repeal until 1969 and did not offer organizational support for the national effort until 1973 (Staggenborg 1991, 15). The National Association for the Repeal of Abortion Laws (what is now NARAL) had just 651 individual members in January 1972 (Southard 1972). And while the National Organization for Women (NOW; founded in 1966), endorsed repealing abortion restrictions in 1967, the topic internally divided the organization's delegates.[11] First-wave feminists wanted to maintain organizational focus on economic equality, while younger members pushed endorsing abortion repeal (Greenhouse and Siegel 2012, 36). Some of the earliest feminists, including Planned Parenthood founder Margaret Sanger, opposed legalized abortion (Critchlow 1999, 135). Coupled with a lack of resources, the internal fracture precluded NOW from becoming a powerful abortion advocate before *Roe* (Staggenborg 1991, 20). Still further, pro-choice groups (as well as pro-life groups) struggled financially in early years (Freeman 1975, 91).

The bottom line is that the pro-choice movement, particularly as a woman's right movement, had yet to gain financial or organizational strength prior to *Roe*. However, just as preexisting opinion enabled the Christian Right to articulate pro-life views in a web of conservative causes, latent opinion facilitated framing pro-choice issues in a web of liberal causes. When Betty Friedan, then leader of the nascent NOW, pronounced that abortion access was a woman's civil right (Greenhouse and Siegel 2012, 38–39), she was expressing two ideas that already seemed to go together in the mass public.

Politicians

Like abortion activists, pro-life politicians came from both sides of the aisle, and many politicians changed their policy positions as abortion became increasingly salient (Karol 2009). The resulting equilibrium among politicians—one where pro-life views migrated to the Republican Party—mirrored the prevailing cleavage already found at the mass level. Although difficult to paint a complete portrait, I argue that issue overlap in the mass public created an environment that made it easier for Republicans (Democrats) to pursue anti-abortion (pro-abortion) voters, even when those positions ran contrary to interest groups' demands.

Republicans

Abortion first emerged as a national campaign issue, although in a comparatively small manner, in 1972. President Nixon, like most politicians of the time, had stayed largely quiet on abortion in the late 1960s and early 1970s. Other prominent Republicans, most notably Nelson Rockefeller, were strong advocates for abortion reform. This changed in the lead-up to the 1972 campaign. In 1971, Nixon instructed military hospitals to abide by state abortion laws, a directive that reversed federal policy allowing abortions when pregnancy endangered the mother's mental or physical health, even if states in which the military hospitals resided had laws prohibiting these abortions (Karol 2009, 60). In Nixon's statement of this new policy, he also expressed his personal opposition to abortion (Greenhouse and Siegel 2012, 198).

As discussed in chapter 2, Nixon initially opposed abortion in the years leading up to the 1972 campaign in an effort to appeal to blue-collar Catholic voters, a constituency that had traditionally supported Democratic candidates (Karol 2009, 59–60; Greenhouse and Siegel 2012, 157, 215, 291). These blue-collar Catholic voters, once solidly Democratic, had become unmoored from the party by civil rights and what they viewed as the excesses of liberalism in the 1960s. By undoing the Department of Defense's permission of abortion at military hospitals, an aide advised Nixon, he was employing a "rising issue and a gut issue with Catholics" (qtd. in Greenhouse and Siegal 2012, 287). Nixon and his aides realized that issue overlap between abortion, Vietnam, aid to minorities, and marijuana legalization meant that opposing abortion rights would reinforce existing divides between Nixon and the leftward-shifting Democratic Party (Buchanan 1971; Greenhouse and Siegel 2012, 215–18). Nixon saw abortion, like government aid to minorities, as a tool to attract culturally traditional Democrats into the Republican fold.

Yet Nixon ultimately dropped abortion as a campaign issue. After conducting a poll in August 1972, pollster Robert Teeter told Nixon's chief of staff, "The idea that the President's increased support among Catholics results directly from his abortion stand is . . . not supported by the data." Catholics had already supported Nixon before his abortion appeals, Teeter noted (Teeter 1972b). Public opinion data showed that race and Vietnam, not abortion, drove Catholics to Nixon (Greenhouse and Siegel 2012, 292n122; Finkelstein 1971). Without the benefit of attracting further Catholic support and to avoid offending other voters, Teeter advised that Nixon should not discuss abortion. As a result of this poll, Nixon dropped the issue and expressed privately to aides that the federal government should stay out of setting abortion policy (Kotlowski 2001, 252).

Nixon's experience underscores several key points. First, abortion conservatives had been entering the Republican coalition even without explicit appeals on the issue. Second, patterns among ordinary voters, not pressure from interest groups, sparked Nixon's shifting positions. Indeed, early conservative activists wondered what compelled Nixon's sudden fealty toward their issue. Paul Weyrich, who many credit for organizing the

anti-abortion movement into Republican politics, wrote, "Nixon's statement on abortion was surprising, in my view, because we are unaware of
any strong anti-abortion input among his close associates" (Weyrich 1971).
Likewise, James McHugh—the director of the Family Life Division at the
US Catholic Conference and a prominent leader of the early anti-abortion
movement—hypothesized that Nixon's stance was to "court favor with the
Church" (McHugh 1971). This fits with Krimmel's (2017, 158) work arguing that politicians sought organized interests to act as intermediaries to
communicate with voters they were targeting. Rather than interest groups
generating party positioning, interest group–party building in the case of
abortion was the result of Nixon trying to cement the conservative New
Majority voter coalition.

   Four years later, Gerald Ford, like Nixon, took a modestly conservative abortion position that seemed more focused on dividing Democrats
and winning conservative Catholic voters rather than as a response from
conservative policy demanders. Abortion can make "inroads into the traditionally Catholic Democratic constituency, as well as the equally Democratic Southern fundamentalist one," a memo to a Ford aide advised. "The
abortion controversy is attractive to the President," the memo continues
because it "is more divisive to Democrats than Republicans" (Melady and
Lee 1976). Another aide advised the president's staff more bluntly: the
anti-abortion Catholics "vote and are presently unenthusiastic about Carter" (Cashen 1976). Many pro-life groups ultimately supported Ford, but
only after Reagan and Democratic candidates George Wallace and Ellen
McCormack lost in the primaries.

   By the 1980 election, Reagan had long opposed abortion beyond trau-
matic circumstances and opposed government funding for abortions (Williams 2016, 80–84, 118). Although Reagan reluctantly signed moderate
abortion reform in 1967 as governor of California, he quickly expressed
regrets and threatened to veto additional measures being considered to further legalize abortion (Williams 2016). By the 1980 election, he had helped
visibly brand the Republican Party as the conservative abortion party.

Democrats

Although feminists had entered the Democratic Party by 1972, the party
also contained large socially conservative constituencies that precluded
Democrats from sending clear signals on abortion through the 1970s
(see Layman 2001, ch. 4; Young 2000; Layman and Carsey 2002, 794). The

Democrats' initial 1972 front-runner, Edmund Muskie, voiced skepticism toward abortion in early 1971, and Hubert Humphrey campaigned explicitly against abortion rights in 1972 (Williams 2011, 520). Even George McGovern, who perhaps apocryphally started the campaign with a liberal position, by May 1972 expressed opposition to abortion and said that states should decide their own policy.[12] In fact, McGovern floor whips successfully squashed pushes at the Democratic National Convention to include pro-choice language in the Democratic platform, fearing it would "siphon off nation-wide votes" (Perlstein 2008, 694; Lader, undated memo B). McGovern's public indifference to abortion rights frustrated feminists (Wolbrecht 2000, 37). Women leaders in the GOP actually pushed the Republican platform committee (tasked with developing the Republican National Convention's policy platform) to adopt a pro-choice position to lure feminists disaffected by McGovern's betrayal (Williams 2011, 523).

Four years later, Jimmy Carter similarly frustrated feminists by taking a milquetoast position. Carter opposed constitutional efforts to overturn *Roe*, but also opposed federal funding for abortion. As on most issues, Carter purposefully adopted a moderate stance to position himself between his more conservative white southern base and the northern liberals who were needed for victory (Eizenstat 2018).

By the mid-1970s, many pro-choice groups believed that Ted Kennedy, the liberal (and Catholic) Democratic senator from Massachusetts, would carry their cause in presidential elections. This is despite Kennedy sending constituent mail opposing abortion until at least 1971 (Douthat 2009). Kennedy's about-face on abortion surprised activists. Indeed, the National Organization for Women was so surprised, they greeted Kennedy's unexpected pro-choice position by creating "a special award" for him (Lynch 1975b). What initiated Kennedy's position change? As chapter 1 details, Kennedy had become "convinced" that a majority of Massachusetts voters supported his view (Lynch 1975a). If Massachusetts was the testing ground in a "Church-Kennedy test on abortion, I am convinced that Kennedy would win," a priest advised Catholic leadership (Hehir 1975). Perhaps as important, Kennedy was eyeing the presidential nomination, and his shift leftward, NARAL cofounder Lawrence Lader concluded, was an effort to appeal to liberal constituencies for the 1976 presidential primary. Kennedy's newfound position on abortion, "coupled with his strong stand on Boston school integration, seems to portend a major bid for liberal support, perhaps the signal for his re-entry into the 1976 campaign," Lader surmised (undated memo A). Kennedy ultimately did not run for president in 1976 and lost to Carter in the 1980 primary.

The abortion examples underscore a detail raised in chapter 2: Democrats, perhaps because they had wielded such a large and ideologically diverse coalition throughout the midcentury, had a more difficult time moving leftward at the pace that Republicans moved rightward. Republicans, especially in the South, were a minority party, and, perhaps consequently, the ascendant conservative wing quickly took control of the party and pushed them to the right on abortion and other issues faster than liberals could push the Democratic Party left. Southern Democrats and other conservative constituencies remained influential until at least the 1990s and perhaps longer. Democrats through the end of the twentieth century delicately balanced this tension, at times downplaying their commitment to liberal abortion positions and other social issues.

Public Intellectuals

As abortion slowly worked its way into the party system in the 1960s and 1970s, it also slowly worked its way into the discourse among liberal and conservative intellectuals. As chapter 1 details, when conservative leaders and thinkers envisioned the rise of the New Majority in the early 1960s, abortion, it seems, was omitted from their vision.

The pages of *National Review* (*NR*), an ideologically conservative magazine, were void of abortion politics until 1965 when they published a series of articles on population control, an issue that provoked discussion of abortion. As part of this series on population control, *NR* published an article by Alan Guttmacher, the president of Planned Parenthood, who cited that Japan's legalization of abortion "worked miracles" for controlling growth of the Japanese population (Guttmacher 1965). While *NR* itself did not endorse abortion specifically, this series sympathized with the population control movement. In 1966, William F. Buckley, the founder of *National Review* and arguably the most prominent conservative opinion leader of the mid-twentieth century, wrote harshly of the Catholic Church's opposition to abortion in *NR*: "There is great pressure to ease the abortion laws, and it is being said that the Catholic Church prevent its being done. If that is the case, the Catholic Church should reconsider its position." Buckley, himself a Catholic, wrote that labeling a fetus as a person with human rights "is a vision so utterly unapproachable as to suggest that the requirements of prudence and of charity intervene . . ." (Buckley 1966). *National Review* readers, and writers, reacted harshly to his column in the next issue's letters to the editor. Afterward, Buckley remained quiet on abortion, and the next time *NR* mentioned abortion, they adopted a more conservative tone. By 1974, Buckley wrote in favor of a constitutional amendment to overturn *Roe* (Hochman 2022).

Interestingly, the *Wall Street Journal* (*WSJ*) experienced a similar transformation. The *WSJ* actually shifted from being pro-choice in the early 1970s to opposing abortion rights in the 1980s (Noel 2013, 161–62). Robert Bartley, editor of the newspaper, held a compromise position in which he supported legalized abortion but believed it should not be publicly funded (the same position Carter expressed throughout his presidency) (Bartley 1978). While the source of *WSJ*'s shift is unknown, Paul Weyrich and other conservative activists lobbied Bartley to stake a more conservative abortion position. Rather than being opinion makers, the *Wall Street Journal* and *National Review* seemed to react to their political environment by belatedly adopting conservative abortion positions. Indeed, conservative abortion activists were often frustrated by the conservative intellectual class that they saw as too focused on abstract economic principles rather than the social issues that motivated their movement.

Even while conservative outlets began to trend rightward, messaging on the right remained diverse. For example, James J. Kilpatrick, a prominent conservative columnist who among other things opposed desegregation (Bernstein 2010), emphatically expressed that the Catholic Church had no right to impose their abortion views on others (Kilpatrick 1976). Writing in *NR* in 1979, Kilpatrick had not changed his position: "the substantive provisions of Mr. Justice Blackmun's opinion in *Roe v. Wade* represent sound and reasonable public policy. If these provisions had been embodied in a legislative proposal before a state legislature, they would have had my support" (Kilpatrick 1979, 678).

The emergence of abortion messaging on the left was also diverse. As the section on activists above illustrated, many people otherwise known to be liberal were both pro- and anti-abortion. Daniel Williams (2016) argues that the origins of both the pro- and anti-abortion movement emerged in New Deal liberalism and its implications for debates on contraception. New Deal progressives saw contraception as a means to reduce poverty and advance social reforms, while Catholics, also integral supporters of New Deal liberalism, saw contraception as devaluing human life (Williams 2016, 19). More broadly though, liberal public intellectuals, like their conservative counterparts, spoke little of abortion reform in the decades prior to the culture wars of the 1970s. *The Nation* published just three articles about abortion in the 1950s. The first, published in 1952 by Margaret Sanger (founder of Planned Parenthood), *opposed* abortion reforms. "Next to infanticide," Sanger (1952) wrote, "[abortions] are the worst means of checking population increase." *The Nation* did publish a piece in favor of liberalizing abortion laws in 1955, but that same year they also reviewed a book about Sanger that, because she opposed abortion, struck a conservative abortion tone. Not until 1965, would *The Nation* again publish a piece favoring abortion reform.

In the two decades before 1970, the *New Republic* published just five pieces on abortion (including one book review by Lawrence Lader, the cofounder of NARAL). Each of these pieces expressed sympathy for abortion reform, and all were published between 1963 and 1969. Framed differently, by spring of 1966 the liberal *New Republic* and conservative *National Review* had both written only one piece on abortion since 1950, and each piece favored liberalizing abortion laws.

Perhaps the biggest indicator that abortion sat in the liberal intellectual class's periphery was their non-reaction to *Roe v. Wade*. In 1973, the year the Supreme Court ruled on *Roe v. Wade*, the *New Republic* published just one editorial on abortion, and although fairly sympathetic to legalized abortion, they chastised the court's ruling. State legislatures, not the Supreme Court, should decide abortion policy, the *New Republic* wrote: "The question [of legalized abortion] is not for courts, but should have been left to the political process" (1973, 9). *The Nation* published just two articles on abortion in the *two* years following *Roe* (although both were liberal). To place this in perspective, in July 2022 alone, the month after the Supreme Court repealed *Roe*, a search of the *New Republic* for the key word "abortion" yielded twenty-seven articles.

More broadly, many of the earliest calls to reform abortion laws were justified to legally protect doctors or framed as a means to prevent overpopulation. Early advocates did not routinely frame liberalized abortion laws as part of a broader women's rights movement as is conventional today. For example, public intellectuals Lawrence Lader and Garrett Hardin, cofounders of NARAL, initially framed abortion repeal as a means to limit population growth (Williams 2016, 109). Indeed, when feminist Betty Friedan, also a NARAL cofounder, said she wanted NARAL's charter to include a statement that abortion rights were a woman's right to control her body, other leading abortion reformers at NARAL proclaimed, "What have women's rights got to do with abortion?" (Friedan 1976, 122). This discussion raises two points central to this book. First, public intellectuals, at least at the magazines analyzed here, weren't talking about abortion that much, and when they did, they expressed diverse messages through the late 1960s. This limited their ability to meaningfully shape early public opinion. Second, the cases of *National Review* and the *WSJ* illustrate a larger point: the stances taken by media outlets did not emerge out of nowhere, but were efforts to speak to a broader readership. In moments of political change and uncertainty, news producers are inclined to follow as much as they are to lead. For example, in December 1973, Jeffrey Hart, an editor and writer at *National Review*, wrote the magazine's editors, "A vacuum exists in the coverage of religious matters that could be filled by the NR. . . . Would it not therefore be a good move for NR to include a regular religious column or section. . . . I think the NR could appeal to a sizeable audience with such coverage" (Hart 1973).

Conclusion

The alignment of white evangelicals, the pro-life movement, and the Republican Party contrasts what appeared to be true prior to the 1980 election: abortion was a Catholic concern, and Catholics were Democrats. Furthermore, in the 1970s, Democratic identifiers in the mass public held marginally more conservative abortion attitudes than Republicans.

Existing scholarship emphasizes that anti-abortion activists and party elites played the pivotal role in aligning the pro-life movement within the Republican Party. This chapter argues that such views overstate the role of elite influence. While Republican politicians had discretion, they made choices in an environment where anti-abortion attitudes overlapped with conservative policies already adopted by the Republican Party. For example, Nixon did not consider his abortion decision in a political environment defined solely by economic intervention and did not view his coalition as limited to Republican identifiers. Rather, race, Vietnam, and marijuana legalization divided the electorate, and because he had positioned to the right on each of these issues, issue connections among voters made it easier to oppose abortion rights, too. Similarly, while Catholics had historically supported Democrats, the turbulence of the 1960s meant that racially conservative and hawkish Catholics — who happened to be the most conservative Catholics on abortion—had already begun entering the Republican Party before any national politician made anti-abortion appeals. And among activists, the very success of the Christian Right hinged partially on their ability to articulate what many voters already believed. The messages sent by Christian Right leaders were made in an environment where anti-abortion appeals already fit into a web of conservative causes at the mass level.

CHAPTER SEVEN

The Partisan Divide on Immigration

Following their loss in the 2012 presidential election, conservatives in-side and outside the Republican Party scrambled to appeal to Latino voters. Latinos, a large and quickly growing demographic, had voted over-whelmingly for Obama in the prior election cycles, and leading operatives feared that without the Latino vote, Republicans would continue to strug-gle to win presidential elections.

Senator Marco Rubio, then thought to be a leading contender for pres-ident in 2016, sponsored comprehensive immigration reform in the US Senate. Among other things, the reform package included a pathway to cit-izenship for undocumented immigrants. Other prominent GOP officehold-ers agreed with Rubio. Republican Speaker of the House John Boehner called immigration reform "long overdue." Future Speaker of the House Paul Ryan, fresh off the campaign trail as Romney's vice-presidential can-didate in 2012, told congressional advocates that immigration reform was "the right thing to do" (MacGillis 2016).

Conservative media figures, either out of perceived strategic foresight or personal conviction, also joined the effort to overhaul the immigration system. Rupert Murdoch, owner of the conservative Fox News channel and himself an advocate for immigration reform, agreed to hold back conserva-tive media personalities from attacking Rubio's immigration bill (Horowitz 2016). Sean Hannity, perhaps the public face of the Fox News channel, ex-pressed that his positions on immigration had evolved: "If people are here, law-abiding, participating for years, their kids are born here, you know, first secure the border, then pathway to citizenship, done" (Weinger 2012). Leading GOP activists were also open to reform. In 2013, the *New York Times* reported that "many of the most powerful and well-financed forces in the party are moving to provide cover for [Rubio] and Republicans like him who are pushing to overhaul the nation's immigration system" (Peters 2013). This list included the likes of the GOP mega-donors the Koch brothers and Grover Norquist, president of Americans for Tax Reform (Preston 2012).

Rubio's immigration bill passed the Senate in 2013, with fourteen Republicans voting in favor. The Republican-controlled House was set to take up the legislation, and by June 2014 *ProPublica* reported that 140 House Republicans, a majority of the Republican House caucus, signaled support for comprehensive immigration reform. The reform package included a mixture of more border security and pathway to citizenship for undocumented immigrants. House leadership signaled willingness to move forward with legislation. And then something happened: Eric Cantor, the House Majority leader (the second most powerful Republican in the House of Representatives), lost his primary election to an insurgent right-wing candidate who painted Cantor as pro–immigration reform. Immigration advocates knew this was bad news. One by one, Republican members of Congress told legislative leaders that despite their previous commitment, this was not the time for them to pursue reform (MacGillis 2016). They worried they would suffer the same fate as Cantor.

Congress never passed immigration reform, and Republican nominees in the lead-up to the 2016 election converged around an anti-immigration position. In fact, Rubio turned his back on his own immigration reform bill and tacked right on immigration to gain a leg up in the 2016 primary field (Miller 2016). And in the general election, Trump employed a strategy that state and congressional Republicans had been doing for years; rather than expanding the party by trying to pick up Hispanic voters using pro-immigration messaging, Trump peeled off conservative Democrats who opposed immigration. In a few years, immigration reform, which had at times enjoyed bipartisan elite consensus, become the most controversial issue at the highest levels of American politics.

*   *   *

While this book focuses on issues that arose and became polarizing in the 1970s and 1980s, the racial realignment also helps illuminate issues that have become highly partisan only much more recently. This chapter analyzes the longer-term structural forces that enabled the rise of anti-immigration candidates in the GOP. Why did Democrats and Republicans polarize in the directions they did? Could elite forces have created an alternative outcome?

I argue that the accelerating partisan divide on immigration that emerged prior to the 2016 election represents, to date, perhaps the longest legacy of the 1960s racial realignment. This chapter shows that the 1964 presidential election sowed the initial partisan divisions on the now-familiar partisan schism on immigration among the mass public: as white southerners defected to Barry Goldwater in 1964, they brought their very conservative immigration attitudes with them, despite immigration not being a partisan, or visible, campaign theme in 1964. This structural shift, like the other issues in this book, is underpinned by the fact that civil rights conservatives, on average, hold more conservative immigration attitudes.[1] This transformation sowed the seeds of a Republican Party willing to elect more restrictionist politicians and created a more fertile environment for pro-immigration groups—most notably Latino civil rights groups—to mobilize in the Democratic Party.[2]

What distinguishes immigration from other culture war issues discussed in this book is that each party's core interest groups—business interests in the GOP and labor unions among the Democrats—held countervailing positions to much of the rank and file. So, too, did prominent ideological voices. Given the cross-pressures of prominent interest groups, the evolution of immigration as a partisan issue presents perhaps the hardest test against a bottom-up theory of party sorting. Yet, as this chapter's opening vignette illustrates, while these elite forces perhaps at times slowed polarization, especially among national party candidates, they ultimately succumbed to the structural forces pushing the parties apart.

The mechanisms ultimately pushing the Republican Party rightward on immigration parallel the forces pushing the party rightward on other culture war issues. First, Republican primary voters held quite conservative immigration views, especially on questions of undocumented immigration. The Voter Study Group shows that by 2012, 71% of Republican primary voters opposed a pathway to citizenship for undocumented immigrants. Many of those voters, four years later, would support Donald Trump in the presidential primary. Given the anti-immigrant sentiment in the Republican primary electorate, supporting immigration reform meant risking being challenged from the right (as happened to House Majority leader Eric Cantor).

In general elections, Republicans—some of whom once saw shifting left on immigration as a means to win Latino voters even after running against immigration reform in the primary—realized that they could expand their general election pool by shifting to the right and peeling off conservative Democrats. Although more racially diverse by the mid-2010s, these voters had the profile of Goldwater, Wallace, and Reagan Democrats that Republicans had been pursuing for decades; people who held more moderate or liberal economic views but who were, in this case, immigration restrictionists (Sides, Tesler, and Vavreck 2019). In many ways, this transformation occurred at the subnational level before it emerged in national politics. Republicans in Congress and in state-level races had used undocumented immigration as a wedge issue to peel off conservative Democrats for some time and realized the perils of pro-immigration stances in primary elections.

This chapter proceeds in four sections. First, I analyze long-term trends on public opinion and immigration. Despite a wide literature on immigration and party politics, no work tracks the over-time partisan divide on immigration attitudes (among the mass public) from the 1950s through the Trump era (most start in the 1990s). This chapter fills that gap in public opinion research. Second, I break down the 1964 racial realignment's effect for the partisan distribution of immigration opinion in the mass electorate. Third, I explore why the racial realignment was a critical juncture that constrained the parties' future immigration positions. Fourth, I argue that Obama's ascendancy to the presidency, which itself was an outgrowth of the racial realignment, further racialized the images of the parties and induced more polarization on immigration that then went into overdrive during the Trump era.

To be clear, the racial realignment alone cannot explain today's immigration divide: many events played out between the 1960s and the Trump era. Rather, I argue that the racial realignment represents a critical juncture that shaped the contours of the partisan debate to come. The shifting electoral cleavages, and the partisan-group building that occurred slowly for decades, enabled the rapid polarization of the last decade.

Background: Immigration and the Party System

At polarization's low point in the 1950s, the contemporary alignment of anti-immigration forces in the Republican Party seemed unlikely. First, midcentury surveys showed that Democrats in the electorate were slightly more conservative than Republicans on immigration. Second, the national party platforms throughout the mid-twentieth century contained similar language on immigration, and the question of undocumented immigration was absent from either party's national platform until the 1972 Republican platform, which included a single sentence on the topic (UCSB Presidency Project). In fact, more congressional Republicans than Democrats voted in favor of the 1965 Immigration and Nationality Act, sweeping legislation that removed nation-based immigrant quota systems. Finally, the landscape of interest groups in the 1950s suggested that Republicans, not Democrats, were primed to hold the pro-immigration banner: labor unions had historically opposed immigration because they perceived that foreign workers threatened domestic wages, and for that same reason, business groups generally pushed for more expansive policies.

Intellectual thinkers also expressed diverse views. In the late 1970s, the ideologically liberal magazine *New Republic* published several articles arguing that migrant labor from Mexico would undercut US labor and contribute to population growth and food shortages. The "United States must do something to stop illegal immigration," the *New Republic*'s lead column exclaimed weeks after the 1980 election (TRB from Washington 1980). Conversely, prominent conservative intellectuals and media outlets in the 1980s embraced relaxing immigration laws, believing open borders and the free flow of labor aligned with the tenets of free markets (Tichenor 1994, 342). In fact, the *New Republic* called the editorial writers at the *Wall Street Journal*, an otherwise conservative newspaper, "an extreme school of [unauthorized immigrant] inclusionists" (Kondracke 1987).

Attitudes toward Racial Equality and Immigration

In each year with available data (as done in chapter 3), I compare attitudes toward immigration levels and measures of black racial equality.[3] While survey firms have long asked about attitudes toward immigration and refugee policy, the nature of those questions and the types of immigration the questions asked about vary widely. This is because the constantly changing nature of immigration debates means pollsters asked different questions in different eras. For example, in 1965, survey firms asked about removing nation-based quotas, a question they stopped asking after Congress passed the Hart-Celler Act, which removed these quotas. As a result, available public opinion is difficult to compare as the questions asked often changed.

To measure immigration attitudes over time, I use a question that survey firms have asked consistently, with only slight variations, since 1955: *Do you want immigration levels to be increased, decreased, or kept about the same?* While the debate over immigration levels has taken different forms (e.g., family based or skill based; documented and undocumented) this question captures broad support for immigration. Furthermore, and perhaps most importantly, because it is the only question consistently asked over a long period of time, it is the best available tool to analyze shifting opinions on immigration. The American National Election Study began asking this question in 1992, and so I use the ANES data after 1992. Before 1992, I use every possible dataset that asks this question (totaling six surveys).

Of course, there are limitations for using this measure. While this question has consistent wording, which allows for the best available comparison over time, it may capture different elements of the debate at different times. For example, in 1955, when immigration flows were effectively zero, someone who wanted immigration levels to stay the same could represent a conservative position given the conservative status quo. Yet in the 1980s, when immigration rates were increasing, keeping immigration levels the same may represent a liberal position. However, between 1955 and 2016, public opinion on immigration levels is remarkably consistent despite drastic changes in immigration rates.[4]

Figure 7.1 shows the over-time correlation between racial and immigration attitude pairs: restrictionist immigration opinion and opposition to black racial equality have gone hand in hand among ordinary voters dating to the earliest public opinion polls, which include questions on both immigration levels and black racial equality. For non-statistically oriented readers, recall that a correlation measures how much two variables vary together. The positive values in figure 7.1 show that people who hold more conservative immigration views tend to also hold more conservative racial views. For example, in the first point in figure 7.1, 59% of respondents who opposed the Civil Rights Act wanted to lower immigration levels compared to just 32% of respondents who supported the Civil Rights Act (levels are similar for white and non-white respondents). The correlation between racial attitudes and immigration levels are strikingly consistent across time. Between 1964 and 2012, the trend line remains almost flat before rapidly increasing in 2016 and 2020.

Unfortunately, surveys asking about both general immigration levels and black racial equality date only to 1964, but examining questions on refugees (as opposed to general immigration levels) reveals a similar

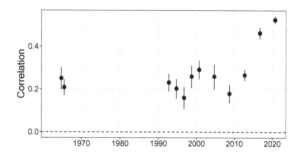

FIGURE 7.1. Correlation: Attitudes toward Immigration and Race. Each point is the correlation between immigration levels (defined by whether a respondent wants immigration levels to increase, decrease, or stay the same) and black racial equality. Positive coefficients mean that more conservative attitudes on immigration correspond with more conservative attitudes toward black racial equality. Lines represent 95% confidence intervals.

TABLE 7.1. **Attitudes toward African American Racial Equality and Refugees**

	% Oppose Refugees
1957 Gallup Survey: US	
Support school desegregation	45%
Oppose school desegregation	60%
1948 Survey: Elmira, NY	
Disagree: African Americans are "lazy and ignorant"	53%
Agree: African Americans are "lazy and ignorant"	71%

Note: Table shows relationship between attitudes toward school desegregation (top panel)/black racial prejudice (bottom panel) and refugee levels. The question from 1957 asks: "Under the present immigration laws, the Hungarian refugees who came to this country after the revolts last year have no permanent residence and can be deported at any time. Do you think the law should or should not be changed so that these refugees can stay here permanently?" The 1948 Elmira question asks: "Congress has passed a bill to admit 200,000 refugees to the United States in the next four years. Do you approve or disapprove of this?"

pattern that dates back further (table 7.1). A 1957 Gallup survey (poll #589) asked respondents whether they believed Hungarian refugees (who had come to the United States after a failed uprising against Soviet rule in Hungary) should be allowed to stay in the United States permanently. The survey also asked respondents whether they supported the Supreme Court case to integrate schools. Those who supported school integration were 15 percentage points more supportive of allowing Hungarian refugees to stay than those opposed to school integration. A survey of residents in Elmira, New York (Bureau of Applied Social Research 1948), finds a similar pattern in 1948: respondents who expressed that African Americans are "lazy and ignorant" were about 18 percentage points more likely to disapprove of allowing refugees into the country.[5]

These data suggest that the relationship between black racial equality and immigration attitudes stretches across both time and type of immigration. To further investigate immigration type and its relationship to black racial prejudice, I use data from a 1981 survey conducted by *ABC News/Washington Post* (1981), which asks about both racial prejudice and whether the respondent would encourage immigration from various countries. Correlations between racial prejudice and immigrant attitudes, presented in figure 7.2, are strongest when asked about immigration from countries with people of color (e.g., Iran, Haiti) and weakest toward immigration from Western Europe. But the correlations point in the same direction. *That is, regardless of the country source of immigration, conservative racial attitudes correspond with more restrictionist views.*[6]

That immigration and attitudes toward racial equality are intertwined is not surprising. Immigration attitudes map onto broader feelings of ethnocentrism, a predisposition that closely tracks feelings around black racial equality in the United States (Kinder and Kam 2009; Kinder and Mendelberg 2000; Valentino, Brader, and Jardina 2013). Furthermore, immigration debates often strike implicit, if not explicit, racial overtones.

While this chapter's argument extends across types of immigration, debates over immigration in the last sixty years have been particularly race-based because immigrants have become more racially diverse. The Immigration and Nationalization Act, which Congress passed in 1965,

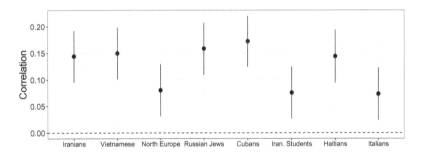

FIGURE 7.2. Correlation: Racial Prejudice and Immigrant Nationality. Each point is the correlation between (1) whether a respondent agrees with the following statement: "If blacks would try harder, they could be just as well off as whites"; and (2) whether the respondent would encourage immigration to the United States of each of the groups listed on the x-axis. Positive coefficients mean more conservative attitudes on immigration correspond with higher racial resentment.

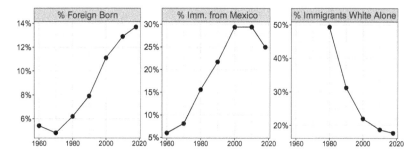

FIGURE 7.3. Immigration Levels and Demographics. Data are from Pew Research Center (Budiman et al. 2018).

removed nation-based quotas, and in doing so, scholars argue, both expanded the foreign-born population living in the United States and diversified the racial composition of those immigrants (Tichenor 2016; Gjelten 2015; Abrajano and Hajnal 2015, 29). As figure 7.3 shows, the percentage of the foreign-born US population rose from 4.7% of the population in 1970 to 10% in 2000 and sat around 14% in 2018. In 1960, about 13% of the foreign born were from Asia or Latin America and 84% from Europe ·or Canada. By 2000, 74% of the foreign born were from Asia or Latin America, and just 19% of the foreign born were from Europe or Canada (Gutierrez 2019).

Furthermore, starting in the 1970s, the presence of undocumented immigrants, many from Mexico and Central America, substantially increased. While difficult to precisely measure the number of undocumented immigrants, Pew estimates there were approximately 3.9 million undocumented immigrants in the United States in 1990. Just a decade later, that number was estimated to be 8.6 million. By 2005, that number had reached nearly 11 million (Passel and Cohn 2019; Schildkraut 2010; Hopkins 2010). The racial diversification of immigrants following 1965 has meant that identity and ethnicity have heavily defined immigration debates, even if material concerns also shape immigration attitudes (Citrin et al. 1997; Valentino, Brader, and Jardina 2013).[7] Furthermore, scholars argue that people's perceptions of immigrants violating American norms and traditions shape hostile views of immigration (e.g., Schildkraut 2010; Citrin, Reingold, and Green 1990).

As with other issues discussed in this book, partisan messaging cannot explain the persistence of the issue bundles before the late 1970s. In the early 1960s, the parties expressed similar positions on immigration. In fact, more congressional Republicans than Democrats voted for the 1965 Hart-Celler Immigration Act. And although Lyndon Johnson, a Democrat, signed the bill into law, Truman, Eisenhower, and Kennedy each supported removing immigration quotas (TRB from Washington 1965b). Likewise, messaging from public intellectuals was sparse, and the ideological source did not always predict the message in the 1960s and 1970s. The liberal *New Republic*, like organized labor, saw immigration as a threat to the goals of labor unions (e.g., jobs, maintaining high wages) and would continue to oppose liberalized immigration efforts through the early 1980s. The *New Republic* also opposed the 1965 immigration reform law and published three columns expressing their disapproval: "We try not to be prejudiced against the Administration's liberalized immigration law. But a lot of arguments for it leave us cold. The bill would let more people in at a time when millions are already unemployed" (TRB from Washington 1965a).

Conservative magazine *National Review*, by my search, published only one column on the 1965 immigration act, which opposed increasing immigration levels (Haag 1965). This was just the second article *National Review* published on immigration since the magazine's founding in 1955, and the first since 1956. And as discussed in the introduction, the *Wall Street Journal* and other conservative intellectuals, in the spirit of free markets and open borders, often supported liberalized immigration, including undocumented immigration from Central America.

Partisan Immigration Divides

Despite immigration representing a long-standing issue in US politics, for the reasons discussed above, there exists (to my knowledge) no long-term over-time analysis of partisan trends toward issues of immigration that starts *before* the 1990s. This section explores partisan divides on immigration attitudes before and after the 1964 racial realignment.

The earliest poll that asks about immigration attitudes (using the measure defined above) and party identification, in September 1964, shows that Republicans are slightly left of Democrats (first point of panel A in figure 7.4). By spring of 1965 (second data point in panel A), the difference remains small and statistically insignificant, but the order has switched, such that Republicans are 2 percentage points to the right of Democrats. Between 1965 and the early 2000s, the difference between Republican and Democratic identifiers stays remarkably constant at around 2 to 3 percent-

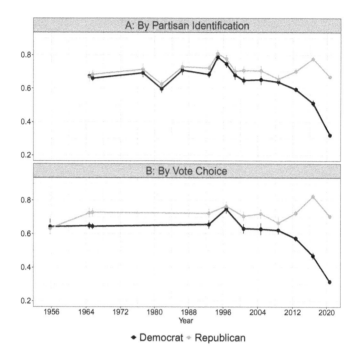

FIGURE 7.4. Attitudes toward Immigration Levels. The top panel (A) tracks immigration attitudes by partisan identification — meaning people who call themselves Democrats or Republicans. The bottom panel (B) tracks immigration attitudes by presidential vote choice. Immigration opinions are measured using a three-point scale of whether respondent wants immigration levels to decrease (coded 1), stay the same (coded 0.5), or increase (coded 0). Higher values are more conservative.

age points. The divide opens slightly in 2000 and 2004 to about 5 percentage points. By 2012, Democrats and Republicans are split by 11 percentage points, and in 2016 that number rises to 26 percentage points. The gap grows even larger in 2020, driven entirely by Democrats moving further to the left.

Next, the bottom panel of figure 7.4 tracks immigration attitudes between 1955 and 2020 by vote choice in presidential elections. (The 1955 survey asks about vote choice, but not partisan identification, which extends the analysis nine years earlier.) The first data point, in 1955, shows effectively no difference in immigration attitudes between Dwight Eisenhower (the Republican presidential candidate) and Adlai Stevenson (the Democratic presidential candidate) supporters. Indeed, Stevenson voters are slightly more conservative than Eisenhower voters. By 1964, though,

Barry Goldwater (Republican) supporters are clearly to the right of Lyndon Johnson (Democrat) supporters.

A simple cross-tab of the percentage of voters who want to decrease immigration levels illustrates the magnitude of difference that emerged between 1955 and 1964 (the figure plots an average of the three-point scale). In 1955, Stevenson voters are 7 percentage points more likely to favor decreasing immigration levels (47% to 40%). In 1964, Goldwater voters are 12 percentage points more likely to say they want immigration levels to decrease (50% to 38%). This represents a 19 percentage-point swing on immigration positions between 1955 and 1964. The partisan divides measured by vote choice are larger than partisan divides measured by party identification because of split-ticket voters and Independents (a fact the next section explores).

The divide that emerged in 1964 persists the next time vote choice and immigration levels are asked in 1992. It shrinks in 1996 at the height of anti-immigration fervor, but then returns to 1992 levels in the early 2000s and then explodes in 2012 and 2016.

The Partisan Immigration Divide Emerges in 1964

Over-time attitudes toward immigration show that between 1955 and 1964, vote choice became a significant predictor of immigration attitudes. This is puzzling because the parties did not send divergent signals on immigration in 1964. I argue that this emerging partisan divide is the result of white southerners and other racial conservatives who abandoned the Democratic Party to vote for Goldwater in 1964 on account of civil rights and brought their restrictionist immigration attitudes with them.

While panel data spanning the 1964 election do not exist, a Gallup poll in September 1964 asks about vote choice in both 1960 and 1964. Vote recall is a noisy measure for actual voting behavior (Himmelweit, Biberian, and Stockdale 1978), but provides a reasonably accurate estimate for preferences. (For example, a panel of respondents in 1972 and 1976 shows that only about 7% of respondents in 1976 recall voting for a candidate other than what they reported in 1972.) Although imperfect, this data enables analysis of immigration cleavages by vote choice in 1960 and 1964 *among the same pool of voters*. As a reminder, in 1960 Nixon and Kennedy had overlapping civil rights positions, but in 1964 Johnson and Goldwater had divergent civil rights positions. This allows analysis of how party switchers between 1960 and 1964 differed on the question of immigration.

However, because the data are from only one point, this analysis requires two assumptions: (1) that the primary reason voters defected from Nixon and voted for Goldwater in 1964 is the Democratic Party's adoption of a strong civil rights program; and (2) voters did not change their opinions toward immigration between 1960 and 1964. With respect to the latter point, overall attitudes on immigration between the 1955 and 1964 surveys are remarkably constant (see appendix figure A.2). Furthermore, immigration was not a salient campaign issue to voters in this era, a usual prerequisite for large-scale opinion change. Among thirty-nine public opinion polls between 1960 and 1965, in only one poll did even a single respondent say immigration was the most important issue (in that poll, conducted in September 1964, 0.89% of respondents said it was the most important issue).

For this same reason, it is unlikely people changed parties between 1960 and 1964 *because* of immigration. To my knowledge, there exists no literature that argues immigration propelled southern realignment in 1964. Rather, and as discussed in chapter 2, scholarship shows the primary reason for southern defection is civil rights. In the Gallup poll presently being analyzed, nearly three-quarters of the 1960 JFK voters who defected to Goldwater in 1964 opposed the civil rights bill (compared to less than a quarter who stayed with the Democrats), all of the defectors are white, and 49% of the switchers are from the South (despite southerners representing only 26% of the sample). Each of these suggest that civil rights is a major factor in the reported vote switching.

But how are partisan divides on immigration affected by Goldwater Democrats' defection? Panel A of figure 7.5 dissects support for *decreasing* immigration levels by 1960 and 1964 vote choice. In 1960, Kennedy voters are 4 percentage points to the left of Nixon voters, although the difference is not statistically different from zero. By 1964, the gap opens up to 12 percentage points (and is statistically different from 0).

Panels B and C show that the South entirely drives this shift. In the South, Kennedy voters are 1 percentage point to the right of Nixon voters in 1960. But in 1964, Johnson voters are 15 percentage points to the left—a net swing of about 16 percentage points. In the non-South, the partisan differences are parallel: about 5 percentage points divide the parties by both 1960 and 1964 vote choice. These data align with the book's core thesis: as racially conservative voters in the South abandoned the Democratic Party on account of civil rights, they brought their already conservative immigration attitudes with them, *even without the parties taking visibly polarizing positions on immigration.*

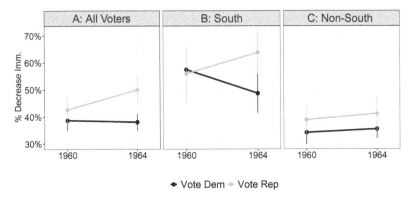

FIGURE 7.5. Immigration Attitudes by Vote Choice in 1960 and 1964 Presidential Elections. The graph shows immigration opinion (higher values are more conservative) by reported presidential vote choice in 1960 (between JFK and Nixon) and 1964 (between Goldwater and LBJ). Data are from a Gallup survey in September 1964 that asked about vote choice in both 1960 and 1964.

The Racial Realignment as a Critical Juncture (Again)

The previous section shows that electoral coalitions newly divided by civil rights also became more polarized on immigration, too, even without candidates making appeals on those issues. The 1964 realignment generated the initial partisan divide in public opinion that persisted until after the 2008 election. Absent a racial realignment, the fights over immigration that occurred in the latter part of the twentieth century would have occurred in a different partisan environment. This mattered for party polarization on immigration in the decades leading up to Trump's nomination.

Democrats and Immigration

When polarization sat at its low point in the 1950s, an analysis of interest groups would suggest that if the parties polarized on immigration, Democrats would favor restricting immigration and Republicans would favor expanding immigration. Business groups aligned with the GOP often supported increased immigration while organized labor, closely aligned with the Democratic Party, opposed loosening immigration standards from the nineteenth through mid-twentieth century. This extended across different types of immigration, including undocumented immigration across the US-Mexico border. Democrats' opposition to immigration in the midcentury United States mirrored the concerns of immigration restrictionists today: undocumented immigration undercut domestic employment and depressed wages. These concerns were not restricted to old-school conservative Democrats, but emerged among leading figures of the progressive movement as well.

The racial realignment shifted this equilibrium by bringing groups and voters into the Democratic Party that were sympathetic to a multicultural democracy and would support loosened immigration levels. This, as discussed above, became perhaps even more pronounced by the fact that immigration struck an increasingly racial tone in the 1960s, and by the 1970s, immigration was becoming increasingly tied to undocumented immigration from Mexico and other parts of Central America. A 1977 Roper poll (Poll #77-9), the first to ask both about undocumented immigrants and Hispanic identity, finds that 57% of Hispanic voters supported amnesty for undocumented immigrants compared to just 43% among non-Hispanic respondents. Attitudes toward civil rights groups were a strong predictor of non-Hispanic respondents' views toward undocumented immigration. Just 34% of non-Hispanic respondents who believed civil rights groups had too much power supported some sort of amnesty for undocumented immigrants compared to 58% of non-Hispanic respondents who believed civil rights groups had not enough power.

The very fact that the Democrats embraced civil rights made it difficult to have a message of opposition to immigration. Immigration scholar Dan Tichenor writes, "The pro-immigration impulses of the Left were richly informed by a universal rights zeitgeist that gained ascendance among progressive Democrats in the postwar era" (2002, 255). Lyndon Johnson immediately felt the constraints of this zeitgeist during the 1965 push to remove national quotas. Johnson expressed initial reluctance to remove the quota system because he believed the political challenges of reforming immigration would hinder his other policy priorities. Yet Johnson ultimately embraced the agenda because, as one of Johnson's former advisers remembered: "LBJ could not ignore the obvious connections between immigration reform and the administration's most important foreign and civil rights goals" (qtd. in Tichenor 2016, 695). Critics viewed the national quota system, which systematically restricted immigration of people of color, as racist. It would be awkward to advocate for black civil rights but then uphold an immigration system that favored white European immigrants.

Perhaps the racial realignment's greatest effect on Democratic positioning toward immigration in the latter part of the twentieth century was

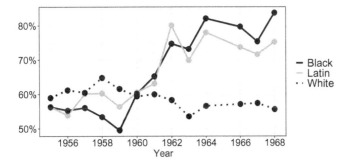

FIGURE 7.6. Texas Percentage Democrat: By White, Black, and Latin Respondents, 1954–1968. Figure shows the percentage of Democrat identifiers among black (solid black line), white (dashed line), and Latin (solid gray line) respondents in Texas. Respondents choose between Democrat, Independent, Republican, Other/Don't Know. Polls conducted multiple times per year are averaged together.

that it brought Latino civil rights groups and voters into the Democratic Party, which would prove to be crucial for pushing the party leftward on immigration. While it is difficult to pinpoint the effect of the racial realignment on shifting loyalties of Latino groups and voters, evidence suggests that the early 1960s was a turning point. A series of Texas state polls in the 1950s and 1960s (produced by Belden Associates), a state with a sizable Latino population in the midcentury United States, consistently asked about partisanship and whether respondents were "anglo, negro or latin."[8] Most Latinos in the Southwest in this era were of Mexican origin or descent, so trends are not nationally representative, but are instructive and, to my knowledge, have not been previously shown. Moreover, people of Mexican nationality or descent were a majority of the Latino vote in the 1970s–1980s United States (Francis-Fallon 2019, 357).[9] Also, Mexican American voters and interest groups pushed for liberalized immigration laws in ways that other Hispanic constituencies, notably Cubans, would not.

Figure 7.6 shows that Democratic partisanship among Texas Latin voters skyrockets in the early 1960s and moves in lockstep with African American partisanship. The speed of racial polarization in the Texas electorate in the early 1960s is staggering: In 1960, white, black, and Latin respondents were each about equally likely to identify as Democrats; by 1964, Latin and black respondents were 25 percentage points more likely than white respondents to identify as Democratic.

While it's impossible to say why Latin voters moved rapidly to the Democratic Party in this period, the parties' changing messaging on civil

rights was a major factor. "Viva Kennedy" groups—Hispanic organizations that advanced Kennedy's candidacy in 1960—messaged voters that
Democrats and liberals were the party most likely to secure racial and
economic justice for Hispanics (Garcia 2000, 56). Racial discrimination in
policing, schooling, wages, and living conditions deeply affected Hispanic
communities and underscored liberal attitudes on these issues among Latin
people (Garcia 2000, 53; Vargas 2005). For example, a Texas Poll in the early
1960s (Belden Associates) showed that only 18% of white respondents
believed Texas schools should be immediately desegregated, compared to
48% of Latino and black voters who wanted immediate desegregation.[10]
Increasing partisan identification with the Democrats was also the result
of John Kennedy's (and then Bobby Kennedy's) relationship with Cesar
Chavez and the United Farm Workers, which generated loyalty among
many Mexican and Mexican American workers to the Kennedys and, by
extension, the Democratic Party.

To be clear, in the 1960s, immigration policy, including undocumented
immigration, being framed as an issue that affected Latinos had yet to
emerge in the context that it does today, and to the extent it bubbled onto
the agenda, Democrats were antagonistic. In other words, Latino voters
were not moving to the Democratic Party *because* of undocumented immigration at this time. Rather, when undocumented immigration from Mexico
began to gain salience in the 1970s, many Hispanic voters were already
aligned with the Democratic Party, which then constrained the positions
the party could take.

The racial realignment mattered for the Democrats' future ability to
position on immigration not simply because it predisposed Latino voters
to the Democratic Party, who would be some of the most liberal voters on
questions of undocumented immigration, but because it also predisposed
Latino civil rights groups, focused on ameliorating racial injustices faced by
Latinos, into the Democratic Party. Again, group-party building between
the Democratic Party and Latino groups initially occurred over Latino
group demands for racial and economic equality. However, Latino civil
rights groups' existing ties to the Democratic Party were central to efforts
to push the Democratic Party leftward on immigration when the issue
gained salience in the 1970s and 1980s as a "Hispanic" issue. "We've always
given our votes to the Democratic Party," one Latino activist proclaimed
before the 1980 election. "Now we have to make that party responsive to
us" (qtd. in Francis-Fallon 2019, 340).

While white liberals and even Hispanic public opinion toward undocumented immigration was mixed at times, Latino civil rights groups consistently pushed for what is today considered liberal immigration policy (Applebome 1986). The Mexican American Legal Defense and Educational Fund, League of United Latin American Citizens, and National Council of La Raza played prominent roles in pushing the party leftward on immigration in the 1980s and 1990s (Gimpel and Edwards 1998, 49–50; Wong 2006). For example, during a 1984 presidential debate, the debate moderator pressed Democratic presidential nominee Walter Mondale for flipping his position on immigration reform to satisfy Hispanic leadership groups that had become newly prominent in the party. Just fifteen years earlier, Mondale had expressed concern that the entrance of undocumented immigrants across the southern border threatened key Democratic initiatives. Mondale also proposed legislation in the Senate that banned the hiring of undocumented immigrants (Presidential Debate 1984; Fine and Tichenor 2009, 104; Greene 1969).

As with other issues in this book, the pressures pushing Democrats leftward came through both the general and primary elections. In 1976, 82% of Hispanic voters supported Jimmy Carter in the general election, which placed pressure on his administration to attend to Latino interests and representation. Carter, as did Kennedy in 1960, saw Hispanic voters as essential to win southern states to counterbalance the exodus of white voters to the Republican Party. But after making bold promises, Carter disappointed many Hispanic groups during his first term. Carter did make efforts at immigration reform, including proposing legislation that offered amnesty, but he also supported employer restrictions—fines levied on businesses that hired undocumented immigrants—which upset many Hispanic civil rights groups. Hispanic leaders were also upset at Carter for a lack of Hispanic representation in his administration and for his failure to protect undocumented immigrants (Tolchin 1979).

As his first term wound down, Carter realized he needed to bolster his appeal to Hispanic groups. Not only would Hispanic voters be important for the general election, but they would be crucial in the primary election to ward off Ted Kennedy's insurgent run from the left. Kennedy's primary campaign pushed Carter leftward on immigration. Kennedy, partially because of his older brothers' involvement with Cesar Chavez and the United Farm Workers, had long enjoyed support from the Mexican American community (Burns 1976, 207–8) and fervently campaigned for their vote during the 1980 primary cycle (Ayres 1980b).[11] To stave off Kennedy's challenge from the left and to prevent losing Mexican American voters to him, Carter created the Office of Hispanic Affairs, which, Carter said, would advise him "on many things, one of which is how to get votes" (Francis-Fallon 2019, 334). Carter toured the country trying to shore up support among Hispanic Americans in advance of his reelection, a constituency that could be the deciding vote margin in both the primary and general election.

The racial realignment affected Democratic positioning on immigration for other reasons, too. For one, it meant most minority members of Congress, who became important advocates for immigration reform, were elected in the Democratic, rather than the Republican, Party. For example, while both the AFL-CIO and NAACP favored employer restrictions—a policy that criminalized the hiring of undocumented immigrants—many black and Hispanic members of Congress, who were overwhelmingly concentrated in the Democratic Party, opposed employer restrictions. These members of Congress feared employer restrictions would lead to racial profiling of all minorities and opposed them (Gimpel and Edwards 1998, 117, 237–38; Wong 2006, 119).[12]

Finally, the racial realignment mattered for the Democrats' immigration positions both because of the voters and groups it brought into the coalition, but also because of voters it pushed away; primarily southern Democrats. In Congress, members from the US South, which had been represented almost exclusively by Democrats through the mid-twentieth century, consistently opposed liberalizing immigration laws (Gimpel and Edwards 1998). For example, more Republican than Democratic members of Congress voted for the 1965 Hart-Celler Act. This is because many southern Democrats opposed the bill. Of eighteen senators who opposed Hart-Celler, thirteen were Democrats elected in former Confederate states. Southern opposition to the national quotas struck a particularly racial overtone. North Carolina Democrat Sam Ervin, a segregationist, believed the United States should be a primarily European country: "With all due respect to Ethiopia . . . I don't know of any contributions that Ethiopia has made to the making of America" (qtd. in Gjelten 2015).[13] As the regional composition of the parties shifted, the anti-immigrant forces within the Democratic Party shrank.

Republicans and Immigration

While the racial realignment predisposed Latinos to the Democratic Party, it cut off much of the Republican Party as a viable alternative for the Latino groups that would push for looser immigration restrictions. The ascen-

THE PARTISAN DIVIDE ON IMMIGRATION

dant conservative wing in the Republican Party hampered Gerald Ford's response to growing undocumented immigration from Central America. Members of his administration adopted harsh rhetoric to protect Ford from the party's right flank, and Ford himself messaged that the White House was "cognizant of the adverse impact that illegal aliens have on employment opportunities for American citizens" (Ford Press Conference 1975; Francis-Fallon 2019).

While Carter won over 80% of the Hispanic vote in 1976 and between 65–70% of the Hispanic vote in 1980, the Reagan administration viewed their improved showing in the 1980 election as a possibility that Latino voters could be lured into the GOP (Francis-Fallon 2019, 365). Reagan did well among Cuban voters and sought out the non-Cuban Hispanic population, which, if captured, would be a boon for Republican fortunes. In many regards, Reagan viewed the Hispanic vote as Nixon had eight years earlier. Nixon believed "Spanish-speaking" voters could be lured into the Republican Party through the appeals that worked with conservative (non-Hispanic) white people: by appealing to anti-blackness and a host of other traditional social values (Francis-Fallon 2019, 231–32).

In the 1972 election, in a landslide win, Nixon did fairly well with His-panic voters, especially Cuban Americans and middle- and upper-class Latinos. But it would be difficult to replicate. The Republican Party had moved to the right during the 1970s, and attracting new Hispanic voters without alienating its existing support among white racial conservatives would prove difficult. This was exacerbated by the fact that undocumented immigration, an issue that had become important for many voters of Mex-ican descent during the 1970s, was less popular among the Republicans' growing conservative wing. Still further, many Mexican American voters, whom Reagan's efforts targeted, identified as liberal and viewed the Rea-gan administration coldly. Historian Benjamin Francis-Fallon writes that Reagan's "attempt to roll back the limited welfare state laid down in the New Deal and the multicultural democracy born during the civil rights era" ran into a wall against the mission of many national Hispanic organizations (2019, 366). Elizabeth Dole, then adviser to President Reagan, expressed similar concern: "Hispanics are beginning to view the Administration as racist and as one with little concern for the poor." A survey of Mexican Americans in East Los Angeles and San Antonio showed that they over-whelming approved core Democratic policies such as extending the Voting Rights Act (which was up for renewal and which Reagan wanted to water down), bilingual education, and the Equal Rights Amendment. Dole's staff

158 CHAPTER SEVEN

expressed that "the Mexican-American is more progressive than expected" (qtd. in Francis-Fallon 2019, 370–72). And while the Republican Party, as is true today, enjoyed more support from Cuban constituencies, this potentially alienated the Republican Party from making further gains into the non-Cuban Hispanic base (Francis-Fallon 2019, 377).

Nevertheless, Reagan, like other national Republican figures in the years to come, made efforts to push the party left on immigration. In 1980, in the spirit of unfettered global markets pushed by conservative economic thinkers and business groups, Reagan expressed support for free trade of goods and people across borders. Furthermore, Reagan, as former governor of California, also had ties with agricultural growers, a powerful lobby that opposed employer restrictions and wanted guest-worker programs as a means for cheap labor (Tichenor 2002, 255).

Electoral considerations also factored into Reagan's stance. In an effort to woo Mexican Americans in Texas, a state Carter barely won in 1976, Reagan endorsed the idea that immigrant laborers should be allowed to enter the country "for whatever length they want to stay" (Raines 1980). During his first term, Reagan saw opposing employer restrictions as an opportunity to win Mexican American voters without alienating conservative interests. Hispanic groups opposed employer restrictions because they feared it would lead to discriminatory hiring practices, while businesses and market conservatives saw them as an undue government regulation. The Reagan administration secretly planned to veto an immigration reform bill that included harsh employer restrictions in an effort to "score a political coup" with Hispanic Americans. Congressional Democrats caught wind of Reagan's plan and tabled the bill (Tolchin 1983).

In the 1984 presidential debate, Reagan went further: "I believe in the idea of amnesty for those who have put down roots and who have lived here" (Presidential Debate 1984). And in 1986, Reagan acted on these words, signing the Immigration Reform and Control Act, which included amnesty for undocumented immigrants in the United States before 1982. In 1987, the Reagan administration issued an executive order that expanded the number of people whom the act would grant amnesty (Tichenor 2002). Reagan's successor, George H. W. Bush, signed immigration reform in 1990, which expanded entry of *legal* immigration (an update on the 1965 act) and, like Reagan, also signed an executive order to shield deportation of children of immigrants who had been given legal status by the 1986 bill (Noferi 2014).

Perhaps the most concerted effort to push the GOP left came during

George W. Bush's candidacy and then presidency. One impetus for reform came from business groups, which were a powerful motivator for George W. Bush's immigration reform efforts in the early 2000s (Tichenor 2009, 16). But electoral factors also pushed Bush to tack leftward. The Republican Party was coming off a bruising loss in the 1996 presidential election. At the height of anti-immigrant fervor in the mid-1990s, Republican presidential candidate Bob Dole took a firm anti-immigrant stance and, perhaps as a result, was the first Republican to lose Florida since Ford in 1976. Bush, among others, believed Republicans would have to soften their position to keep the party viable among the growing Latino population. Bush pushed for a guest-worker program and for creating a path to amnesty for the millions of undocumented immigrants already living and paying taxes in the United States.

However, Bush's efforts stalled. Not only was Bush directly pushing against Republican voters who were hostile to immigration, but he was also challenging many congressional and state Republicans who opposed immigration reform and saw restrictionist positions as electorally profitable. At least by the 1980s, even while national Republicans were liberal on immigration, some Republican candidates for Congress and other subnational offices, especially in border states with a large number of undocumented immigrants, realized that running on anti-immigrant sentiment was a means to secure nomination in the primary and that it served as a wedge issue to attract anti-immigrant blue-collar voters from the Democrats in the general election (Tichenor 2002, 285). In other words, Republicans realized that rather than moving left on immigration to pick up Latino voters, who were proving difficult to mobilize into the GOP, they could tack right and win the Goldwater/Wallace Democrat-type voters (and those with a similar profile), who, as the previous section shows, held quite conservative immigration views.

Elton Gallegly was one such congressional Republican. In the 1992 midterms, Gallegly faced a tough reelection fight in a redrawn district in Southern California. Gallegly, a leading immigration restrictionist in Congress, campaigned for the seat on a hard-line immigration position despite a third of his newly redrawn congressional district being Hispanic. The district's demographics made anti-immigrant positions risky, Gallegly admitted. But the issue also generated political capital: "Immigration messaging has hit hot buttons out there," one strategist noted of Gallegly's campaign (Soble and Miller 1992). "Racial polarization is good politics. It wins," another strategist commented (Kelley 1991). Gallegly won reelection in 1992. His

Democratic opponent's campaign manager acknowledged that Gallegly's victory was a result of his ability to successfully create "wedge issues" on immigration (Soble 1992).

Perhaps the most visible use of immigration as a wedge-issue strategy was Republican California Governor Pete Wilson's signing on to Proposition 187, a state ballot initiative that would cut off state funds for Medicaid and education to undocumented immigrants. Wilson, the incumbent Republican governor, had been trailing the Democratic challenger by double digits in the 1994 governor's race. In a desperate effort to close the gap, Wilson doubled-down on opposition to immigration and embraced Proposition 187 to lure in conservative Democrats. It worked: Pete Wilson won a second term (Wilson 2019).

Gallegly and Wilson were not immigrant outliers among state and congressional Republicans. An amendment to remove amnesty for undocumented immigrants from the 1986 immigration reform bill cut deeply along partisan lines: 76% of House Republicans opposed amnesty compared to just 30% of Democrats. Of the sixty-eight Democrats who opposed amnesty (and voted for the amendment), forty-three came from states of the former Confederacy. This is an important point: this amendment vote reveals that the issue of amnesty for undocumented immigrants — a central tenet of immigration reform and political debates in the years to come — was already quite a polarizing issue among Congress even while national Republican candidates sought moderate-to-liberal immigration reform.

Not only were general election forces pushing some Republicans rightward, but primary contests did as well, even by the 1980s. Candidates for California's Republican Senate primary in 1986 converged around a hard line against undocumented immigrants and leveled charges that others were soft on the issue (Cervantes 1986; Associated Press 1986). One candidate filmed a campaign commercial at the US-Mexico border with migrants illegally crossing the border in the background (Roderick 1986). These messages did not come out of nowhere: a 1986 Field Poll of California voters showed that 87% of voters registered in the Republican primary thought undocumented immigration in California was a "very serious" or "somewhat serious problem."

Furthermore, the lack of Hispanic voters in the Republican primary electorate meant that avoiding the issue presented little upside and potentially great risk. Republican candidates seemed to take notice. In the 1988 presidential primary, the League of United Latin American Citizens (LULAC), a leading Hispanic civil rights group, hosted presidential candidates at their convention in Texas. Seven Democratic candidates but only one Republican, former Buffalo Bills quarterback and Congressman Jack Kemp, attended. This was because of electoral considerations: only 2% of Hispanic voters voted in the Texas Republican primary. "I like what [Kemp] said, but I'm not a Republican," one attendee said, "And Republicans are the ones who are going to tell [Kemp] what to do" (Applebome 1987).

The political opportunism of moving right to gain a leg up in the Republican primary, and the perils of embracing the alternative, was realized at the highest level of politics. National and subnational Republican politicians who once favored liberalized immigration issues tacked to the right in the heat of competitive primaries in the decades to come.

George W. Bush's popularity within the party in 2000 and 2004 meant that although his pro-immigration appeals did not resonate strongly with the party, he did not have to worry about being "primaried." Bush's successors were not given such a luxury. In 2008, Republicans nominated Arizona Senator John McCain, who, by all accounts, was an immigration reformer.[14] Yet when McCain entered the 2008 GOP primary, he faced a reality that to win the nomination, he must abandon his reformist sympathies: "As boos and hisses from angry Republican conservatives grew louder at campaign events," *Politico* writes, "he switched course and vowed to 'first' secure the borders" (Martinez 2008). Mitt Romney followed a somewhat similar trajectory. In 2005, Romney supported bipartisan immigration reform that provided a pathway to citizenship but tacked to the right when seeking the Republican nomination just a few years later. In 2012, Romney outflanked his GOP rivals during the primaries, including conservative firebrand Newt Gingrich, whose conciliatory immigration plan Romney criticized as "amnesty" (Balz 2012).

The polarization of the 2016 general election candidates represents the ascendancy of a strategy that had been simmering in subnational politics for some time. The core difference between Trump, compared to Romney and McCain, is that the latter two largely dropped their opposition to immigration when they got to the general election. When pressed on immigration positions in the summer of 2012, the *New York Times* stated that Romney had become "rubber-kneed" (Edsall 2012). This was perhaps out of both political considerations—Republicans believed they could make inroads with Hispanic voters—and personal politics: neither Romney nor McCain seemed to hold the personal anti-immigrant convictions as Trump did. The Trump campaign, similar to congressional Republicans like Elton

Gallegly, tapped into a reservoir of anti-immigrant sentiment sitting in the electorate, including at the edges of the Democratic Party, to win public office.

A great deal has been written about Trump and immigration, but it is worth highlighting two points that align with a bottom-up view of polarization. First, Trump's ascendancy did not meaningfully change his supporter's opinions on immigration (e.g., Sides, Tesler, and Vavreck 2019; Hopkins and Washington 2020). Figure A.6 in this book's appendix compares public opinion among a panel of the same Trump voters, interviewed in both 2011 and 2016, on immigration policy, racial resentment, and feelings toward various minority groups (data from the Democracy Fund Voter Study Group). Public opinion among those who voted for Trump between 2011 and 2016 is almost constant. Only on feelings toward *legal* immigration do Trump voters shift rightward.

Perhaps more surprisingly, Trump did not raise salience of the issue among his supporters. Figure 7.7 compares the salience of immigration to Trump voters in both 2011 and 2016 (note: because this is a panel, the same respondents were interviewed in both 2011 and 2016, allowing direct comparison). Before Trump arrived on the scene, a large segment of the Republican electorate felt strongly about immigration. This number changed little between when respondents were first interviewed in 2011 and 2016. Indeed, of Trump voters who said immigration was very important to them in 2016, 80% of those voters had said immigration was very important to them in 2011.

This highlights a core theme of the book: for an issue to gain political

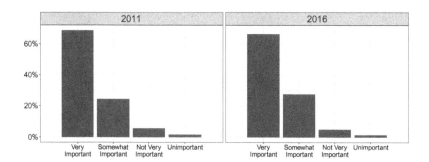

FIGURE 7.7. Trump Voters: Issue Importance, 2011 and 2016. Each panel shows the percentage of Trump voters who thought immigration was a very important/somewhat important/not very important/unimportant issue. The left-hand panel shows those voters in 2011. The right-hand panel shows those same voters in 2016.

salience, it, almost by definition, needs an elite mouthpiece. But rather than changing minds or making the issue salient among voters, it seemed that Trump's campaign, at the highest level of politics, simply unveiled opinion on the ground. To be sure, media personalities like Rush Limbaugh and other conservative leaders inside and outside of the Republican Party apparatus had been speaking about immigration for some time: but these appeals did not emerge out of nowhere. As this chapter shows, among ordinary voters, Republicans had been to the right of Democrats on immigration since the 1960s, and restrictionist immigration views had been tied to black racial conservatism since the earliest polling in the 1940s. Efforts to push the Republican Party right on immigration, from the highest levels of politics, ran up against structural forces that had been shaping the Republican Party since the racial realignment.

The Partisan Immigration Divide Widens: The 2010s

The previous sections show that an initial partisan divide on immigration, as measured by vote choice, emerged in 1964 and remained remarkably constant until the early 2000s. But in Obama's first term, as figure 7.4 shows, the partisan immigration debate widens. Obama's term offered several flash points on immigration: Obama announced plans to defer deportation for Dreamers in 2012, and debates flared up over Arizona's state immigration laws in the summer of 2010. Democrats and Republicans in the electorate polarized on the issue.

However, widening partisan divides were not simply a consequence of more visible partisan messaging on immigration. Obama was fairly quiet on immigration during the first part of his term, and he initially tried to crack down on immigration to gain negotiating capital with congressional Republicans. Despite this, many anti-immigrant Democrats might already have been alienated from Obama's coalition. This is because Obama's race, a powerful heuristic for some voters, pushed anti-immigrant voters out of the Democratic Party even before immigration flared up in Obama's first term. Racially conservative Democrats, turned off by the party's nomination of a black man, were also quite conservative on immigration.

Tesler (2016) argues that Obama's race vividly sharpened the racial images of the parties in the public's mind. In 2004, just about half of respondents knew that Democrats stood to the left of Republicans on racial policy; at the end of Obama's first term, that number had risen to around 75%. For voters with less formal education, a demographic that swung from Democrats to Republicans in the 2010s, the perceptions of the parties' positions on race changed even more.

Were anti-immigrant voters pushed away from Obama because of his race? To isolate the effect of Obama's race on growing partisan divides on immigration, I use "trial" election match-ups posed to voters early in the 2008 primary (fielded in February by the 2008–9 ANES panel study). These "trial" election questions asked voters who they would vote for in hypothetical Obama-McCain and Clinton-McCain match-ups. Intended vote choice early in the primary season is more likely to capture heuristics available to voters given the newness of campaigns and the fact that primary candidates (within the same party) often hold similar policy positions and any differences are unclear early on. Obama's race, rather than his policy views, was a salient heuristic for early vote choice (Tesler 2016). How do people who say they will vote for Clinton over McCain compare with those who say they would support McCain over Obama? The former race features two white candidates, the latter one white and one black candidate. Did racially conservative Democrats defect to McCain when Obama was on the ticket? Did those same voters hold conservative positions on immigration, too?

Figure 7.8 compares the opinions of people who would vote for both Clinton or Obama (the stayers) with those who would vote for Clinton but would defect to McCain if Obama was on the ballot (the defectors). I also show opinion attitudes among those who said they would vote for McCain in both match-ups. (These hypothetical match-ups were presented in February 2008.) Unsurprisingly, voters who defected from the Democrats when Obama rather than Clinton was on the ticket expressed significantly more racial resentment (as measured by a four-question racial resentment scale; see Kinder and Sanders [1996] for explanation). Perhaps more surprisingly, figure 7.8 shows that people who defected from the Democrats when Obama was on the ticket also hold significantly more conservative attitudes toward granting amnesty for undocumented immigrants (the immigration-levels question used in the previous sections was not available). These divisions are especially interesting because the ANES asked respondents where they perceived Clinton and Obama to stand on immigration, and people perceived Clinton's and Obama's immigration positions to be similar. (In fact, data from this survey show that voters perceived Obama and Clinton to hold similar positions across marquee campaign issues like health care spending and gay rights.) In other words, any vote switching at this point in the campaign was unlikely to be tied to

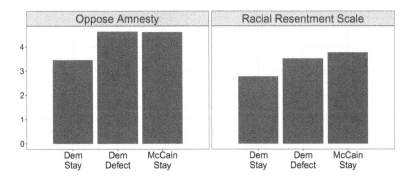

FIGURE 7.8. Attitudes of Clinton/Obama Switchers (Hypothetical Vote). Respondent attitudes are listed on the y-axis. The "Dem Stay" column are those respondents (in a hypothetical match-up) who would vote for both Obama and Clinton. Those in the "Dem Defect" column are those who would vote for Clinton, but not for Obama (and would vote for McCain). Those in the "McCain Stay" column are those who would vote for McCain against either Democratic candidate. Data are from the ANES 2008–2009 Panel Study.

policy differences between the Democratic candidates as voters did not see differences between Clinton and Obama.

The early timing (February 2008) also reduces the possibility of other alternative explanations for why conservative Democrats abandoned the Democrats when Obama was on the ticket, such as the Tea Party or health care reform. Likewise, other non-policy explanations, such as conspiracies of Obama's birth country or that Obama was a secret Muslim, had yet to emerge in force by the spring of 2008.[15] While the immigration debate engulfed the parties and fanned the partisan divide on immigration, these trends suggest that Obama's race — before he took up the immigration issue — had already accelerated partisan polarization on immigration. This finding also helps contextualize why immigration polarized so rapidly in the 2010s. Obama himself was seen as an out-group member to some conservatives, and when Obama messaged pro-immigration stances, he further calcified partisan identities.

Research by Daniel Hopkins (2021) dovetails with this finding. Using panel data that includes pre-Trump campaign measures of prejudice, Hopkins finds that anti-black rather than anti-Latino prejudice more robustly predicted future Trump vote choice. Hopkins speculates that because conflict over equality and rights for African Americans has been such a long-standing partisan division, Trump's rhetoric activated those cleavages despite his focus on groups alongside African Americans. In other words, anti-Latino prejudice (or immigration) followed the path well worn by decades of partisan fights over civil rights, including the racialized Obama presidency.

Conclusion

Even though immigration was not a major campaign theme in 1964, the contest between Lyndon Johnson and Barry Goldwater changed the partisan trajectory of immigration conflict in the United States. As immigration restrictionists left the Democratic Party to vote for Goldwater, the now-familiar partisan divide on immigration emerged. This generated decades of sometimes quiet, sometimes visible, party building that has generated massive partisan divides on immigration.

Let's return to Elton Gallegly, the anti-immigration Republican in Southern California discussed earlier in this chapter. In 1986, Gallegly replaced Republican Bobbi Fiedler, who vacated the district to run for the US Senate. Local news coverage showed that Fiedler, unlike Gallegly, talked little about immigration during her congressional campaigns, but was a prominent opponent of busing children to desegregate schools. When Fiedler first ran for Congress in 1980, her opponent was a twenty-year incumbent liberal Democrat, James Corman, who characterized Fiedler as a "demagogue on one-issue (busing)." Corman's district, according to the *Los Angeles Times*, was a largely working-class district in which 60% of voters were registered Democrats (Merl 1980a). Fiedler beat Corman, a racial liberal, by peeling off union voters whose economic sympathies perhaps lay with Democrats but were upset by busing in local schools (Merl 1980b; Bernstein 2001).

When Gallegly replaced Fiedler in 1986, he frequently talked about immigration but rarely mentioned busing. He did not need to. Anti-immigration and anti-busing issues spoke to the same voters; as busing fell off the agenda, Gallegly mobilized the conservative, although once-Democratic, white base by emphasizing anti-immigration positions instead. This was fertile ground as many Californians felt strongly about immigration. A 1986 Field Poll shows that among likely Republican primary voters, 63% said they believed unauthorized immigration was a "very serious" problem. Gallegly and other congressional and statewide Republicans offered representation for an already deeply held sentiment within their primary electorate. This was the same playbook as on abortion, guns, and the other social issues discussed earlier.

Undocumented immigration polarized the parties at the subnational level even while Reagan, Bush, and other national leaders tried to push the party left. For example, while Reagan signaled support for amnesty for undocumented immigrants in the mid-1980s, 76% of congressional Republicans voted to strike amnesty from the 1986 immigration reform bill. And on the 1996 Illegal Immigration and Reform Responsibility Act, only 5 of 234 House Republicans who voted on the bill opposed it.

The evolution of immigration as a partisan issues aligns with scholarship arguing that members of Congress (or other subnational officeholders) are especially attuned to the grassroots and constantly test new messages, which, if successful, work their way throughout the party (Jenkins, Peck, and Weaver 2010; Chen 2007; Schickler 2016). This meant that not only were high-profile efforts to push the Republican Party left running up against their own voters, but they were also running up against members of Congress, who perhaps better realized the electoral ramifications of moving left. For example, when Republican Paul Ryan became Speaker of the House in 2015, he did so with the promise he would not bring immigration reform, which he previously had expressed support for, to the floor. This was the immigration reform that Rubio, Boehner, and prominent conservative interests advocated for. "I need your assurance that you will not use the Speaker's position to advance your immigration policies . . . because there is a huge gap between your immigration position and the wishes of the American citizens I represent," Republican and House Freedom Caucus member Mo Brooks wrote Ryan (Plott 2015). To be sure, crosscutting pressures of economic interest groups slowed polarization on immigration compared to the other culture war issues, particularly among national leaders, but the structural roots of polarization were too strong. The parties' electoral bases were pushing elected officials apart.

CHAPTER EIGHT

Beyond the United States

Although the contours and timing of the racial realignment is unique to the United States, the 1964 racial realignment parallels change that has occurred in other parts of the world; it marked the transformation of a party system that cleaved primarily along attitudes toward economic issues to a party system also divided along attitudes toward race and ethnicity.[1]

This chapter draws on data from across the globe to explore three questions that parallel this book's analysis of the United States. To academics studying comparative politics, these themes are likely familiar (e.g., Bakker et al. 2014; Hooghe and Marks 2018; Marks, Wilson, and Ray 2002; Marks and Wilson 2000; Inglehart 1977; Wheatley and Mendez 2019); this chapter is an effort to contextualize the party system in the United States with party systems across the globe.

This chapter first explores whether people, in other national contexts, who hold more conservative views on race and ethnicity also hold more conservative views on what are considered culture war issues in the United States.[2] By conservative views on race and ethnicity, I mean those who have relatively more ethnocentric attitudes.[3] Using data from the World Values Survey, I find that the package of issues observed in the US electorate (see chapter 3) are found across other Organisation for Economic Co-operation and Development (OECD) countries.

This chapter's second section explores the clusters of issues among parties in the European Union. Similar patterns emerge among party elites in the EU that emerged in the post-1970s United States: parties with diverging positions toward ethnic minorities also hold diverging views on other social issues, too. The fact that these issue bundles (along the racial axis) are observed across the world, in both the mass public and among parties in office, casts doubt on a core claim of an existing scholarship on US parties:

that party platforms are contingent choices made by party leaders and then messaged down to voters (e.g., Bawn et al. 2012; Carmines and Stimson 1989). The ubiquitousness of these issue bundles suggests structural forces are shaping public opinion and parties along this dimension.

Indeed, while literature on parties in the United States focuses on party alignment across different issues as disparate events, the literature on European party systems tends to conceive of party conflict on two dimensions: a left-right economic dimension that encompasses political fights over regulation and economic redistribution, and an authoritarian dimension that captures "post-materialist" conflict over racial and gender equality, crime, and environmental concerns (e.g., Inglehart 1984; Marks et al. 2006). This post-material dimension of conflict is sometimes referred to as the GAL/TAN dimension (Green, Alternative, and Libertarian versus Traditional, Authoritarian, and Nationalist) in the comparative politics literature. The GAL side support issues like abortion and same-sex marriage while the TAN side favors tradition and order (e.g., Barquero et al. 2022). In the United States, the racial realignment brought the authoritarian dimension (the GAL/TAN dimension), which previously had crosscut party lines, into the partisan fold.

This chapter's third section explores what happens when party systems that are divided along economic lines start to polarize on views toward race and ethnicity. Chapter 2 argues that had the United States held overlapping positions on civil rights and remained divided only by economic issues, the parties would have been less polarized, or sorted differently, on issues like abortion or gay rights because the economic cleavage did not act as a countervailing force. Indeed, in the 1950s and 1960s, when the party cleavages were primarily defined by New Deal economic loyalties, Democrats and Republicans, to the extent they had positions at all, held overlapping positions on culture war issues. A similar pattern emerges in European party systems. Party systems in the EU that are divided along economic lines tend to hold crosscutting positions on religion, the environment, "social-lifestyle" policies, and immigration as well. Likewise, public opinion along the economic axis in other parts of the world mirrors trends in the United States: economic attitudes are not a strong predictor of views on other social issues. Malka, Lelkes, and Soto (2019) analyze issue bundles in the mass public in dozens of national contexts and find that people on the economic left hold crosscutting attitudes on sexual morality, immigration, and women's role in society.

But what happens when European parties, once divided along economic lines, polarize on race and ethnicity? Do their voters polarize on other issue dimensions as well? Using Sweden as a case study, I argue that they do. The Swedish party system, which remained divided rigidly along economic lines into the early twentieth century, experienced the rapid growth of a Far Right anti-immigrant party, the Sweden Democrats, in the first decade of this century. The Sweden Democrats transformed from almost nonexistence at the turn of the century to the third largest party in the Swedish parliament following the 2014 election. I find that voters moved to the Sweden Democrats because of their anti-immigration views, but also brought their conservative attitudes on other issues like abortion or gay rights with them, too. This parallels change that occurred in the United States in the 1960s and 1970s: as voters sorted between parties based on their attitudes toward race and ethnicity, they were sorting along other issue dimension as well.

The bottom line is that the US party system, at both the elite and mass level, in important ways looks like party systems and public opinion in other parts of the globe. If the bundle of positions found in the US party system were bargained by interest groups or contingent on the choices of party leaders, it is difficult to understand why so many other countries, at least in the ways highlighted in this chapter, look similar to the United States.

Issue Bundles Around the Globe

This book focuses on an enduring feature of US public opinion: people who are more conservative on questions of civil rights have long held conservative positions on a range of other issues including abortion, gun control, immigration, and the environment. These patterns persist to the earliest public opinion polls and predate the national parties dividing on those issues. But to what extent do we see these linkages in other parts of the globe?

In the US analysis, I focus on black civil rights and racial equality as it represents a long-standing conflict in US politics. And while many other countries have racial conflict, such as fights over Aboriginal rights in Australia or Native land use in Canada, these vary from country to country. To consistently measure ethno-racial attitudes across the globe, I use two questions from the World Values Survey (WVS) (Inglehart et al. 2014). First, in several years, the WVS asked respondents which groups they "would not like to have as neighbors." On this list are "people of a different race." The second question asks about ethnic diversity: "Turning to the question of ethnic diversity, with which of the following views do you agree? Please use this scale to indicate your position." Respondents can then choose on a scale from 1 to 10, where the left-most response is "Ethnic diversity enriches life" and the right-most response is "Ethnic diversity erodes a country's unity." I recode both of these variables from 0 to 1, where 1 represents the conservative (more ethnocentric) value, and average them together.

I am interested in how these attitudes toward race and ethnic diversity correlate with some of the culture war issues explored earlier in the book. The WVS includes five questions that broadly parallel these political issues:

1. *Abortion:* "Please tell me for each of the following actions whether you think it can always be justified, never be justified, or something in between: Abortion."

2. *Gay rights:* "Please tell me for each of the following actions whether you think it can always be justified, never be justified, or something in between: Homosexuality."

3. *Women's rights:* "When jobs are scarce, men should have more right to a job than women."

4. *Environment:* "Which of [these statements] comes closer to your own point of view? (a) Protecting the environment should be given priority, even if it causes slower economic growth and some loss of jobs. (b) Economic growth and creating jobs should be the top priority, even if the environment suffers to some extent."

5. *Immigration:* I indexed two questions asked by the WVS: (1) "When jobs are scarce, employers should give priority to [fill in respondent's nationality] people over immigrants." And (2) "How about people from other countries coming here to work. Which one of the following do you think the government should do? (a) Let anyone come who wants to? (b) Let people come as long as there are jobs available? (c) Place strict limits on the number of foreigners who can come here? (d) Prohibit people coming here from other countries?"

I recode each one of these variables from 0 to 1 and then regress these attitudes on the index of racial tolerance and ethnic diversity. For countries in which the question is asked in multiple years, I include a year fixed effect (which controls for factors that change across time). Figure 8.1 plots the bivariate regression between attitudes on the index of racial openness/ethnic diversity and five issues relevant to the culture wars in the United States among OECD countries with available opinion data. Conservative racial attitudes are almost uniformly bundled with what are considered

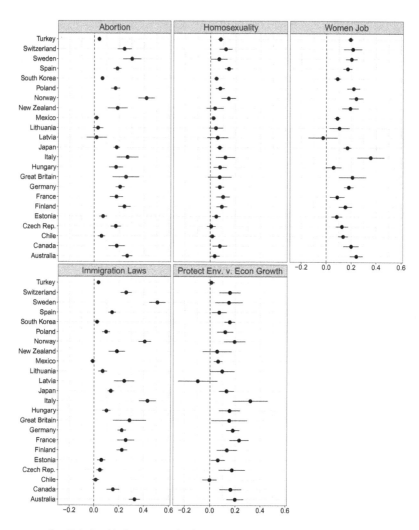

FIGURE 8.1. Relationship between Attitudes on Race/Ethnic Diversity and Other Issue Attitudes in OECD Countries. Each coefficient shows the bivariate relationship of regressing attitudes on abortion (top left), homosexuality (top center), women's role to fill open jobs (top right), an index of openness to immigration (bottom left) and protecting the environment (bottom center) on an index of racial openness and acceptance of ethnic diversity. See text for wording details. Positive coefficients mean conservative attitudes on race correspond with conservative attitudes on the respective issue. I restrict the results to OECD countries with available data.

conservative positions on abortion, gay rights, immigration, the environment, and gender equality. The persistence of these issue bundles across
the developed world parallels what was observed in the United States
(discussed in chapter 3).

The persistence of these issue bundles across the world complicates
elite-driven narratives that dominate the literature on US politics. If party
platforms are driven by contingent choices of elites or activists, and these
preferences are then passed down to voters, why do a similar bundle of
issues exist across the globe?

A skeptical reader might wonder whether US politics leaks across borders. Other countries might adopt themes, messages, and packages of policy
positions that originated in the United States. This certainly happens, yet
data from the 1970s in the United Kingdom and Australia—which predates the American parties dividing on these issues—shows these issue
bundles already emerging in foreign countries (see appendix figure A.7).
The earliest data from the United Kingdom (1974) shows that people who
supported racial equality were also more likely to be liberal on abortion,
gender equality, and laws to protect the countryside (Crewe, Robertson,
and Sarlvik [1974] 1977). Australia in 1979 (Aitkin [1979] 2004), the year
of the earliest available data, shows similar trends: Australians who believe
Aborigines (Australia's native population) should get special support from
the government are more likely to hold liberal attitudes on marijuana,
abortion, and gay rights. Rather than these issue bundles existing because
they have been packaged together by elites, a more likely explanation is
that attitudes in many developed countries are clustered together because
of shared micro-foundations, as discussed in chapter 3.

Parties Across Europe

What then are the implications of these bundles? A core contention of the
book is that had the United States remained divided primarily along economic
lines—and civil rights had continued to crosscut the parties—Democrats and
Republicans would have been less polarized on other culture war issues like
guns or abortion when they became salient in the 1970s. This section contextualizes this claim by analyzing party positions in the European Union.

To get a broader picture of party cleavages, I use data from the 2014
Chapel Hill Expert Survey (CHES), which asks European political experts
where they believe European political parties—referring to the parties'

candidates—stand across issue dimensions (Polk et al. 2017). While not a perfect measure of party positions, they offer a useful comparison of party positions across countries (Bakker et al. 2014). The 2014 survey has the positions of 245 parties spread across 26 countries in the European Union. To measure economic cleavages, I use a question on the CHES that asked experts to place parties' position on "improving public services vs. reducing taxes." I then use four questions from the survey that broadly mirror the culture war questions used in the analysis of the United States: the parties' position on (1) the "role of religious principles and politics"; (2) "social lifestyle (e.g., homosexuality)"; (3) "the environment"; and (4) "immigration policy." Figure 8.2 plots the parties' positions (across the parties in the 26 EU countries) on spending versus taxation (along

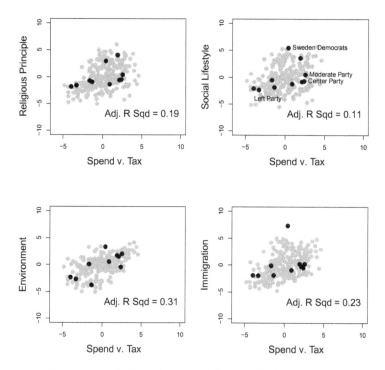

FIGURE 8.2. European Party Positions by Economic Positions. Each gray point represents the coordinate between a party's position on the issues listed along the x-axis and y-axis. Data are from the 2014 Chapel Hill Expert Survey (Polk et al. 2017) and include party positions from 245 parties in the EU. Higher values equal more conservative values. Data are de-meaned by country. The Swedish parties, for comparison, are highlighted in black. The adjusted R-squared measures how much of the variation in the y-axis variable (e.g., religious principles) can be explained by the variable on the x-axis (tax and spending).

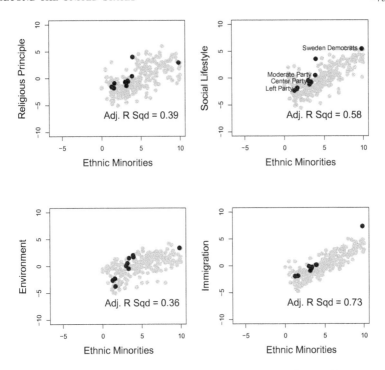

FIGURE 8.3. European Party Positions by Ethnic Minorities Position. Each gray point represents the coordinate between a party's position on the two issues listed along the x-axis and y-axis. Data are from the 2014 Chapel Hill Expert Survey (Polk et al. 2017). Higher values equal more conservative values. Data are de-meaned by country. The Swedish parties, for comparison, are highlighted in black.

the x-axis), and each of these four issues (measured on the y-axis). These economic divisions (reflected along the x-axis) do not cleanly separate the parties along other policy dimensions (y-axis). Consider the Swedish parties, which are highlighted in black on the graph. On economic issues, the Moderate Party and Center Party are the parties furthest to the right on economic issues. The party furthest to the economic left is the Left Party. Despite being polarized on economic issues, they vary little on religion, social-lifestyle issues, the environment, or immigration.

Contrast this with parties polarized by attitudes toward race. To measure attitudes toward ethnic or racial cleavages, I use a question on the expert survey that asks about parties' support or opposition for "rights for ethnic minorities." I repeat the same analysis as before, this time with divisions toward ethnic minorities reflected along the x-axis. Figure 8.3 shows that parties polarized by views on ethnic and racial minorities are much more polarized on attitudes toward each of the other issues. To illustrate this, again consider the Swedish parties (highlighted in black). The Far Right anti-immigration Swedish party, the Sweden Democrats, are much more conservative on ethnic minorities than the Left Party (as reflected on the x-axis). But they are also much more conservative on religion, social-lifestyle issues, immigration, and the environment as well (as reflected on the y-axis).

To compare the cleavages differently, I plot the adjusted R-square between the variables listed on each graph. Higher R-squared values means the variation in the variable on the y-axis can be better predicted by variation in the variable on the x-axis. For example, the adjusted R-squared value between party positions on religion and taxation is 0.19. This is less than half the R-squared value for the relationship between religion and ethnic minorities (0.39). Parties divided by their positions on race and ethnicity are much more divided by their positions on religion when compared to parties divided by economic issues.

This cross-national trend in Europe contextualizes the patterns seen in the United States. Figure 8.2 suggests that parties polarized on economic positions can and do take a range of positions on immigration and gay rights. This parallels the United States in the mid-twentieth century: When the US parties were divided primarily along economic lines forged by the New Deal, they took crosscutting positions on culture war issues. The United States was not an outlier. However, figure 8.3 suggests that parties divided by their positions toward racial minorities tend to also be divided on issues like religion or the environment. This aligns with the experience in the United States and this book's core argument: When the parties in the United States divided by civil rights, they developed a constellation of polarized positions on other culture war issues as well. Again, the United States was not an outlier, but fit a pattern of party systems that arose across Europe.

One core difference, though, is that the electoral systems of many European countries allow for multiparty competition, while the "first past the post" system in the United States facilitates two-party competition. In multiparty systems, this may allow Far Right parties to splinter off and fight along the "TAN" dimension, while other parties continue to fight along the economic axis. In the United States, a similar flexibility is not afforded since both economic and non-economic interests are fighting for representation within two parties.

The Rise of the Sweden Democrats

This section focuses on Sweden, and the rise of the Sweden Democrats, a Far Right anti-immigrant populist party, that was effectively nonexistent in the first decade of the 2000s but became the third largest party in the Swedish parliament following the 2014 election. Until the Sweden Democrats' rise, party conflict in Sweden, like the United States prior to the 1960s, was defined heavily along economic lines. This economic cleavage was so strong that even while Far Right populist parties grew across Europe in that same time frame, Sweden largely resisted their rise. Indeed, throughout the 1990s and first decade of this century, Sweden's lack of a Far Right (anti-immigration) party was such an anomaly that it generated a wave of scholarship as to why Sweden was the exception. Among other things, this scholarship cites that the relative low salience of cultural issues such as immigration enabled sustained class-based voting in Sweden (Rydgren 2002; Dahlstrom and Esaiasson 2011).

However, the Syrian refugee crisis changed this equilibrium. Across Western Europe, the electorates of countries that received an influx of refugee applications polarized; right-wing citizens became more anti-immigrant while left-wing citizens became more accepting (Brug and Harteveld 2021). Sweden seemed no longer to be the exception. Perhaps more telling, Swedes saw immigration as an increasingly salient issue. The percentage of Swedes who believed immigration was an important issue in the 1990s fluctuated around 10–12% (Rydgren and Meiden 2019, 444–45). By 2010, it had spiked to 19%, and by 2015, in the midst of the Syrian refugee crisis, this number soared to 53%.

Through immigration, the Swedish electorate has become much more diverse. For example, the two largest foreign-born groups in Sweden are Syrians and Iraqis, who together total 350,000 people. In 1990, only about 15,000 Syrian or Iraqi nationals lived in Sweden. In a country of 10 million people, this represents a rapidly changing demographic (and is part of a broader influx of immigrants into Sweden; about 20% of Sweden is non-native born, nearly double that of just two decades ago) (Statistics Sweden). In Sweden, noncitizens can and do vote in subnational elections, and Sweden also has a relatively easy process to become naturalized and thus gain the right to vote in all elections (Bevelander and Hutcheson 2022, 431). Immigrants to Sweden, their children, and their political allies are demanding political and economic rights.

In some ways, this mirrors the transformation of the United States into a multiracial democracy in which African Americans became a voting bloc that demanded civil, political, and economic rights. Although the United States has been a multiracial country since its founding, African Americans were excluded from politics through slavery and then Jim Crow. Scholars argue that removing black civil rights as an issue from the political agenda, which itself is done by diluting African American political power, reduced polarization in the midcentury United States (Levitsky and Ziblatt 2018). The rise of black political power first outside the South and then in former Confederate states in the 1950s and 1960s upended that equilibrium.

Although the source of change is different, Sweden has become much more racially/ethnically heterogeneous, and its politics are reacting in a similar manner. Like in the midcentury United States, economic cleavages that had long structured the Swedish party system weakened in the face of ethno-racial tensions.[4] The Far Right anti-immigrant party, the Sweden Democrats, which had received limited support and no parliamentary seats in the 1990s, became a major political force. While Sweden Democrats received only 0.4% of the vote in the 1998 elections, that number increased to 2.9% in the 2006 election and nearly doubled to 5.7% by the 2010 election. By the 2018 election, Sweden Democrats received 17.5% of the vote, sixty-two parliamentary seats, and had become Sweden's third largest party. Racially conservative Swedes abandoned the working-class Social Democrats and migrated to the Far Right Sweden Democrats, just as racially conservative white people abandoned the working-class Democrats in the 1960s.

In a short period of time, the Sweden Democrats effectively developed as a one-issue party focused on restricting immigration (Dahlstrom and Esaiasson 2011, 348; *BBC News* 2018). Thus, the rise of Sweden Democrats allows us to analyze a central theme: As voters moved toward the Sweden Democrats, are they doing so based on their immigration views? And does movement toward or away from the Sweden Democrats then generate sorting on other issues, too?

To answer these questions, I use panel data from the Swedish Election Studies between the 2006 and 2010 Swedish elections, which spans part of the dramatic rise in support for the Sweden Democrats (Holmberg, Oscarsson, and Statistics Sweden 2014). Between 2006 and 2010, the Sweden Democrats nearly doubled their vote share and for the first time gained parliamentary seats. Panel data allows analysis of the same voters before and after the Sweden Democrats' rise. In Sweden, several substantive empirical trends would place race and ethnicity—specifically immigration—as the primary cause of voters abandoning old party allegiances and supporting the Sweden Democrats (at least in terms of policy issues). First, Sweden Democrats initially built their brand on the single issue of opposing immigration (Dahlstrom and Esaiasson 2011, 348; *BBC News* 2018). Second, supporters of the Sweden Democrats overwhelmingly rank immigration as the most important issue (Erlingsson, Vernby, and Ohrvall 2014, 208). Third, and perhaps most importantly, people associate the party with opposition to immigration more than any other issue. When asked what issue people associated with the party, 69% of voters identified that the Sweden Democrats emphasize immigration. There was a precipitous drop to the next issue: about 8% say Sweden Democrats emphasize pensions and social welfare, and only 6% say Sweden Democrats emphasized law and order (these are the next highest mentions after immigration). Other issues, such as Euro-skepticism, gender equality, and family values, which are often associated with right-wing populist parties, received effectively no mentions. These factors combined suggest that Swedish voters migrating to the Sweden Democrats were doing so because of their immigration views.

This leads to the next point of interest: Were voters who moved toward the Sweden Democrats already more conservative on policy issues like abortion or gay marriage? To measure party sorting, I use a 0–10 feeling thermometer toward the Sweden Democrats that was conducted in both 2006 and 2010. A feeling thermometer measures how coldly (0) or warmly (10) a respondent feels toward, in this case, the Sweden Democrats. Presumably, because the Sweden Democrats' vote share was so small in 2006, the survey did not ask whether people voted for them in that year. Figure 8.4 plots the average policy position, *measured in 2006*, of people who grew warmer to the Sweden Democrats between 2006 and 2010. What did these voters think about policy issues before Sweden Democrats rose to prominence? Because these attitudes are measured in 2006, the explanation that Sweden Democrats caused people to have conservative attitudes on these issues can be ruled out.

To facilitate comparison, each attitude is standardized to have an average of 0 and standard deviation of 1. As might be expected, prior conservatism on questions of refugees strongly correlates with increased affect toward the Sweden Democrats four years later. People who moved toward the Sweden Democrats are 0.63 of a standard deviation more conservative on refugee policy than the average Swede in 2006. But future pro–Sweden Democrat voters were already more conservative on other social issues,

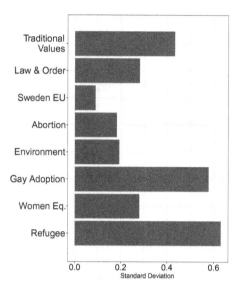

FIGURE 8.4. 2006 Policy Views of People Who Became More Favorable toward Sweden Democrats between 2006 and 2010. Each bar represents the average opinion, measured in 2006, of people who became more favorable to the Sweden Democrats between 2006 and 2010 as measured in 2006. The data have been de-meaned and standardized such that the average respondent has an attitude of 0. Higher values represent more conservative opinions.

too. On many of the issues that animate culture war fights in the United States—like gay rights, abortion, or gender equality—people who moved toward the Sweden Democrats already held significantly more conservative positions on these issues. This is despite virtually no voters expressing that issues like Swedish identity, gender equality, family policy, the environment, or morality were core issues for the Sweden Democrats at this early point.

While the Sweden Democrats rose to prominence as a result of immigration, public opinion shows that voters who moved to support the Sweden Democrats already held conservative views on abortion, gay rights, and traditional values. This potentially offers an explanation for why Sweden Democrats, as the party evolved, picked up conservative cultural positions on other issues. For example, Sweden has some of the most liberal abortion laws in the world, and because abortion had not been a source of political conflict, it had long been absent in party manifestos (Backlund 2011, 13). But Sweden's liberal abortion laws came under attack by the Sweden Democrats in the 2010s (Mulinari and Neergaard 2014, 47). One explanation is that as a by-product of their anti-immigration positions, the Sweden Democrats have pooled together a mass of conservative abortion voters, too. This gave political capital for party leaders to stake anti-abortion positions. Prior to the Sweden Democrats' rise, these voters were scattered among parties.

This explanation parallels what happened in the United States in the 1960s: the racial realignment pooled voters who were worried about changing cultural norms into a single party. The initial cause of this shift was changing racial relations (in Sweden's case immigration), but politicians soon realized that their base had increasing numbers of people worried about changing gender norms or gay rights as well.

Conclusion

Exploring party systems and public opinion in developed democracies across the globe provides context for the trends observed in the United States. First, the issue bundles observed along the racial axis in the United States are found in many OECD countries. Likewise, in parties across the European Union, parties that are more hostile toward ethnic minorities are also more conservative on the environment, religion, immigration, and social-lifestyle issues. There are, of course, exceptions. For example, Geert Wilders, leader of Holland's Far Right party, favors expanding women's rights and LGBTQ rights, but frames this support in the context of Islam being seen as a threat to these groups (and Dutch society more generally) (Pieters 2017). However, figure 8.3 suggests that Wilders, who had long been a one-man party, is the exception rather than rule.

In this context, the trends observed in the United States are not anomalous. What does this mean for bottom-up versus top-down theories of party sorting? If the party coalitions or platforms are elite bargained, why do similar coalitions exist with respect to the racial axis across the European Union? With respect to the racial axis, why are similar issue bundles observed in public opinion across OECD countries? One explanation is that party types spread across borders; it is possible that other countries learn from the United States. But similar issue bundles existed in Great Britain by at least 1974 and Australia by 1979, which predates coalition building in the United States, so intercountry learning cannot be the sole explanation. Rather than an elite-driven phenomenon, it is likely that the

micro-foundations and underlying values shaping public opinion and electoral coalitions in the United States are found in many other nations (e.g.,
Inglehart 1977).

Public opinion and party systems around the globe also shed other light
on the implications for the racial realignment in the United States. Parties
polarized by economic positions across the globe hold crosscutting positions on religion, immigration, the environment, and social-lifestyle questions. Scholars observe a similar pattern in public opinion (Malka, Lelkes,
and Soto 2019). It is worth thinking what this might mean for a path not
taken in the US party system. In the midcentury United States, the parties
were divided primarily by economic lines and held overlapping views on
civil rights. They also held overlapping views on immigration, women's
equality, the environment, and, to the extent they were on the agenda,
abortion and gun control.

Claims that the parties could have gone either way on issues like abortion or women's rights in the 1970s are often made with this equilibrium in
the background: when the parties were divided primarily along economic
lines, party positioning on abortion was up in the air (Adams 1997; Noel
2013). This is perhaps correct; party systems that are polarized along economic lines do hold a range of positions on non-economic social issues.
But by the time abortion and gun control became salient political fights
in the 1970s, the parties had already polarized on civil rights. The EU data
suggests that parties divided by their positions toward ethnic minorities
tend to polarize on other social issues, too. The United States fits this trend.

CHAPTER NINE

Conclusion

The threat of polarization to the very existence of US democracy has become abundantly clear. In their book *How Democracies Die*, Levitsky and Ziblatt (2018) argue that intense partisan polarization erodes institutions and norms required for democratic governing. Without common ground, parties see the opposition as illegitimate. In the contemporary United States, the sense of illegitimacy has reached the point that state legislatures and Congress have seriously considered substituting the popular vote in presidential elections with a legislatively determined winner. Democracy is, at the very least, on life support.

Levitsky and Ziblatt pinpoint the 1960s racial realignment as fundamental to norm-eroding polarization because polarization, over time, sorted the parties by race. In the 1950s, a similar proportion of the Democratic and Republican parties was non-white. By 2012, 44% of Democrats were non-white, but only 10% of Republicans were people of color. A party system divided between racial groups, Levitsky and Ziblatt argue, generates greater "intolerance and hostility than traditional policy issues such as taxes and government spending" (2018, 171–72).

This book highlights another reason the racial realignment has eroded common ground: views toward racial equality have long overlapped views on a range of other deeply held beliefs. When the parties polarized by civil rights in the 1960s, the electorate was also quietly dividing, along partisan lines, on issues like immigration, abortion, and gun control. This relationship is not one-to-one; there are many people who are racially liberal but oppose abortion or people who dislike gun control but want equality for people of all races. But on average, the attitudinal divides on race overlap attitudinal divides on issues like women's rights, gay rights, and immigration. This trend has been present for as long as public opinion data have been available.

This is a crucial point: if democratic erosion results from opposing camps lacking common ground, polarization in and of itself is not the driving force. As this book discusses, parties can be deeply polarized on economic issues, but might overlap on questions of immigration or religion. Indeed, chapter 8 shows that European parties that are deeply divided on the question of government taxation and spending often hold crosscutting positions on cultural issues like gay marriage. That is, parties that oppose each other on economic issues often find common cause on other issues. The opportunity for partisan animosity, and thus democratic erosion, is lessened. However, when the parties are divided by race and attitudes toward racial equality, not only is this itself an explosive issue, but it is often accompanied by divisions on other, deeply held beliefs on other issues like abortion or gun control.

As more and more issues get locked into the party system, this continues to foment already deep partisan identities. That is, contemporary polarization is so deep because people's views are increasingly stacked upon each other (e.g., Republicans are conservative on race *and* abortion). This creates disdain for the other side, which then further reinforces cleavages.

The composition of the parties' existing coalitions continue to shape their ability to position on new issues when they arise. When new issues like transgender rights enter the political arena, they reinforce existing battle lines that characterize contemporary politics. For example, people who are more liberal on transgender rights also hold liberal views on many other issues already absorbed into the Democratic coalition. Likewise, the values and traits predicting conservatism on gay rights, abortion rights, and women's rights, like moral traditionalism and authoritarianism, also predict views on transgender rights (Taylor et al. 2018, 100). By 2011, in one of the first polls on partisanship and views toward transgender people, Democratic voters already held more liberal views than Republicans (Tadlock 2015, 41).

Elites then reinforced these nascent cleavages. For example, in 2012, the Democratic platform had zero mentions of transgender people, but the Democrats' 2020 platform mentioned transgender rights fifteen times. This also occurred at the state level. In a study of executive orders by US governors, Sellers (2014) finds that Democratic governors are more likely than Republican governors to extend protections to transgender individuals because it signaled support of more socially liberal policies desired by liberal constituencies (Taylor and Haider-Markel 2014, 275). Among activists, the growing alliance between the transgender movement and gay and lesbian movement by the 1990s allowed the transgender movement to utilize the gay and lesbian community's existing ties to the Democratic Party (Taylor, Lewis, and Haider-Markel 2018, 296). As a consequence, transgender rights activists found it easier to ally with Democrats. On the Republican side, Religious Right groups like the Family Research Council, which had become essential to the Republican coalition by the time transgender rights gained attention, were hostile to the transgender movement (Taylor and Haider-Markel 2014).

This book's argument—the fueling of polarization by overlapping issues positions aligned in the party system—overlaps Mason's (2018) argument that contemporary polarization can be explained by a series of overlapping identities (e.g., race, religion) that have created a mega-partisan identity. While this book focuses on overlapping issue cleavages, rather than identities, it sheds light on *why* racial and religious identities are aligned in the party system—the racial realignment.

One possible implication of this book is that contemporary views of partisanship as a mega-identity are largely fueled by racial identification (Zhirkov and Valentino 2022). The Trump era supercharged this because Trump himself represented such a clear out-group that it brought the left's issue positions on race and ethnicity further into line and contributed to the Democrats' massive leftward swing on immigration and race between 2016 and 2020. This raises the question: If polarization is rooted in the racial realignment, how then can it be undone? A central theme of this book is that political elites—including politicians, interest groups, and the media—had less discretion in building party coalitions than current scholarship suggests. If polarization were simply a product of politicians or interest groups, it might be relatively easy to come undone. Politicians simply need to reach across the aisle. But if the source of polarization runs deep in the electorate, the space for working across the aisle shrinks. For example, chapter 7 documents a decades-long struggle of leading Republicans and interest groups trying to push the party leftward on immigration. But these efforts failed, I argue, because campaigning on liberal immigration laws rang hollow in a GOP that had become anchored by racial and cultural conservatives.

Indeed, politicians and interest groups are more flexible in their willingness to take positions or enter coalitions than voters might be. Politicians want to win elections and are often willing to take any policy position that achieves that goal. As one activist noted: "Politicians take a position for

one of two reasons: because of personal conviction, or because it is easier
politically to take that position than the other" ("Political Planning of the
Corporation," n.d.). Most politicians, though, even on highly salient issues,
lack conviction. Karol (2009) finds that politicians routinely changed positions on newly salient issues as they realized their initial position was out
of step with their broader coalition. Interest groups and social movements
are flexible in a different way: many issue-oriented activists care deeply
about their issue and are thus willing to align with strange bedfellows to
achieve policy goals. Chapter 6 argues that diffuse public opinion guided
many pro-life activists to the Republican Party despite their initial preference to align with the Democrats.

To be sure, interest groups and politicians feed the flames of polarization. But their ability to transform the political system is constrained by
the forces underneath them. The 2016 nomination of Donald Trump illustrates this sensitivity between the cues politicians are willing to give and
the perceived preferences of ordinary voters. For example, Levitsky and
Ziblatt (2018, 71) raise a common refrain with respect to Trump in 2016:
"Had Republican leaders publicly opposed Trump, the tightly contested,
red-versus-blue dynamics of the previous four elections would have been
disrupted. The Republican electorate would have split—some heeding the
warnings of the party leadership and other sticking with Trump. . . . Instead,
the election was normalized. The race narrowed. And Trump won." Not a
single Republican senator or governor, and only one retiring member of
the House, endorsed Clinton in 2016. In other words, the party gatekeepers
did not gate keep, allowing Trump to secure the nomination.

The lack of Republican elite signals opposing Trump probably did shape
public opinion at the edges. But mass-level forces deeply influenced why
these gatekeeping signals were never sent. Steve Israel (2020), a former
Democratic member of Congress, humorously illustrates this point:

> I remember a House Republican who once told me he thought Donald Trump
> would destroy his party. Then, in the summer of 2016, I ran into him at an airport.
> He told me he'd just received the results of a poll. "Who do you think is the most
> popular candidate in my district?" he asked. "You?" I responded. (Congressional
> protocol requires consistent flattery.) "Nope. Donald Trump." And so he began
> to shift his position.

If the party system is to change, it will be the result of a changing electorate, and the political class will respond to changing incentives. The

United States has depolarized before, and it stands to reason that it will depolarize again, although when, and what might happen before such a realignment occurs, is difficult to guess. The rapidly changing demographics of the country offer one opportunity for depolarization. At some point, the GOP will need to expand itself beyond a nearly all-white party if it is to stay competitive (perhaps surprisingly, the Trump elections actually marked racial depolarization between the parties). However, the Electoral College map and single-member districts may slow the impetus for change. The GOP regularly receives a minority of the vote but continues to hold power through institutional advantages. Since 1992, Republicans have won the popular vote for president only once (Bush's 2004 reelection), but the Electoral College placed both George W. Bush and Donald Trump in the White House in 2000 and 2016, respectively.

In the Senate, equal representation of seats means Republicans can hold a majority of the chamber's seats (or be in the slim minority) despite receiving vastly fewer votes. The reason? Republicans tend to dominate in small states like Wyoming, while Democrats perform better in large states like New York or California. Population distribution across states will worsen: by 2040, 70% of the population will live in fifteen states. This means 30% of the population will be represented by 70% of the Senate.[1] And perhaps further slowing any change is the fact that in state legislatures (and the US House of Representatives), Republicans consistently win majorities in the legislature despite failing to win a plurality of the state's vote. While gerrymandering exacerbates this trend, it has widely arisen because of the contours of political geography where liberals (Democrats) are packed into cities while conservatives are more evenly distributed across suburban and rural districts (Rodden 2019).

Another roadblock for depolarization is that, for example, while the Latino population is growing and the GOP may need non-white voters to remain competitive, it is unclear if Latino voters will slow polarization. While immigrants and their children tend to be liberal on immigration, subsequent generations, with stronger ties to the United States, are less so (Corral and Leal 2020). Thus, the GOP could remain hawkish on immigration and depolarize the parties on racial lines as third-plus generations of Latino voters expand among the electorate. The 2016 and 2020 election are modest evidence of this trend (Stanton 2020).

Another potential cause of depolarization may be that economic despair rearranges partisan loyalties, as happened during the Great Depression. But there is reason to doubt this. The COVID crisis—which brought about unprecedented disruption to daily life, massive casualties, and an economic crisis—only fomented polarization. Research shows that in eras of polarization, people's perceptions of the economy are heavily tainted by whether their party is in power (Freeder 2020). Thus, even in the wake of a long-lasting depression, it is not clear it would be widely perceived as such.

Perhaps depolarization will occur because racial attitudes and other policy views are decoupled. Black and Latino voters, even Democrats, have historically been more conservative on salient social issues. As the Latino population grows, this may dampen the religious schism between the parties. Alternatively, prior to the New Deal era, race and economic issues were less consistently tied together. These issues may again be decoupled. A growing black or Latino middle class may be one such impetus for change. But for the time being, the electorate tightly clusters issues together, and partisan polarization runs deep.

Acknowledgments

This book started as an email draft that I never sent one afternoon as I sat at Café Milano, a coffee shop across the street from Berkeley's campus. I worked on it throughout graduate school, and eight years later, it is finally done.

Many people have helped me with this project, and many conversations, even in passing, have proved valuable for developing this manuscript. First, I want to thank Eric Schickler, Gabe Lenz, Rob Van Houweling, and Sarah Anzia for reading and rereading so many drafts and guiding me through this process; thank you for all your help.

I had the fortune of being at UC Berkeley with a large cohort of graduate students who read and discussed many iterations of this project. Chris Carter, Justine Davis, Natalia Garbiras Diaz, Elizabeth Elder, Jake Grumbach, Elizabeth Herman, Laura Jakli, Brad Kent, Nick Kuipers, Andrew McCall, Catlan Reardon, Alexander Sahn, and Joseph Warren provided invaluable feedback on drafts and discussion on this project at many stages.

I want to also thank my colleagues Craig Parsons and Dan Tichenor at the University of Oregon for providing valuable feedback on later chapters and Alison Gash for helping get the book proposal across the finish line. Thank you also to Andrew Proctor for generously reading the first chapters and offering helpful comments. Various parts of this manuscript also benefited from conversations throughout the years with Terri Bimes, Allison Grossman, Jim Guth, Marika Landau-Wells, Geoffrey Layman, Tom Mann, Quinn Mecham, Whitney Mello, Rob Mickey, Cecilia Mo, Hans Noel, Laura Olson, Justin Phillips, Paul Pierson, Daniel Schlozman, Laura Stoker, and especially Jack Citrin. Drew Collins-Burke provided excellent research assistance.

Thank you to Kelsie Norek and Kathleen Weldon at the Roper Center for helping me navigate and making data in their collection available.

Thank you also to Sara Doskow at the University of Chicago Press for shepherding this project through to completion, Erin DeWitt for copyediting the manuscript, and Frances Lee for her support.

Finally, I want to thank my family, old and new, to whom this book is dedicated, for being such great cheerleaders. Especially my parents, for their unconditional support of their children, and my beautiful wife, Sarah, who makes every day the best day.

Appendix

Chapter 3: Issue Connections in the Mass Public

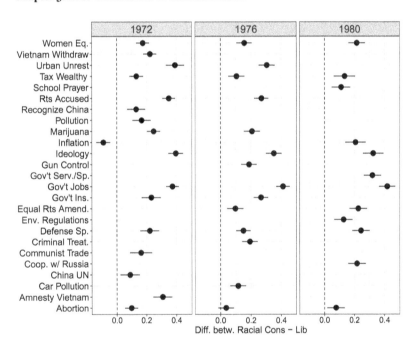

FIGURE A.1. Issue Bundles (Standardized, No Recode). The figure replicates figure 3.2 in the manuscript without recoding variables. To enable comparison across panels, I standardize the variables to have a mean of 0 and a standard deviation of 1. Measure of racial attitudes are aid to minorities.

TABLE A.1. **Issue Bundles, Controlling for Demographic Variables (1972 Data)**

	(1) Vietnam	(2) Defense	(3) Amnesty	(4) Communist Trade	(5) China UN	(6) Recognize China	(7) Jobs	(8) Insurance	(9) Tax Rate	(10) Pollution	(11) Inflation	(12) Women Eq	(13) Abortion	(14) Urban Unrest	(15) Rts Accuse	(16) Marijuana
Aid Black	0.167***	0.173***	0.237***	0.138**	0.107**	0.111***	0.277***	0.164***	0.085**	0.148***	-0.052*	0.151***	0.107***	0.303***	0.306***	0.203***
	(0.026)	(0.039)	(0.036)	(0.042)	(0.033)	(0.027)	(0.027)	(0.042)	(0.029)	(0.027)	(0.025)	(0.025)	(0.027)	(0.033)	(0.027)	(0.025)
Rural	-0.027	0.069	0.015	-0.032	0.013	-0.045	-0.035	0.095*	0.051	-0.018	-0.049	0.043	0.116***	-0.027	0.064*	0.110***
	(0.026)	(0.038)	(0.035)	(0.044)	(0.034)	(0.028)	(0.027)	(0.040)	(0.029)	(0.028)	(0.025)	(0.026)	(0.027)	(0.034)	(0.027)	(0.025)
South	0.086**	0.118**	0.066	0.057	0.044	0.029	0.055	0.094*	0.035	0.008	-0.008	0.006	0.110***	0.133***	-0.020	0.100***
	(0.029)	(0.044)	(0.040)	(0.050)	(0.039)	(0.032)	(0.031)	(0.046)	(0.033)	(0.032)	(0.028)	(0.029)	(0.031)	(0.039)	(0.031)	(0.029)
Catholic	0.024	-0.003	-0.004	-0.034	-0.006	-0.016	-0.029	-0.057	0.017	-0.017	0.045	0.002	0.190***	-0.036	-0.042	0.044
	(0.029)	(0.044)	(0.040)	(0.048)	(0.037)	(0.031)	(0.031)	(0.047)	(0.032)	(0.030)	(0.028)	(0.029)	(0.031)	(0.038)	(0.031)	(0.029)
Income	0.005	0.006	0.015	-0.013	-0.059***	-0.038**	0.052***	0.083***	0.013	-0.003	-0.020	-0.030**	-0.041***	-0.030*	-0.021	-0.028**
	(0.011)	(0.017)	(0.015)	(0.018)	(0.014)	(0.012)	(0.012)	(0.018)	(0.012)	(0.012)	(0.011)	(0.011)	(0.012)	(0.014)	(0.012)	(0.011)
BA	-0.039	-0.199***	-0.136**	-0.227***	-0.108*	-0.087*	0.000	-0.100	-0.123**	-0.039	-0.070*	-0.071*	-0.094*	0.013	-0.101**	-0.250***
	(0.035)	(0.051)	(0.047)	(0.054)	(0.044)	(0.037)	(0.036)	(0.053)	(0.038)	(0.036)	(0.034)	(0.034)	(0.037)	(0.045)	(0.037)	(0.034)
White	0.037	0.024	0.211***	-0.013	-0.171**	-0.083	0.227***	0.017	0.051	-0.050	-0.097*	-0.033	-0.087*	0.058	0.049	-0.097*
	(0.040)	(0.060)	(0.055)	(0.068)	(0.053)	(0.043)	(0.041)	(0.063)	(0.044)	(0.042)	(0.038)	(0.039)	(0.041)	(0.050)	(0.042)	(0.038)
Rep	0.055	0.096	0.081	-0.044	0.008	-0.015	0.043	0.148*	0.044	0.057	-0.032	-0.036	-0.004	0.011	0.030	0.049
	(0.039)	(0.060)	(0.055)	(0.064)	(0.051)	(0.041)	(0.041)	(0.064)	(0.044)	(0.041)	(0.038)	(0.039)	(0.041)	(0.049)	(0.042)	(0.038)
Dem	-0.102**	-0.069	-0.098	-0.035	0.008	-0.031	-0.053	0.018	-0.024	0.042	-0.006	-0.054	-0.013	-0.057	-0.071	-0.026
	(0.037)	(0.058)	(0.054)	(0.063)	(0.049)	(0.040)	(0.039)	(0.063)	(0.042)	(0.039)	(0.037)	(0.037)	(0.039)	(0.047)	(0.040)	(0.037)

Constant	0.188***	0.437***	0.354***	0.386***	0.477***	0.308***	−0.023	−0.059	0.226***	0.082	0.976***	0.351***	0.588***	0.154*	0.360***	0.662***
	(0.057)	(0.085)	(0.079)	(0.103)	(0.078)	(0.063)	(0.059)	(0.090)	(0.064)	(0.062)	(0.055)	(0.056)	(0.059)	(0.072)	(0.061)	(0.055)
N	1,408	696	654	541	633	652	1,359	620	1,306	690	1,316	1,428	1,452	678	1,352	1,412
adj. *R2*	0.069	0.108	0.185	0.059	0.081	0.057	0.163	0.108	0.028	0.038	0.024	0.043	0.083	0.154	0.142	0.151
	(1) Vietnam	(2) Defense	(3) Amnesty	(4) Communist Trade	(5) China UN	(6) Recognize China	(7) Jobs	(8) Insurance	(9) Tax Rate	(10) Pollution	(11) Inflation	(12) Women Eq	(13) Abortion	(14) Urban Unrest	(15) Rts Accuse	(16) Marijuana
Busing	0.163***	0.250***	0.306***	0.100	0.073	0.057	0.282***	0.106	0.110*	0.080*	−0.088*	0.123***	0.136***	0.195***	0.245***	0.259***
	(0.037)	(0.058)	(0.053)	(0.060)	(0.047)	(0.040)	(0.041)	(0.057)	(0.044)	(0.037)	(0.036)	(0.035)	(0.037)	(0.054)	(0.045)	(0.035)
N	1,988	921	887	789	946	975	1,862	950	1,815	1,044	1,854	2,199	2,233	843	1,713	2,180
	(1) Vietnam	(2) Defense	(3) Amnesty	(4) Communist Trade	(5) China UN	(6) Recognize China	(7) Jobs	(8) Insurance	(9) Tax Rate	(10) Pollution	(11) Inflation	(12) Women Eq	(13) Abortion	(14) Urban Unrest	(15) Rts Accuse	(16) Marijuana
Civil Rts Movement	0.127**	0.140*	0.299***	0.222**	0.034	0.047	0.251***	0.113	0.112*	0.117**	−0.080*	0.191***	0.149***	0.189**	0.224***	0.309***
	(0.042)	(0.065)	(0.054)	(0.068)	(0.054)	(0.048)	(0.046)	(0.064)	(0.047)	(0.044)	(0.040)	(0.041)	(0.041)	(0.062)	(0.050)	(0.037)
N	1,216	565	540	475	574	589	1,112	594	1,084	617	1,105	1,328	1,359	488	1,029	1,325

Note: Each column represents a multivariate regression including demographic controls. The primary variable(s) of interest are Aid Black, Busing, and Civil Rts Movement (same as fig. 3.2). The relationship shown in figure 3.2 holds even after controlling for multiple demographic variables. Each cell is the regression coefficient, with the standard errors in parentheses. The first portion of the table shows the full model for government aid to African Americans. The main coefficient, only, for busing and whether the civil rights movement is moving too quickly—the same measures used in the text—are included at the bottom in bold (control variables omitted).

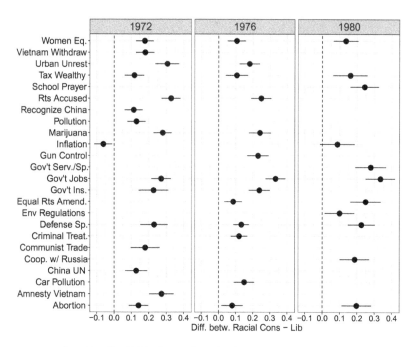

FIGURE A.2. Issue Bundles (White Respondents Only). Replicates figure 3.2 among white respondents only. The measure of racial attitudes are aid to minorities.

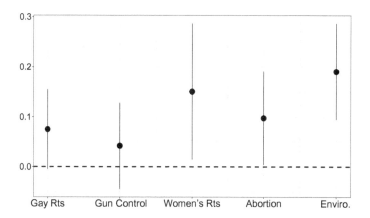

FIGURE A.3. Black Respondents Only. Data from 1982 and 1987 General Social Survey that oversampled black people. Positive coefficients mean more conservative racial attitudes correlate with more conservative views on each of the policy positions listed along the x-axis.

Chapter 7: The Partisan Divide on Immigration

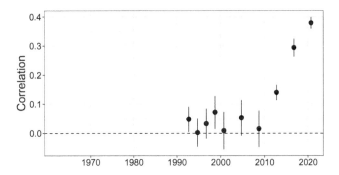

FIGURE A.4. Correlation: Immigration Levels and Economic Attitudes. Each point represents the correlation between support for immigration levels (increase, keep same, decrease) and index of economic attitudes.

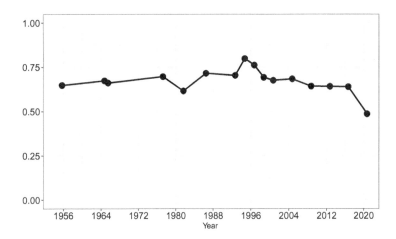

FIGURE A.5. Public Opinion: Immigration Levels by Year. Higher values represent more restrictive immigration positions. The question used asks respondents whether they want immigration increased (coded o), kept the same (coded as 0.5) or decreased (coded as 1).

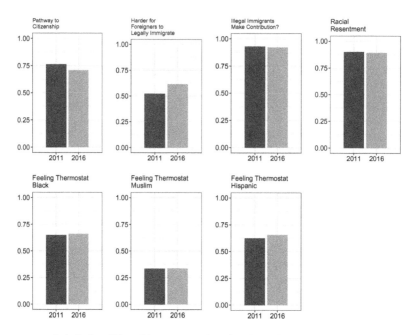

FIGURE A.6. Attitudes of Trump Voters, 2011 and 2016. Each panel shows support for the specific policy/measure listed above among Trump voters when interviewed in 2011 and 2016.

Chapter 8: Beyond the United States

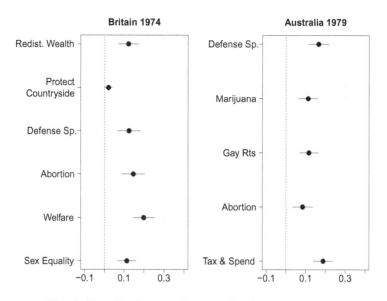

FIGURE A.7. Historical Issue Bundles, United Kingdom (1974) and Australia (1979).

Notes

Chapter One

1. Ted Kennedy, at the time, said that while he personally opposed abortion, he supported liberalizing abortion laws. This was a common refrain among Democratic politicians into the 1990s and 2000s.

2. The gay rights movement of the 1970s focused on lesbian and gay rights; bisexual and transgender people were not included at this time. Gay and lesbian activists made deliberate attempts to keep the movement focused on gay and lesbian rights as they organized in the 1970s. Thank you to Andrew Proctor for this clarification.

3. A distinction between the parties' 1968 platform is that the GOP emphasized state regulations.

4. See https://www.govtrack.us/congress/votes/90-1968/s558.

5. Available at https://avalon.law.yale.edu/18th_century/fed57.asp.

6. Most scholarship on top-down theories of opinion leadership acknowledge that "easy issues" like abortion or race dampen the power of elite cues (Lenz 2012, 222; Converse [1964] 2006, 46). However, despite the public's varying willingness to accept elite cues, top-down theories of party positioning and sorting are applied to highly charged emotional issues including abortion, civil rights, gun control, and women's rights (e.g., Carmines and Stimson 1989; Adams 1997; Karol 2009; Bawn et al. 2012).

7. And while a common understanding of political conservatism is that government should stay out of people's (economic) affairs, the values underpinning conservatism on non-economic issues are different from those underpinning economic issues. As shown above, economic attitudes in the mid-twentieth century had little to do with views toward issues of women's rights.

8. Although on many racial policies, the right-tail of answers on black racial equality is much smaller.

Chapter Two

1. This prompted Strom Thurmond, a Democratic segregationist senator from South Carolina, to lead a revolt of southern delegates from the convention. But unlike a few decades later, white segregationists had no place to go in the two-party system (although Thurmond ran as a third party-candidate in some states in 1948).

2. To be sure, it was not always social issues that drove the South from the Democratic Party. Choi et al. (2021) show that Clinton's signing of the North American Free Trade Agreement (NAFTA) hurt employment in southern counties that traditionally voted Democrat in the 1990s. The economic threat posed by free trade accelerated the decline of Democratic loyalties in the region as protectionist Democratic policies were one of the few issues that kept socially conservative Democrats inside the party.

3. In fact, Reagan served as the California state chair for Goldwater's 1964 campaign (Perlstein 2008).

4. While Reagan ultimately chose Bush to be his vice president, it was only after Bush promised to commit to Reagan's platform "without exceptions" (Allen 2000). Eight years later, Bush himself became president by appealing to socially conservative voters he had been inattentive to earlier in his career.

5. This was not all Catholics. Nixon's team recognized that "there is a deep division in the Catholic community. We should be working the Catholic social conservatives—the clear majority" (Buchanan 1971).

Chapter Three

1. The question asked whether the respondent favors a law to imprison local police officers who failed to protect a prisoner from a lynch mob and make the county where a lynching occurred pay a $10,000 fine to the victim and their family.

2. The bill was sponsored by North Carolina congressman Robert Doughton, who like most members of Congress from the South in this era opposed anti-lynching legislation and other civil rights measures (Lewis et al. 2023). This legislation was aimed at curbing organized crime (and endorsed by the International Association of Chiefs of Police!) (Collier 1938).

3. For example, if a survey asks two questions on abortion, I standardize each variable and then average the two together, and then re-standardize the variable.

4. For example, asking whether "homosexuals" as a group "are helpful or harmful," as Harris did in the late 1960s–1970s, imprecisely measures whether someone supports government policy to protect discrimination based on sexual orientation. However, prejudice against gay people overlaps and informs individual opposition to government policies that protect gay rights.

5. I define conservative as taking a right-of-center position. Because most questions on the ANES asked respondents on a seven-point scale, I code respondents who indicate a response between 1 and 3 as liberal and between 5 and 7 as conservative. To test the robustness of this classification, I also standardize the variables to have a mean of 0 and standard deviation of 1 and run the regressions without recoding variables. Results persist. See appendix figure A.1.

6. This is represented by the following regression model: $Abortion_i = \alpha + \beta_1 Aid\text{-}black_i + \varepsilon_i$.

7. Limiting inflation is usually interpreted as conservative because it benefits creditors (i.e., the wealthy), but Nixon aggressively pursued price controls to keep inflation down. Both Carter and Reagan took measures to fight inflation, too.

8. Appendix table 11.1 controls for demographic variables. Appendix figures A.2 and A.3 shows results among white and black respondents, only.

9. See https://www.census.gov/content/dam/Census/library/working-papers/2002/demo/POP-twps0056.pdf.

10. In some years, the ANES simply asks which party, for example, favors more defense spending.

11. Those respondents who place the Republican Party to the right of the Democratic Party are consistently more educated and perceived by ANES interviewers as being more knowledgeable.

12. As Sanger's quote alludes, the earliest conversations about abortion were often in context of population control, a concern at the time, rather than an issue of women's rights as it is today.

13. Unfortunately, the dataset's codebook has been lost, and only these newspapers can be identified.

14. As measured by government aid to African Americans, excluding the question on inflation.

Chapter Four

1. This differs from exploring whether race causes policy views on other issue dimensions (but see Mendelberg 2001; Tesler 2012).

2. Tesler (2012) finds similar patterns in the Obama era.

3. Scholars debate what feeds into ideological identification and find that both issues and political symbolism influence ideological self-placement (e.g., Jacoby 1991; Conover and Feldman 1981).

Chapter Five

1. This said, Johnson's unexpected ascendancy almost certainly hurt Goldwater from doing better in the South. Johnson was a southerner, and had Kennedy lived

and run in 1964, historians and contemporaneous observers wondered if Kennedy would have ceded more southern ground to the Republicans in 1964.

2. See https://timesmachine.nytimes.com/timesmachine/1963/11/28/issue.html.

3. Question text: Do you think abortion operations should or should not be legal in the following cases: (a) "health of the mother is in danger," (b) "child may be deformed," (c) "where the family does not have enough money to support another child."

4. While it is possible that Nixon switchers are more liberal on abortion because Kennedy was a Catholic, Kennedy did not campaign on abortion and there were few Catholic voters in the South in this era. Repeating this analysis with non-Catholics produces similar results.

5. It is possible that people associate support for prayer with liberals through, for example, the 1962 Supreme Court ruling that prevented prayer in public schools. However, knowledge of Supreme Court rulings are low (e.g., Zaller 1992).

6. Nixon and Humphrey differed little on gun control; both supported the gun control act that was before Congress, although Humphrey charged that Nixon was trying to evade the issue (Karol 2009, 87).

Chapter Six

1. This chapter is adapted from N. O'Brian, "Before Reagan: The Development of Abortion's Partisan Divide," *Perspectives on Politics* 18, no. 4 (2020): 1031–47. © American Political Science Association 2019, published by Cambridge University Press. Reprinted with permission.

2. The National Catholic Welfare Conference in the late 1960s split into two separate institutions, the NCCB and USCC. Prior to this split, the NCWC led anti-abortion efforts within the Catholic Church.

3. By this, Fink likely meant pursuing increasingly hard-line positions and tactics on abortion.

4. "Southern Baptist Convention Resolutions on Abortion," https://www.johnstonsarchive.net/baptist/sbcabres.html.

5. Valentine's views varied. Valentine pushed the 1971 plank on abortion but made clear that he opposed "abortion on demand." Furthermore, he rejected labeling the CLC as either a "pro-life" or "pro-choice" organization (Hollis 1976).

6. Criswell later recanted this view.

7. Some evangelical leaders appeared to not have realized that their laity opposed abortion because it was commonly associated with Catholics.

8. Paul Weyrich and other socially conservative activists had been trying to mobilize around abortion for decades. This story likely refers to Baptist ministers, including Jerry Falwell, whom Weyrich had brought into the political arena. The nonreligious leaders of the Religious Right, including Weyrich, had been talking about abortion for some time.

9. The DNC's plank in 1976 is rather moderate, but slightly to the left of the Republican platform.

10. Like others, Robertson believed Carter's religiosity meant he would be more conservative than he ultimately was.

11. Although it has since become a famous organization, NOW had only 1,200 members in November 1967 (Freeman 1975, 80).

12. McGovern's opponents labeled him as an abortion supporter to paint him as an extremist. See Wolbrecht 2000; Young 2000; Perlstein 2008, 652.

Chapter Seven

1. This relationship persists across decades as well as types of immigration: documented and undocumented immigration, as well as immigration from Europe, the Middle East, or Central America (e.g., Gimpel and Edwards 1998).

2. As discussed later in this chapter, Latino civil rights groups initially gravitated toward the Democrats because of civil rights, not immigration.

3. In years in which more than one question on racial equality is asked, I create an index.

4. Appendix figure A.2 shows the average public opinion toward immigration spiked in the conservative direction in the mid-1990s, but remained remarkably constant between 1955 and 2016, before trending in the liberal direction in 2020. This is not surprising given that work suggests that immigration attitudes react to national salience of the issue rather than localized flows (Hopkins 2011; although these may correlate at times).

5. Congress passed legislation in 1948 to allow displaced persons in Europe (as a result of World War II) into the United States. Both major parties' presidential candidates in 1948 believed the legislation did not go far enough in allowing refugees into the United States.

6. Gimpel and Edwards (1998) present similar survey results from this survey.

7. Midcentury immigration debates also often focused on immigration to the United States from people fleeing communist countries. Attitudes on black racial equality correlate with support for immigration from communist countries, too.

8. Little work explores the evolution of partisan ties of Latino voters in the mid-twentieth century. This is partially because "Latino" as a pan-ethnicity had yet to develop, and partially because on the national level, people of Latin American origin were a fairly small proportion of the population and not tracked in national polls.

9. The 1980 Census shows that about 60% of the US Hispanic population was of Mexican origin or descent.

10. Other options were to slowly desegregate the schools or to resist desegregation.

11. Kennedy's commitment to a broader suite of socially liberal issues (economic justice, civil rights) helped Kennedy appeal to Mexican American voters.

12. In 2015, 90% of elected Latino official identified as Democrats (Abrajano and Hajnal 2015, 42).

13. Ervin, unlike most southern Democrats, eventually supported the bill.

14. In 2004, McCain won reelection to the Senate with support from two-thirds of Arizona's Hispanic population (Martinez 2008).

15. The same ANES panel used above, in February 2008, asked respondents how typical Obama was of most black people. Democratic defectors and stayers perceive Obama's blackness similarly: 24% of switchers saw Obama as "not typical at all" of African Americans compared to 21% of Democratic stayers. Finally, while switchers were more likely to think Obama was a Muslim, a minority of switchers held this belief (28%).

Chapter Eight

1. Although ethnic cleavages have long been deterministic of party cleavages in some parts of the globe.

2. By culture war issues, I mean issues like abortion, gay rights, gender equality, and so on.

3. In this chapter, I measure racial attitudes using questions on whether people are accepting of people of other races and their affect toward ethnic diversity more generally.

4. In the United States, this cleavage was civil rights for African Americans, while in Sweden it was attitudes toward Syrian refugees.

Chapter Nine

1. Norman Ornstein has highlighted this trend. See Bump (2018).

References

ABC News/Washington Post. 1981. "#1981-875602: Race Relations, Chilton Research Services." Roper Center for Public Opinion Research, Cornell University, Ithaca, NY. Dataset, https://doi.org/10.25940/ROPER-31086603.

Abrajano, Marisa, and Zolton Hajnal. 2015. *White Backlash: Immigration, Race, and American Politics*. Princeton, NJ: Princeton University Press.

Achen, Christopher, and Larry Bartels. 2017. *Democracy for Realists: Why Elections Do Not Produce Responsive Government*. Princeton, NJ: Princeton University Press.

Adams, Greg. 1997. "Abortion: Evidence of an Issue Evolution." *American Journal of Political Science* 41 (3): 718–37.

Adorno, Theodor W., Else Frenkel-Brunswik, Daniel Levinson, and Nevitt Sanford. 1950. *The Authoritarian Personality*. New York: Harper and Brothers.

Agadjanian, Alexander. 2021. "When Do Partisans Stop Following the Leader?" *Political Communication* 38 (4): 351–69.

Aitkin, D. (1979) 2004. "Macquarie University Australian Political Attitudes Survey, 1979" [computer file]. Canberra: Australian Data Archive, Australian National University.

Aldrich, John H. 2011. *Why Parties? A Second Look*. Chicago: University of Chicago Press.

Allen, Richard. 2000. "George Herbert Walker Bush; The Accidental Vice President." *New York Times Magazine*, July 30. https://www.nytimes.com/2000/07/30/magazine/george-herbert-walker-bush-the-accidental-vice-president.html.

American National Election Studies (ANES). Various years, 1948–2020. University of Michigan and Stanford University. https://electionstudies.org/.

American National Election Studies (ANES). 2008–2009 Panel Study. University of Michigan and Stanford University. https://electionstudies.org/.

Ammerman, Nancy. 1990. *Baptist Battles: Social Change and Religious Conflict in the Southern Baptist Convention*. New Brunswick, NJ: Rutgers University Press.

Ansolabehere, Stephen, Jonathan Rodden, and James Snyder. 2008. "The Strength of Issues: Using Multiple Measures to Gauge Preference Stability, Ideological Constraint, and Issue Voting." *American Political Science Review* 102 (2): 215–32.

Apple, R. W. 1975. "The Dilemma of the Republicans." *New York Times*, March 10. https://www.nytimes.com/1975/03/10/archives/the-dilemma-of-the-republicans -minority-is-torn-by-centrists.html.

Applebome, Peter. 1986. "On Border, Doubts about Curbing Alien Flow." *New York Times*, October 29. https://www.nytimes.com/1986/10/29/world/on-border-doubts -about-curbing-alien-flow.html.

Applebome, Peter. 1987. "Democrats Vying for Hispanic Votes." *New York Times*, June 29. https://www.nytimes.com/1987/06/29/us/democrats-vying-for-hispanic -votes.html.

Arnold, E. Douglas. 1992. *The Logic of Congressional Action*. New Haven, CT: Yale University Press.

Associated Press. 1964a. "'Bama Goes Republican." *Macon (AL) Telegraph*, November 4. Accessed via www.newspapers.com.

Associated Press. 1964b. "Connally Reverses Rights Act Views." *New York Times*, December 22. https://www.nytimes.com/1964/12/22/archives/connally-reverses -rights-act-views.html.

Associated Press. 1986. "Fiedler Rebuffs Ed Davis." *Chico (CA) Enterprise-Record*, February 13. Accessed via www.newspapers.com.

Ayres, Drummond B. 1980a. "On the Issues: Edward M. Kennedy." *New York Times*, March 20. https://www.nytimes.com/1980/03/20/archives/on-the-issues-edward -m-kennedy-activist-for-underprivileged-a-shift.html.

Ayres, Drummond B. 1980b. "Kennedy Courting Mexican-Americans." *New York Times*, April 30. https://nyti.ms/3Ytiz1G.

Babcock, Charles. 1982. "Religious Right Decries Shift on Tax Exemptions." *Washington Post*, January 28.

Backlund, Anders. 2011. *The Sweden Democrats in Political Space—Estimating Policy Positions Using Election Manifesto Content Analysis*. Master's thesis, Sördertörn University.

Bakker, Ryan, Erica Edwards, Seth Jolly, Jonathan Polk, Jan Rovny, and Marco Steenberg. 2014. "Anchoring the Experts: Using Vignettes to Compare Party Ideology across Countries." *Research and Politics* 1 (3). https://doi.org/10.1177/ 2053168014553502.

Balmer, Randall. 2006. *Thy Kingdom Come: How the Religious Right Distorts the Faith and Threatens America*. New York: Basic Books.

Balz, Dan. 2012. "Mitt Romney's Immigration Problem." *Washington Post*. June 26. https://www.washingtonpost.com/politics/romneys-immigration-problem/2012/ 06/26/gJQA2HXu4Vstory.html.

Barber, Michael, and Jeremy Pope. 2019. "Does Party Trump Ideology? Disentangling Party and Ideology in America." *American Political Science Review* 113 (1): 38–54.

Barquero, Pablo Ortiz, Antonia María Juiz Jiménez, and Manuel Tomás González-
Fernández. 2022. "Ideological Voting for Radical Right Parties in Europe." *Acta
Politica* 57: 644–61.

Bartley, Robert. 1978. Letter to Paul Weyrich, December 12. Box 38, Folder 18, Paul
M. Weyrich Papers. American Heritage Center, Laramie, WY.

Bawn, Kathleen, Martin Cohen, David Karol, Seth Masket, Hans Noel, and John
Zaller. 2012. "A Theory of Political Parties: Groups, Policy Demands and Nomi-
nations in American Politics." *Perspectives on Politics* 10 (3): 571–97.

BBC News. 2018. "Sweden Democrats Tap into Immigration Fears." September 25.
https://www.bbc.com/news/world-europe-29202793.

Belden Associates. "The Texas Poll." August 1954, November 1954, May 1955, August 1955, November 1955, May 1956, August 1956, May 1957, November 1957,
May 1958, August 1958, November 1958, May 1959, August 1959, November
1959, February 1960, May 1960, August 1960, November 1960, May 1961, August
1961, February 1962, March 1962, November 1962, May 1963, August 1963, November 1963, February 1964, May 1964, August 1964, October 1964, November
1964, July 1966, November 1966, January 1967, August 1967, October 1967, January 1968, April 1968, June 1968. Roper Center for Public Opinion Research,
Cornell University, Ithaca, NY. https://ropercenter.cornell.edu/ipoll/.

Bernstein, Adam. 2001. "James Corman Dies at 80." *Washington Post*, January 5.

Bernstein, Adam. 2010. "James J. Kilpatrick, Conservative Commentator, Dies."
Washington Post, August 16.

Bevelander, Pieter, and Derek S. Hutcheson. 2022. "Voting Behavior of Immigrants
and Their Children in Sweden." *Journal of Immigrant & Refugee Studies* 20 (3):
427–33.

Blackwell, Morton. 1982. Letter to Elizabeth Dole, December 3. Box 4, Folder 7,
Paul M. Weyrich Papers. American Heritage Center, Laramie, WY.

Bobo, Lawrence. 1983. "Whites' Opposition to Busing: Symbolic Racism or Realistic
Group Conflict?" *Journal of Personality and Social Psychology* 45 (6): 1196–210.

Bowen, Michael. 2010. *Roots of Modern Conservatism: Dewey, Taft, and the Battle
for the Soul of the Republican Party*. Chapel Hill: University of North Carolina
Press.

Boyd, James. 1970. "Nixon's Southern Strategy: It's All in the Charts." *New York
Times*, May 17. https://www.nytimes.com/1970/05/17/archives/nixons-southern
-strategy-its-all-in-the-charts.html.

Brand, Spencer. 1980. "Republican Leadership for Black America." Box 83, Folder
3, Paul M. Weyrich Papers. American Heritage Center, Laramie, WY.

Briggs, Ed. 1989. "Plagiarism by Criswell Charged; He Denies Claim." *Baptist Press*,
July 12. Box 37, Folder "Southern Baptist Convention Controversy, 1988–1989,"
Richard Land Collection. Southern Baptist Historical Library and Archives,
Nashville, TN.

Brilliant, Mark. 2010. *The Color of America Has Changed: How Racial Diversity*

Shaped Civil Rights Reform in California, 1941–1978. New York: Oxford University Press.

Brug, Wouter van der, and Eelco Harteveld. 2021. "The Conditional Effects of the Refugee Crisis on Immigration Attitudes and Nationalism." *European Union Politics* 22 (2): 227–47.

Buchanan, Pat. 1971. Letter to Ehrlichman, Haldeman, and Colson, September 23. Box 3, Folder 52. White House Special Files. Richard Nixon Presidential Library.

Buckley, William F. 1966. "The Catholic Church and Abortion." *National Review*, April 5.

Buckley, William F. 1972. Letter to Bob Jones. Box 121, Folder 6, William A. Rusher Papers, 1940–2010. Library of Congress, Washington, DC.

Budiman, Abby, Christine Tamir, Lauren Mora, and Luis Noe-Bustamante. 2018. "Facts on US Immigrants, 2018." Pew Research Center. https://www.pewresearch .org/hispanic/2020/08/20/facts-on-u-s-immigrants-trend-data/.

Bump, Philip. 2015. "When Did Black Americans Start Voting so Heavily Democratic?" *Washington Post*, July 7. https://www.washingtonpost.com/news/the-fix/ wp/2015/07/07/when-did-black-americans-start-voting-so-heavily-democratic/.

Bump, Philip. 2018. "In about 20 Years, Half the Population Will Live in Eight States." *Washington Post*, June 18. https://www.washingtonpost.com/news/ politics/wp/2018/07/12/in-about-20-years-half-the-population-will-live-in-eight -states/.

Bureau of Applied Social Research, Columbia University. 1948. "BASR Poll: 1948 Voting Study—Elmira, N.Y." Roper Center for Public Opinion Research, Cornell University, Ithaca, NY. https://doi.org/10.25940/ROPER-31090308.

Burns, James McGregor. 1976. *Edward Kennedy and the Camelot Legacy*. New York: W. W. Norton.

Byers, Bo. 1970. "Referendum: Little Meaning." *Kilgore (TX) News Herald*, February 26. Accessed via www.newspapers.com.

Campbell, Angus, Philip Converse, Warren Miller, and Donald Stokes. 1960. *The American Voter*. Chicago: University of Chicago Press.

Carmines, Edward, and James Stimson. 1982. "Racial Issues and the Structure of Mass Belief Systems." *Journal of Politics* 44 (1): 2–20.

Carmines, Edward, and James Stimson. 1989. *Issue Evolution: Race and the Transformation of American Politics*. Princeton, NJ: Princeton University Press.

Carmines, Edward G., and James Woods. 2002. "The Role of Party Activists in the Evolution of the Abortion Issue." *Political Behavior* 24 (4): 361–77.

Carsey, Thomas, and Geoffrey Layman. 2006. "Changing Sides or Changing Minds? Party Identification and Policy Preferences in the American Electorate." *American Political Science Review* 50 (2): 464–77.

Cashen, Henry. 1976. Letter to Michael Duval, July 14. Box 27, Folder "Republican Party Platform—Catholic Issues," Michael Raoul-Duval Files. Gerald R. Ford Presidential Library and Museum, Ann Arbor, MI.

Caughey, Devin. 2018. *The Unsolid South: Mass Politics and National Representation in a One-Party Enclave*. Princeton, NJ: Princeton University Press.

CBS News. 1978. "Education Poll." Roper Center for Public Opinion Research, Cornell University, Ithaca, NY. https://doi.org/10.25940/ROPER-31090619.

CBS News/New York Times Poll. 1976. "Massachusetts Primary Exit Poll." Roper Center for Public Opinion Research, Cornell University, Ithaca, NY. https://doi.org/10.25940/ROPER-31091112.

CBS News/New York Times. 1986. "National Election Day Exit Poll." Roper Center for Public Opinion Research, Cornell University, Ithaca, NY. https://doi.org/10.25940/ROPER-31091244.

Cervantes, Niki. 1986. "GOP Hopefuls Sheath Claws." *Modesto (CA) Bee*, June 1.

Chamberlain, John. 1980. "Moral Issues Will Attract Non-Voters." *New Haven (CT) Register*, October 8. Box 4, Folder 6, Paul M. Weyrich Papers. American Heritage Center, Laramie, WY.

Chen, Anthony. 2007. "The Party of Lincoln and the Politics of State Fair Employment Practices Legislation in the North, 1945–1964." *American Journal of Sociology* 112 (6): 1713–74.

Chen, Anthony, Robert Mickey, and Robert Van Houweling. 2008. "Explaining the Contemporary Alignment of Race and Party: Evidence from California's 1946 Ballot Initiative on Fair Employment." *Studies in American Political Development* 22 (2): 204–28.

Choi, Jiwon, Ilyana Kuziemko, Ebonya Washington, and Gavin Wright. 2021. "Local Economic and Political Effects of Trade Deals: Evidence from NAFTA." *NBER Working Paper*. http://www.nber.org/papers/w29525.

Citrin, Jack, Donald Green, Christopher Muste, and Cara Wong. 1997. "Public Opinion towards Immigration Reform: The Role of Economic Motivations." *Journal of Politics* 59 (3): 858–81.

Citrin, Jack, Beth Reingold, and Donald Green. 1990. "American Identity and the Politics of Ethnic Change." *Journal of Politics* 52 (4): 1124–54.

Collier, Rex. 1938. "Firearms Control: An Interview of the Honorable Homer Cummings, Attorney General of the United States." https://www.justice.gov/sites/default/files/ag/legacy/2011/09/16/04-25-1938.pdf.

Colson, Chuck. 1970. Memo to Richard Nixon, October 16. Box 3, Folder 51, Contested Materials Collection. Richard Nixon Presidential Library.

Conover, Pamela. 1984. "The Influence of Group Identifications on Political Perception and Evaluation." *Journal of Politics* 46 (3): 760–85. Conover, Pamela, and Stanley Feldman. 1981. "The Origins and Meaning of Liberal/Conservative Self Identifications." *American Journal of Political Science* 25 (4): 617–45.

Converse, Philip E. (1964) 2006. "The Nature of Belief Systems in Mass Publics." *Critical Review* 18 (1–3): 1–74.

Converse, Philip E. 1976. *The Dynamics of Party Support: Cohort Analyzing Party Identification*. Beverly Hills, CA: Sage.

Converse, Philip E. 2000. "Assessing the Capacity of Mass Electorates." *Annual Review of Political Science* 3: 331–53.

Corral, Alvaro J., and David L. Leal. 2020. "One in Four Latinos Voted for Trump Last Time. They'll Likely Do So Again." *Washington Post*, November 2. https://www.washingtonpost.com/politics/2020/11/02/about-quarter-latinos-voted-trump-four-years-ago-theyll-likely-do-so-again/.

Cort, David. 1959. "Arms and the Man." *The Nation*, May 23, EBSCOhost.

Cramer, Katherine. 2012. "Putting Inequality in Its Place: Rural Consciousness and the Power of Perspective." *American Political Science Review* 106 (3): 517–32.

Crewe, I. M., D. R. Robertson, and B. Sarlvik. (1974) 1977. *British Election Study, October 1974*. Colchester, Essex: UK Data Archive [distributor].

Critchlow, Donald. 1999. *Intended Consequences: Birth Control, Abortion, and the Federal Government in Modern America*. New York: Oxford University Press.

Critchlow, Donald. 2018. *Phyllis Schlafly and Grassroots Conservatism*. Princeton, NJ: Princeton University Press.

Dahlstrom, Carl, and Peter Esaiasson. 2011. "The Immigration Issue and Anti-Immigrant Party Success in Sweden, 1970–2006: A Deviant Case Analysis." *Party Politics*, 19 (2): 343–64.

Decision Making Information. 1975. "Attitudes towards Gun Control: Overview of a National Survey of the American Electorate." Box 16, Folder "Gun Control File," John Vickerman Files. Gerald R. Ford Presidential Library and Museum, Ann Arbor, MI.

Deitch, Charlie. 2020. "On Roe v. Wade Anniversary, Primary Challenger Calls out Rep. Mike Doyle for Backing Hyde Amendment." *Pennsylvania Capital-Star*, January 23. https://www.penncapital-star.com/government-politics/on-roe-v-wade-anniversary-primary-challenger-calls-out-rep-mike-doyle-for-backing-hyde-amendment/.

Delli Carpini, Michael X., and Scott Keeter. 1996. *What Americans Know about Politics and Why It Matters*. New Haven, CT: Yale University Press.

Democracy Fund Voter Study Group. 2018. "Views of the Electorate Research Survey, May 2018." Washington, DC: Democracy Fund Voter Study Group [producer]. www.voterstudygroup.org.

Denier, Greg. 1980. Letter to Francis J. Lally, February 19. Box 64, Folder "NCCB: Ad Hoc Committee: Pro-Life Activities 1980 Jan.–March," NCCB Papers. Catholic University of America Archives, Washington, DC.

Douthat, Ross. 2009. "A Different Kind of Liberal." *New York Times*, August 30. https://www.nytimes.com/2009/08/31/opinion/31douthat.html.

Edsall, Thomas B. 2012. "Playing It Dangerously Safe." *New York Times*. July 1. https://archive.nytimes.com/campaignstops.blogs.nytimes.com/2012/07/01/playing-it-dangerously-safe/.

Edsall, Thomas B., and Mary Edsall. 1992. *Chain Reaction: The Impact of Race, Rights, and Taxes on American Politics*. New York: W. W. Norton.

Eizenstat, Stuart. 2018. Personal interview with author, August 31.

Elder, Elizabeth Mitchell, and Neil O'Brian. 2022. "Social Groups and Political Belief Systems: Fresh Evidence on an Old Theory." *American Political Science Review* 116 (4): 1407–24.

Elving, Ron. 2015. "Abortion Vote Shows How Much Democrats' World Has Changed." *National Public Radio*, January 26. https://www.npr.org/sections/ itsallpolitics/2015/01/26/381472527/abortion-vote-shows-how-much-democrats -world-has-changed.

Engel, Randy. 1974. Letter to NRLC Board of Directors, March 30. Box 8, Folder "NRLC 1975 (6)," ACCL Papers. Gerald R. Ford Presidential Library and Museum, Ann Arbor, MI.

Engelhardt, Andrew. 2021. "Racial Attitudes through a Partisan Lens." *British Journal of Political Science* 51 (3): 1062–79.

Erlingsson, Gissur, Kare Vernby, and Richard Ohrvall. 2014. "The Single-Issue Party Thesis and the Sweden Democrats." *Acta Politica* 49: 196–216.

Fenno, Richard. 1977. "U.S. House Members in Their Constituencies: An Exploration." *American Political Science Review* 71 (3): 883–917.

Field Poll. January 1966, June 1966, April 1967, August 1966, July 1986. https://dlab .berkeley.edu/data/california-public-opinion-polls.

Filindra, Alexandra, and Noah J. Kaplan. 2016. "Racial Resentment and Whites' Gun Policy Preferences in Contemporary America." *Political Behavior* 38: 255–75.

Fine, Janice, and Daniel Tichenor. 2009. "A Movement Wrestling: American Labor's Enduring Struggle with Immigration, 1866–2007." *Studies in American Political Development* 23 (1): 1–30.

Fink, Judy. 1974a. Letter to NCHLA, November 25. Box 67, Folder "NCHLA Jan– March 1975," NCCB Papers. Catholic University of America Archives, Washington, DC.

Fink, Judy. 1974b. Letter to Joe Lampe, December. Box 15, Folder "ACCL Organization from Late 1974," ACCL Papers. Gerald R. Ford Presidential Library and Museum, Ann Arbor, MI.

Finkelstein, Arthur. 1971. Letter to Robert Marik, December 16. Box 45, Folder 14, Contested Materials Collection. Richard Nixon Presidential Library.

Fiorina, Morris P., Paul E. Peterson, D. Stephen Voss, and Bertram Johnson. 2004. *The New American Democracy*. New York: Longman Pearson.

Fisher, Paul. 1978. "Union Chief Meany Links Prolife with the Ultra Right." *National Catholic Register*, April 9. American Heritage Center. Paul M. Weyrich Papers, Box 24, Folder 2, Laramie, WY.

Flint, Jerry. 1968. "Lemay Supports Legal Abortion." *New York Times*, October 24. https://www.nytimes.com/1968/10/24/archives/lemay-supports-legal-abortions -tells-yale-audience-he-also-is-in.html.

Fordham, Benjamin. 2007. "The Evolution of Republican and Democratic Positions on Cold War Military Spending: A Historical Puzzle." *Social Science History* 31 (4): 603–36.

Ford Press Conference. 1975. "Transcript of President's News Conference on Domestic and Foreign Matters." *New York Times*, February 27. https://www.nytimes .com/1975/02/27/archives/transcript-of-presidents-news-conference-on-domestic -and-foreign.html.

Francis-Fallon, Benjamin. 2019. *The Rise of the Latino Vote: A History.* Cambridge, MA: Harvard University Press.

Franklin, Charles, and Liane Kosaki. 1989. "Republican Schoolmaster: The U.S. Supreme Court, Public Opinion, and Abortion." *American Political Science Review* 83 (3): 751–71.

Freeder, Sean. 2020. "It's *No Longer* the Economy, Stupid: Selective Perception and Attribution of Economic Outcomes." Unpublished manuscript. https:// seanfreeder.files.wordpress.com/2020/12/paper_economy.pdf.

Freeder, Sean, Gabriel S. Lenz, and Shad Turney. 2019. "The Importance of Knowing 'What Goes with What': Reinterpreting the Evidence on Policy Attitude Stability." *Journal of Politics* 81 (1). https://doi.org/10.1086/700005.

Freeman, Jo. 1975. *The Politics of Women's Liberation.* New York: David McKay.

Friedan, Betty. 1976. *It Changed My Life: Writings on the Women's Movement.* New York: Random House.

Frymer, Paul. 2011. *Uneasy Alliances: Race and Party Competition in America.* Princeton, NJ: Princeton University Press.

Gabler, Neal. 2020. *Catching the Wind: Edward Kennedy and the Liberal Hour, 1932–1975.* New York: Crown.

Gallup. Poll numbers 63, 182, 589, 604, 616, 633, 660, 662, 676, 681, 704, 713, 721, 733, 749, 744, 776, 788, 793, 838, 861, 984, 1159G, 1197G, 1202G, 1213, 1238G. Roper Center for Public Opinion Research, Cornell University, Ithaca, NY. https:// ropercenter.cornell.edu/ipoll/.

Gamm, Gerald, Justin Phillips, Matthew Carr, and Michael Auslen. 2022. "The Culture War and Partisan Polarization: State Political Parties, 1960–2018." Presented at the American Political Science Association, 2022.

Garcia, Ignacio. 2000. *Viva Kennedy: Mexican Americans in Search of Camelot.* College Station: Texas A&M University Press.

General Social Surveys. 1972–2018. Investigators: Tom W. Smith, Michael Davern, Jeremy Freese, and Stephen L. Morgan. Sponsored by National Science Foundation. Chicago: NORC, 2019.

Gidding, Lee. 1971. "Executive Director's Report," November 5. Box 15, Folder 2, Lawrence Lader Papers, 1956–1986. New York Public Library Archives, New York, NY.

Gilens, Martin. 1996. "'Race Coding' and White Opposition to Welfare." *American Political Science Review* 90 (3): 593–604.

Gimpel, James G., and James R. Edwards Jr. 1998. *The Congressional Politics of Immigration Reform.* New York: Longman.

Gjelten, Thomas. 2015. "The Immigration Act That Inadvertently Changed America." *The Atlantic*, October 2. https://www.theatlantic.com/politics/archive/2015/10/immigration-act-1965/408409/.

Goldwater, Barry. 1960. *The Conscience of a Conservative.* Shepherdsville, KY: Victor Publishing.

Goldwater, Barry. 1976. Letter to Gerald Ford, May 7. "Selected Documents of the 1976 Presidential Campaign." Gerald R. Ford Presidential Digital Library. https://www.fordlibrarymuseum.gov/library/exhibits/campaign/campaign.asp.

Goldwater, Barry. 2009. "I Sense Here a Realignment of Southern Conservative Democrats." In *Debating the American Conservative Movement, 1945 to Present*, edited by Donald T. Critchlow and Nancy MacLean, 181–82. Lanham, MD: Rowman & Littlefield.

Granberg, Donald. 1981. "The Abortion Activists." *Family Planning Perspectives* 13 (4): 157–63.

Green, Emma. 2016. "The Progressive Roots of the Pro-Life Movement." *The Atlantic*, February 3. https://www.theatlantic.com/politics/archive/2016/02/daniel-williams-defenders-unborn/435369/.

Greene, Sheldon. 1969. "Wetbacks, Growers and Poverty." *The Nation*, October 20, EBSCOhost.

Greenhouse, Linda, and Reva Siegel. 2012. *Before* Roe v. Wade: *Voices That Shaped the Abortion Debate before the Supreme Court's Ruling.* New Haven, CT: Yale Law School.

Grumbach, Jacob. 2022. *Laboratories against Democracy: How National Parties Transformed State Politics.* Princeton, NJ: Princeton University Press.

Gutierrez, Ramon A. 2019. "Mexican Immigration to the United States." *Oxford Research Encyclopedia of American History.* https://oxfordre.com/americanhistory/view/10.1093/acrefore/9780199329175.001.0001/acrefore-9780199329175-e-146.

Guttmacher, Alan. 1965. "How Births Can Be Controlled," *National Review*, July 27.

Haag, Ernest Van Den. 1965. "More Immigration?" *National Review*, September 21.

Hacker, Jacob, and Paul Pierson. 2010. *Winner-Take-All Politics: How Washington Made the Rich Richer—and Turned Its Back on the Middle Class.* New York: Simon & Schuster.

Hager, Elizabeth. 1976. "Rep. Hager Raps Reagan on ERA." Box 39, Folder "Reagan-Women," Nessen Papers. Gerald R. Ford Presidential Library and Museum, Ann Arbor, MI.

Hart, Jeffrey. 1973. Letter to the Editors. December 8. Box 123, Folder "Staff Correspondence 1973," William A. Rusher Papers, 1940–2010. Library of Congress, Washington, DC.

Hartman, Elaine. 1975. Letter to Sheed & Ward Inc., June 4. Box 1, Folder 6, Paul M. Weyrich Papers. American Heritage Center, Laramie, WY.

Hauser, Rita. 1976. Letter to Bob Marrick. March 4. "Reagan on (and off) Abortion." Folder "Voter Groups General," President Ford Committee—Hughes Subject File. Gerald R. Ford Library and Museum, Ann Arbor, MI.

Heffington, Colton, Brandon Beomseob Park, and Laron K. Williams. 2017. "The 'Most Important Problem' Dataset (MIPD): A New Dataset on American Issue Importance." Roper Center for Public Opinion Research, Cornell University, Ithaca, NY. https://doi.org/10.25940/ROPER-31094159.

Hehir, J. Bryan. 1975. Letter to James Rausch, August 14. NCCB Box 67, Folder "July–Dec. 1975." Catholic University of American Archives, Washington, DC.

Hershey, Marjorie Randon. 1984. *Running for Office: The Political Education of Campaigners*. London: Chatham House.

Hetherington, Marc, and Jonathan Weiler. 2009. *Authoritarianism and Polarization in American Politics* New York: Cambridge University Press.

Higgins, Anne. 1976. Letter to the President. November 12. Box C52, Folder "Presidential Handwriting 11/17/1976," Presidential Handwriting File. Gerald R. Ford Presidential Library and Museum, Ann Arbor, MI.

Hillygus, Sunshine, and Todd Shields. 2009. *The Persuadable Voter: Wedge Issues in Presidential Campaigns*. Princeton, NJ: Princeton University Press.

Himmelweit, Hilde, Marianne Jaeger Biberian, and Janet Stockdale. 1978. "Memory for Past Vote: Implications of a Study of Bias in Recall." *British Journal of Political Science* 8 (3): 365–75.

Hitt, Mathew, Kyle Saunders, and Kevin Scott. 2019. "Justice Speaks, but Who's Listening? Mass Public Awareness of U.S. Supreme Court Cases." *Journal of Law and Courts* 7 (1): 29–52.

Hochman, Nate. 2022. "When William F. Buckley Called for Overturning *Roe* in 1974." *National Review*, May 10. https://www.nationalreview.com/corner/when-william-f-buckley-called-for-overturning-roe-in-1974/.

Holbrook, Bob. 1975. "Baptist for Life Background Paper," December 3. Box 86, Folder "Domestic Social Development: Health Affairs: Abortion 1974–76," NCCB Papers. Catholic University of America Archives, Washington, DC.

Hollis, Harry. 1976. Memo, May 27. Box 17, Folder 5, CLC Files 138-5. Southern Baptist Historical Library and Archives, Nashville, TN.

Holmberg, Sören, Henrik Ekengren Oscarsson, and Statistics Sweden. 2014. "Swedish Election Study 2006–2010 Panel." Swedish National Data Service. https://doi.org/10.5878/002092.

Hooghe, Liesbet, and Gary Marks. 2018. "Cleavage Theory Meets Europe's Crises: Lipset, Rokkan, and the Transnational Cleavage." *Journal of European Public Policy* 25 (1): 109–35.

Hopkins, Daniel. 2010. "Politicized Places: Explaining Where and When Immigrants Provoke Local Opposition." *American Political Science Review* 104 (1): 40–60.

Hopkins, Daniel. 2011. "National Debates, Local Responses: The Origins of Local Concern about Immigration in Britain and the United States." *British Journal of Political Science* 41: 499–524.

Hopkins, Daniel. 2021. "The Activation of Prejudice and Presidential Voting: Panel Evidence from the 2016 U.S. Election." *Political Behavior* 43: 663–86.

Hopkins, Daniel, Eric Schickler, and David Azizi. 2020. "From Many Divides, One? The Polarization and Nationalization of American State Party Platforms, 1918–2017." Available at Social Science Research Network. https://papers.ssrn.com/sol3/papers.cfm?abstract_id=3772946.

Hopkins, Daniel, Eric Schickler, and David Azizi. 2022. "From Many Divides, One? The Polarization and Nationalization of American State Party Platforms, 1918–2017." *Studies in American Political Development* 36 (1): 1–20.

Hopkins, Daniel, and Samantha Washington. 2020. "The Rise of Trump, the Fall of Prejudice? Tracking White Americans' Racial Attitudes via a Panel Survey, 2008–2018." *Public Opinion Quarterly* 84 (1): 119–40.

Horowitz, Jason. 2016. "Marco Rubio Pushed for Immigration Reform with Conservative Media." *New York Times*, February 27. https://www.nytimes.com/2016/02/28/us/politics/marco-rubio-pushed-for-immigration-reform-with-conservative-media.html.

Hunt, William. 1984. "Strategic Plan for the ACCL," July 19. Box 30, Folder "Allied Institutional Development Series (5)," ACCL Collection. Gerald R. Ford Presidential Library and Museum, Ann Arbor, MI.

Hunter, James Davidson. 1991. *Culture Wars: The Struggle to Define America*. New York: Basic Books.

Hunter, Marjorie. 1975. "Senate Upholds U.S. Abortion Funds." *New York Times*, April 11, 1975. https://www.nytimes.com/1975/04/11/archives/senate-upholds-us-abortion-funds.html.

Hutchings, Vincent, and Nick Valentino. 2004. "The Centrality of Race in American Politics." *Annual Review of Political Science* 7: 383–408.

Inglehart, Ronald. 1977. *The Silent Revolution: Changing Values and Political Styles among Western Publics*. Princeton, NJ: Princeton University Press.

Inglehart, Ronald. 1984. "The Changing Structure of Political Cleavages in Western Society." In *Electoral Change in Advanced Industrial Democracies: Realignment or Dealignment?*, edited by Dalton Russell, Scott Flanagan, and Paul Allen Beck, 25–69. Princeton, NJ: Princeton University Press.

Inglehart, R., C. Haerpfer, A. Moreno, C. Welzel, K. Kizilova, J. Diez-Medrano, M. Lagos, P. Norris, E. Ponarin, and B. Puranen et al., eds. 2014. World Values Survey: All Rounds—Country-Pooled Datafile Version. Madrid: JD Systems Institute. https://www.worldvaluessurvey.org/WVSDocumentationWVL.jsp.

Israel, Steve. 2020. "How Never Trumpers Fell in Line." *Washington Post*, February 7. https://www.nytimes.com/2020/02/07/opinion/trump-impeachment-congress.html.

Jacoby, William G. 1991. "Ideological Identification and Issue Attitudes." *American Journal of Political Science* 35 (1): 178–205.

Jardina, Ashley. 2019. *White Identity Politics*. Cambridge: Cambridge University Press.

Jefferson, Hakeem. 2023. "The Politics of Respectability and Black Americans' Punitive Attitudes." *American Political Science Review*, 1–17. https://doi.org/10.1017/S0003055422001289.

Jefferson, Mildred. 1976. Letter to Friends for Life, October 15. Box 44, Folder "Carter (1)," ACCL Collection. Gerald R. Ford Presidential Library and Museum, Ann Arbor, MI.

Jenkins, Jeffrey, Justin Peck, and Vesla Weaver. 2010. "Between Reconstructions: Congressional Action on Civil Rights, 1891–1940." *Studies in American Political Development* 24: 57–89.

Karol, David. 2009. *Party Position Change in American Politics: Coalition Management*. New York: Cambridge University Press.

Karol, David. 2019. *Red, Green and Blue: The Partisan Divide on Environmental Issues*. New York: Cambridge University Press.

Katznelson, Ira. 2013. *Fear Itself: The New Deal and the Origins of Our Time*. New York: Liveright.

Katznelson, Ira, Kim Geiger, and Daniel Kryder. 1993. "Limiting Liberalism: The Southern Veto in Congress, 1933–1950." *Political Science Quarterly* 108 (2): 283–306.

Kaufman, Robert. 2000. *Henry M. Jackson: A Life in Politics*. Seattle: University of Washington Press.

Kelley, Daryl. 1991. "Gallegly Urges Stricter Rules for Citizenship." *Los Angeles Times*, October 24.

Kelly, Harry. 1975. "King of the Right Wing Mailing Lists." *Chicago Tribune*, August 13. Box 19, Folder 8, Paul M. Weyrich Papers. American Heritage Center, Laramie, WY.

Key, V. O. 1942. *Politics, Parties and Pressure Groups*, 5th ed. New York: Crowell.

Key, V. O., with Alexander Heard. 1949. *Southern Politics in State and Nation*. New York: Knopf.

Key, V. O. 1955. "A Theory of Critical Elections." *Journal of Politics* 17 (1): 3–18.

Key, V. O. 1959. "Secular Realignment and the Party System." *Journal of Politics* 21 (2): 198–210.

Key, V. O. 1961. *Public Opinion and American Democracy*. New York: Knopf.

Keyssar, Alexander. 2000. *The Right to Vote: The Contested History of Democracy in the United States*. New York: Basic Books.

Killian, Mitchell, and Clyde Wilcox. 2008. "Do Abortion Attitudes Lead to Party Switching?" *Politics Research Quarterly* 61 (4): 561–73.

Kilpatrick, James J. 1964. "Perhaps a Sin; Not a Crime." *Miami Herald*, December 16.

Kilpatrick, James J. 1976. "Abortion Said Poor Issue in Campaign." *Washington Star*,

September 18. Box 45, Folder "Ford Campaign (4)," ACCL Papers. Gerald R. Ford Presidential Library and Museum, Ann Arbor, MI.

Kilpatrick, James J. 1979. "A Comment." *National Review*, May 25.

Kinch, Sam. 1968. "Eggers Claims Texans Fed Up with Tax Increases." *Fort Worth Star-Telegram*, July 12.

Kinder, Donald, and Nathan Kalmoe. 2017. *Neither Liberal nor Conservative: Ideological Innocence in the American Public*. Chicago: University of Chicago Press.

Kinder, Donald R., and Cindy D. Kam. 2009. *Us against Them: Ethnocentric Foundations of American Opinion*. Chicago: University of Chicago Press.

Kinder, Donald, and Tali Mendelberg. 2000. "Individualism Reconsidered: Principles and Prejudice in Contemporary American Public Opinion on Race." In *Racialized Politics: Values, Ideology, and Prejudice in American Public Opinion*, edited by David Sears, Jim Sidanius, and Lawrence Bobo. Chicago: University of Chicago Press.

Kinder, Donald, and Lynn M. Sanders. 1996. *Divided by Color: Racial Politics and Democratic Ideals*. Chicago: University of Chicago Press.

Kinder, Donald, and David Sears. 1981. "Prejudice and Politics: Symbolic Racism versus Racial Threats to the Good Life." *Journal of Personality and Social Psychology* 40 (3): 414–31.

Kingdon, John. 1989. *Congressmen's Voting Decisions*. Ann Arbor: University of Michigan Press.

Klemesrud, Judy. 1976. "Abortion in the Campaign: Methodist Surgeon Leads the Opposition." *New York Times*, March 1. https://www.nytimes.com/1976/03/01/archives/abortion-in-the-campaign-methodist-surgeon-leads-the-opposition.html.

Knox, Neal. 1975. Letter to Max Friedersdorf, July 11. Box 16, Folder "Gun Control (2)," Philip Buchen Files. Gerald R. Ford Presidential Library and Museum, Ann Arbor, MI.

Kondracke, Morton M. 1987. "Moral Borders." *The New Republic*, November 23.

Kotlowski, Dean J. 2001. *Nixon's Civil Rights: Politics, Principle, and Policy*. Cambridge, MA: Harvard University Press.

Krimmel, Katherine. 2017. "The Efficiencies and Pathologies of Special Interest Partisanship." *Studies in American Political Development* 31 (2): 149–69.

Kuziemko, Ilyana, and Ebonya Washington. 2018. "Why Did the Democrats Lose the South? Bringing New Data to an Old Debate." *American Economic Review* 108 (10): 2830–67.

Lacombe, Matthew. 2021. *Firepower: How the NRA Turned Gun Owners into a Political Force*. Princeton, NJ: Princeton University Press.

Lader, Lawrence. n.d. Memo A, "Abortion—A Key Issue in the 1976 Campaign?" Box 21, Lawrence Lader Papers, 1956–1986. New York Public Library Archives, New York, NY.

Lader, Lawrence. n.d. Memo B, "Are Women Really Winning Their Demands

through Political Power?" Box 21, Lawrence Lader Papers, 1956–1986. New York
Public Library Archives, New York, NY.

Lange, Jeva. 2016. "We've Been Asking If the GOP Is Dead since at Least 1936."
The Week, March 14. https://theweek.com/speedreads/612525/weve-been-asking
-gop-dead-since-least-1936.

Lassiter, Matthew. 2006. *The Silent Majority: Suburban Politics in the Sunbelt South.*
Princeton, NJ: Princeton University Press.

Layman, Geoffrey. 1997. "Religion and Political Behavior in the United States:
The Impact of Beliefs, Affiliations, and Commitment from 1980 to 1994." *Public
Opinion Quarterly* 61 (2): 288–316.

Layman, Geoffrey. 2001. *The Great Divide: Religious and Cultural Conflict in American Party Politics.* New York: Columbia University Press.

Layman, Geoffrey, and Thomas Carsey. 2002. "Party Polarization and 'Conflict Extension' in the American Electorate." *American Political Science Review* 46 (4):
786–802.

Layman, Geoffrey C., Thomas Carsey, John Green, Richard Herrera, and Rosalyn
Cooperman. 2010. "Activists and Conflict Extension in American Party Politics."
American Political Science Review 104 (2): 324–46.

Leip, David. 2019. *United States Presidential Election Results.* https://uselectionatlas
.org/RESULTS/index.html.

Lejeune, Anthony. 1957. "Controversy over Wolfenden Report: Can Morality Be
Legislated?" *National Review*, September 28.

Lenz, Gabriel. 2012. *Follow the Leader? How Voters Respond to Politicians' Policies
and Performance.* Chicago: University of Chicago Press.

Levendusky, Matthew. 2009. *The Partisan Sort: How Liberals Became Democrats
and Conservatives Became Republicans.* Chicago: University of Chicago Press.

Levitsky, Steven, and Daniel Ziblatt. 2018. *How Democracies Die.* New York: Crown.

Lewis, Jeffrey B., Keith Poole, Howard Rosenthal, Adam Boche, Aaron Rudkin, and
Luke Sonnet. 2023. *Voteview: Congressional Roll-Call Votes Database.* https://
voteview.com/.

Lind, William S., and Paul Weyrich. 1987. Letter to Richard Neuhaus, March 31. Box
74, Folder 11, Richard John Neuhaus Papers. Catholic University of America
Archives, Washington, DC.

Lindaman, Kara, and Donald P. Haider-Markel. 2002. "Issue Evolution, Political
Parties, and the Culture Wars." *Political Research Quarterly* 55 (1): 91–110.

Lipset, Seymour, and Stein Rokkan. 1967. *Party Systems and Voter Alignments.* New
York: Free Press.

Los Angeles Times. 1926. "Direct Primary in Iowa." June 9. Accessed via ProQuest
Historical Newspapers.

Los Angeles Times. 1985. "Poll #1985-094: The Media." Roper Center for Public
Opinion Research, Cornell University, Ithaca, NY. https://doi.org/10.25940/
ROPER-31092828.

Louis Harris and Associates. Poll numbers: 971, 1431, 1522, 1531, 1561, 1718, 1813, 1880, 1933, 1939, 1970, 2025, 2037, 2047, 2050, 2124, 2215B, 2216, 2314, 2344, 3735, 7490, 792103, P3735, S7581. Accessed via Louis Harris Data Center Dataverse, University of North Carolina at Chapel Hill. https://dataverse.unc.edu/dataverse/harris.

Lowndes, Joseph. 2009. *From the New Deal to the New Right: Race and the Southern Origins of Modern Conservatism*. New Haven, CT: Yale University Press.

Lynch, Robert. 1974a. "The National Committee for a Human Life Amendment, Inc.: Its Goals and Origins." *Catholic Lawyer* 20 (4): 303–8.

Lynch, Robert. 1974b. Letter to NCHLA Board of Directors, November 8. Box 67, Folder "NCHLA 1973–74," NCCB Papers. Catholic University of America Archives, Washington, DC.

Lynch, Robert. 1975a. Letter to Cardinal Medeiros, April 15. Box 67, Folder "April–June 1975," NCCB Papers. Catholic University of America Archives, Washington, DC.

Lynch, Robert. 1975b. Letter to James Rausch, May 27. Box 67, Folder "April–June 1975," NCCB Papers. Catholic University of America Archives, Washington, DC.

MacGillis, Alec. 2016. "How Washington Blew Its Best Chance to Fix Immigration." *ProPublica*. September 15. https://www.propublica.org/article/washington -congress-immigration-reform-failure.

Malka, Ariel, Yphtach Lelkes, and Christopher J. Soto. 2019. "Are Cultural and Economic Conservatism Positively Correlated? A Large-Scale Cross-National Test." *British Journal of Political Science* 49 (3): 1045–69.

Margolis, Michele. 2017. "How Politics Affects Religion: Partisanship, Socialization and Religiosity in America." *Journal of Politics* 80 (1): 30–43.

Marks, Gary, Liesbet Hooghe, Moira Nelson, and Erica Edwards. 2006. "Party Competition and European Integration in the East and West." *Comparative Political Studies* 39 (2): 155–75.

Marks, Gary, and Carole J. Wilson. 2000. "The Past in the Present: A Cleavage Theory of Party Response to European Integration." *British Journal of Political Science* 30: 433–59.

Marks, Gary, Carole J. Wilson, and Leonard Ray. 2002. "National Political Parties and European Integration." *American Journal of Political Science* 46 (3): 585–94.

Marshner, Connie. 1981. Letter to Jack Kemp, February 16. Box 38, Folder "Memo to Congressman Kemp," Paul M. Weyrich Papers. American Heritage Center, Laramie, WY.

Marshner, Connie. 1982. Mayflower Memo, January 24. Box 82, Folder 22, Paul M. Weyrich Papers. American Heritage Center, Laramie, WY.

Marshner, Connie. 2018. Personal interview with author. June 19.

Marshner, Connie. n.d. CRCM speeches. Box 82, Folder 21, Paul M. Weyrich Papers. American Heritage Center, Laramie, WY.

Martin, William. 1996. *With God on Our Side: The Rise of the Religious Right in America.* New York: Broadway.

Martinez, Gebe. 2008. "McCain's Immigration Zigzag." *Politico*, June 20. https://www.politico.com/story/2008/06/mccains-immigration-zigzag-011240.

Mason, Lilliana. 2018. *Uncivil Agreement: How Politics Became Our Identity.* Chicago: University of Chicago Press.

Maxwell, Angie, and Todd Shields. 2019. *The Long Southern Strategy: How Chasing White Voters in the South Changed American Politics.* New York: Oxford University Press.

Maxwell, Rahsaan. 2019. "Cosmopolitan Immigration Attitudes in Large European Cities: Contextual or Compositional Effects?" *American Political Science Review* 113 (2): 456–74.

McCarthy, Colman. 1980. "Some Who Oppose Abortion Now Question One-Issue Politics." *LA Times*, January 2.

McCarty, Nolan, Keith Poole, and Howard Rosenthal. 2016. *Polarized America: The Dance of Ideology and Unequal Riches.* Cambridge, MA: MIT Press.

McCarty, Nolan, and Eric Schickler. 2018. "On the Theory of Parties." *Annual Review of Political Science* 21: 175–93.

McHugh, James. 1971. Letter to Joseph Bernardin, August 26. Box 79, Folder "Social Development: Family Life: Abortion 1971," NCCB Papers. Catholic University of America Archives, Washington, DC.

Mecklenburg, Marjory. 1974a. Memo to NRLC Board of Directors, June 26. Box 8, Folder "Board and Executive Committee (8)," ACCL Papers. Gerald R. Ford Presidential Library and Museum, Ann Arbor, MI.

Mecklenburg, Marjory. 1974b. Letter to Ben Wattenberg, July 12. Box 8, Folder "Board and Executive Committee (9)," ACCL Papers. Gerald R. Ford Presidential Library and Museum, Ann Arbor, MI.

Mecklenburg, Marjory. 1975a. Letter to Shriver for President, September 3. Box 30, Folder "Shriver Campaign Committee (1)," ACCL Papers. Gerald R. Ford Presidential Library and Museum, Ann Arbor, MI.

Mecklenburg, Marjory. 1975b. Letter to Larry Desanto, October 28. Box 30, Folder "Shriver Campaign Committee (1)," ACCL Papers. Gerald R. Ford Presidential Library and Museum, Ann Arbor, MI.

Mecklenburg, Marjory. 1976. Letter to the DNC, May 27. Box 44, Folder, "Republican Party Politics," ACCL Papers. Gerald R. Ford Presidential Library and Museum, Ann Arbor, MI.

Mecklenburg, Marjory. n.d. Meeting notes A. Box 30, Folder "Allied Institutional Development Series (5)," ACCL Papers. Gerald R. Ford Presidential Library and Museum, Ann Arbor, MI.

Mecklenburg, Marjory. n.d. Meeting notes B. Box 45, Folder "Ford (2)," ACCL Papers. Gerald R. Ford Presidential Library and Museum, Ann Arbor, MI.

Melady and Lee. 1976. Memo to Dr. Myron B. Kuropas, June 25. Box 27, Folder "Republican Party Platform—Catholic Issues," Michael Raoul-Duval Files. Gerald R. Ford Presidential Library and Museum, Ann Arbor, MI.

Memo on "Religion." n.d. Box C34, Folder "Special Voter Groups (3)," President Ford Campaign–Political Office. Gerald R. Ford Presidential Library and Museum, Ann Arbor, MI.

Mendelberg, Tali. 2001. *The Race Card: Campaign Strategy, Implicit Messages, and the Norm of Equality*. Princeton, NJ: Princeton University Press.

Merl, Jean. 1980a. "Busing Controversy Dominates Corman-Fiedler Race." *Los Angeles Times*, September 21.

Merl, Jean. 1980b. "Rep. Corman Steps Up Campaign with Brochure Blaming Fiedler for School Woes." *Los Angeles Times*, October 16.

Mickey, Robert. 2015. *Paths Out of Dixie: The Democratization of Authoritarian Enclaves in America's Deep South, 1944–1972*. Princeton, NJ: Princeton University Press.

Miller, Gary, and Norman Schofield. 2003. "The Transformation of the Republican and Democratic Party Coalitions in the U.S." *American Political Science Review* 97 (2): 245–60.

Miller, Zeke. 2016. "Marco Rubio Finds God with Atheist Question in Iowa." *Time*, January 16. https://time.com/4185207/marco-rubio-ted-cruz-iowa-faith/.

Mitchell, Robert Cameron, Angela G. Mertig, and Riley E. Dunlap. 1991. "Twenty Years of Environmental Mobilization: Trends among National Environmental Organizations." *Society of Natural Resources* 4: 219–34.

Morain, Dan. 2014. "Long Ago, a Liberal Republican Helped Win Passage of the Civil Rights Act." *Sacramento Bee*, July 6. https://www.sacbee.com/opinion/opn -columns-blogs/dan-morain/article2602884.html.

Morey, Roy. 1971. Memo to Ken Cole and Ed Harper, September 16. Box 45, Folder 14, Contested Materials Collection. Richard Nixon Presidential Library.

Mulinari, Diana, and Anders Neergaard. 2014. "We Are Sweden Democrats Because We Care for Others: Exploring Racisms in the Swedish Extreme Right." *European Journal of Women's Studies* 21 (1): 43–56.

National Opinion Research Center (NORC). 1955. "NORC Survey #1955-0371: Foreign Affairs." Roper Center for Public Opinion Research, Cornell University, Ithaca, NY. https://doi.org/10.25940/ROPER-31095095.

National Review. 1982. "Catholic Bishops: A Big Problem." December 10.

Naughton, James M. 1976a. "Ford Says Court 'Went Too Far' on Abortion in '73." *New York Times*, February 4. https://www.nytimes.com/1976/02/04/archives/ford-says -court-went-too-far-on-abortion-in-73-but-opposes.html?searchResultPosition=11.

Naughton, James M. 1976b. "Ford-Reagan Race: Similarity in Views." *New York Times*, March 26. https://www.nytimes.com/1976/03/26/archives/fordreagan-race -similarity-in-views.html?searchResultPosition=10.

Naughton, James M. 1976c. "Ford Tells South He Opposes Firearms Registration." *New York Times*, September 27.

NBC/AP. 1981, August. "Reagan/Politics." Roper Center for Public Opinion Research, Cornell University, Ithaca, NY. https://doi.org/10.25940/ROPER -31094609.

Newport, Frank. 2022. "Abortion Moves Up on 'Most Important Problem' List." *Gallup*, https://news.gallup.com/poll/395408/abortion-moves-important-problem -list.aspx.

New Republic. 1936. "Anti-Crime—Or Anti-Labor." February 19, EBSCOhost.

New Republic. 1973. "Abortion." February 10, EBSCOhost.

New York Times. 1975. "The Ford Strategy." November 5. https://www.nytimes.com/ 1975/11/05/archives/the-ford-strategy.html.

New York Times. 1976. "Reagan Affirms Anti-Abortion Stand." February 8. https:// www.nytimes.com/1976/02/08/archives/reagan-affirms-antiabortion-stand.html ?searchResultPosition=5.

New York Times. 1980. "Reagan Gets Backing of Right to Life Group for Stand on Abortion." June 28. https://timesmachine.nytimes.com/timesmachine/1980/06/ 28/113948063.html?pageNumber=7.

Noel, Hans. 2013. *Political Ideologies and Political Parties in America*. New York: Cambridge University Press.

Noferi, Mark. 2014. "When Reagan and GHW Bush Took Bold Executive Action on Immigration." *The Hill*, October 2. https://thehill.com/blogs/congress-blog/ foreign-policy/219463-when-reagan-and-ghw-bush-took-bold-executive-action -on/.

Oakland Tribune. 1966. "Letters to Editor." June 2.

O'Brian, Neil. 2019. "One-Party States and Legislator Extremism in the US House, 1876–2012." *Journal of Politics* 81 (4): 1167–550.

O'Brian, Neil. 2020. "Before Reagan: The Development of Abortion's Partisan Divide." *Perspectives on Politics* 18 (4): 1031–47.

O'Brian, Neil. 2022. "Evangelicals Opposed Abortion Long before Their Leaders Caught Up." *Washington Post*, May 18. https://www.washingtonpost.com/politics/ 2022/05/18/dodds-evangelicals-roe-conservative-opinion/.

Office of Public Opinion Research. 1945. "Roosevelt Survey #52." Roper Center for Public Opinion Research, Cornell University, Ithaca, NY. https://doi.org/10 .25940/ROPER-31095347.

Oxley, Douglas R., Kevin B. Smith, John Alford, Matthew Hibbing, Jennifer Miller, Mario Scalora, Peter Hatemi, and John Hibbing. 2008. "Political Attitudes Vary with Physiological Traits." *Science* 321: 1667–70.

Page, Scott E. 2006. "Path Dependence." *Quarterly Journal of Political Science* 1: 87–115.

Passel, Jeffrey, and D'Vera Cohn. 2019. "Mexicans Decline to Less than Half the U.S. Unauthorized Immigrant Population for the First Time." Pew Research Center. https://www.pewresearch.org/fact-tank/2019/06/12/us-unauthorized-immigrant -population-2017/.

Perkins, Lucy, and Chris Potter. 2021. "U.S. Rep. Mike Doyle Is Retiring from Congress after More than a Quarter-Century in Office." *WESA*, October 18. https://www.wesa.fm/politics-government/2021-10-18/doyle-announces-retirement.

Perlstein, Rick. 2001. *Before the Storm: Barry Goldwater and the Unmaking of the American Consensus.* New York: Hill & Wang.

Perlstein, Rick. 2008. *Nixonland: The Rise of a President and the Fracturing of America.* New York: Scribner.

Perlstein, Rick. 2020. *Reaganland: America's Right Turn, 1976–1980.* New York: Simon & Schuster.

Peters, Jeremy. 2013. "GOP Groups Offering Cover for Lawmakers on Immigration." *New York Times*, July 1.

Phillips, Howard. 1980. Memo to John Lofton, July 25. Box 12, Folder 16a, Howard Phillips Papers, Series 1:1. Jerry Falwell Library, Liberty University, Lynchburg, VA.

Phillips, Kevin. (1969) 2014. *The Emerging Republican Majority.* Princeton, NJ: Princeton University Press.

Phillips, Kevin. 1974. "Conservative Economics." Box 123, Folder "Staff Correspondence 1974," William A. Rusher Papers, 1940–2010. Library of Congress, Washington, DC.

Pieters, Janene. 2017. "Wilders Reiterates Trump Support while Calling for LGBT Rights, Gender Equality." *Netherlands Times News*, January 23. https://nltimes.nl/2017/01/23/wilders-reiterates-trump-support-calling-lgbt-rights-gender-equality.

Pitofsky, Marina. 2019. "Tim Ryan Defends Shift to Supporting Abortion Rights." *The Hill*, June 25. https://thehill.com/blogs/blog-briefing-room/news/450234-tim-ryan-defends-shift-from-pro-life-to-pro-choice-progressive/.

Plott, Elaina. 2015. "Paul Ryan Pledges: No Immigration Reform under Obama." *National Review*, October 27. https://www.nationalreview.com/2015/10/paul-ryan-promises-no-immigration-reform-obama-administration/.

"Political Planning of the Corporation." n.d. Box 4, Folder NRLC (3), ACCL Papers. Gerald R. Ford Presidential Library and Museum, Ann Arbor, MI.

Polk, Jonathan, Jan Rovny, Ryan Bakker, Erica Edwards, Liesbet Hooghe, Seth Jolly, Jelle Koedam, Filip Kostelka, Gary Marks, Gijs Schumacher, Marco Steenbergen, Milada Vachudova, and Marko Zilovic. 2017. "Explaining the Salience of Anti-Elitism and Reducing Political Corruption for Political Parties in Europe with the 2014 Chapel Hill Expert Survey Data." *Research & Politics*, January–March: 1–9.

Presidential Debate. 1984. "Debate between the President and Former Vice President Walter F. Mondale in Kansas City, Missouri." October 21. Ronald Reagan Presidential Library and Museum. https://www.reaganlibrary.gov/archives/speech/debate-between-president-and-former-vice-president-walter-f-mondale-kansas-city.

Preston, Julia. 2012. "Republicans Reconsider Positions on Immigration." *New*

York Times. November 9, 2012. https://www.nytimes.com/2012/11/10/us/politics/
republicans-reconsider-positions-on-immigration.html.

Proctor, Andrew. 2022. "Coming out to Vote: The Construction of a Lesbian and
Gay Electoral Constituency in the United States." *American Political Science
Review* 116 (3): 777–90.

Raines, Howell. 1980. "Reagan Woos the Mexican-Americans." *New York Times,*
September 16. https://www.nytimes.com/1980/09/17/archives/reagan-woos-the
-mexicanamericans.html.

Reichley, Jim. 1976. Letter to Dick Cheney, June 25. Box 2, Folder "Constituency
Analysis," Reichley Files. Gerald R. Ford Presidential Library and Museum,
Ann Arbor, MI.

Roberts, Sam. 2015. "Ben Wattenberg, Neoconservative Author and PBS Host, Is
Dead at 81." *New York Times,* June 29. https://www.nytimes.com/2015/06/30/us/
ben-wattenberg-author-and-commentator-dies-at-81.html.

Roberts, Steven. 1979. "Kennedy Assails Carter in Appeal to Women Voters." *New
York Times,* December 5. https://www.nytimes.com/1979/12/05/archives/kennedy
-assails-carter-in-appeal-to-women-voters.html?searchResultPosition=15.

Rodden, Jonathan. 2019. *Why Cities Lose: The Deep Roots of the Urban-Rural Political Divide.* New York: Basic Books.

Roderick, Kevin. 1986. "Illegal Aliens Add a Dramatic Backdrop to Antonovich
Video." *Los Angeles Times,* May 14.

Rogers, Adrian. 1977. Letter to Foy Valentine, November 28. Box 41, Folder 3, CLC
Staff Files 138-5. Southern Baptist Historical Library and Archives, Nashville,
TN.

Roper Organization. 1977. "Roper Reports 77-9, 1977." Roper Center for Public Opinion Research, Ithaca, NY: Cornell University. https://doi.org.10.25940/
ROPER-31097335.

Rossi Baron, Thea. 2018. Personal interview with author, August 6.

Rudin, Ken. 2009. "When Has a President Been Denied His Party's Nomination?"
National Public Radio, July 22. https://www.npr.org/sections/politicaljunkie/
2009/07/a_president_denied_renominatio.html.

Rusher, William A. 1963. "Crossroads for the GOP." *National Review,* February 12.

Rusher, William A. 1975a. *The Making of the New Majority Party.* New York: Sheed
and Ward.

Rusher, William A. 1975b. "A Marriage of Conservatives." *New York Times,* June 23.
https://www.nytimes.com/1975/06/23/archives/a-marriage-of-conservatives.html.

Rusher, William. 1977. "The Meaning of Coalitionism." *Conservative Advocate,*
March 2. Box 15, Folder 24, Paul M. Weyrich Papers. American Heritage Center, Laramie, WY.

Rydgren, Jens. 2002. "Radical Right Populism in Sweden: Still a Failure, but for How
Long?" *Scandinavian Political Studies* 25 (1): 27–56.

Rydgren, Jens, and Sara van der Meiden. 2019. "The Radical Right and the End of Swedish Exceptionalism." *European Political Science* 18: 439–55.

Safire, William. 1974. "Homosexuals Entitled to Protection of Law." *Miami News*, April 19.

Sanbonmatsu, Kira. 2002. *Democrats, Republicans and the Politics of Women's Place.* Ann Arbor: University of Michigan Press.

Sanger, Margaret. 1952. "Japan Wants Birth Control." *The Nation*, December 13, EBSCOhost.

Scammon, Richard M., and Ben J. Wattenberg. 1970. *The Real Majority.* New York: Coward-McCann.

Schaeffer, Frank. 2007. *Crazy for God: How I Grew Up as One of the Elect, Helped Found the Religious Right, and Lived to Take All (or Almost All) of It Back.* Philadelphia: Perseus Books.

Schattschneider, E. E. 1960. *The Semisovereign People.* New York: Holt, Rinehart & Winston.

Schickler, Eric. 2016. *Racial Realignment: The Transformation of American Liberalism, 1932–1965.* Princeton, NJ: Princeton University Press.

Schildkraut, Deborah. 2010. *Americanism in the Twenty-First Century: Public Opinion in the Age of Immigration.* Cambridge: Cambridge University Press.

Schlozman, Daniel. 2015. *When Movements Anchor Parties: Electoral Alignments in Political History.* Princeton, NJ: Princeton University Press.

Sears, David, and Carolyn Funk. 1999. "Evidence of the Long-Term Persistence of Adults' Political Predispositions." *Journal of Politics* 61 (1): 1–28.

Sears, David, Colette Van Laar, Mary Carrillo, and Rick Kosterman. 1997. "Is It Really Racism? The Origins of White Americans' Opposition to Race-Targeted Policies." *Public Opinion Quarterly* 61 (1): 16–53.

Sears, John. 1976. Letter to Loren Smith, February 25. "Wednesday Morning Quarterbacking–Back Seat Campaign Managing." Box 10, Folder "New Hampshire," Citizens for Reagan. Ronald Reagan Collections, Hoover Institution Archives, Palo Alto, CA.

Sellers, Mitchell D. 2014. "Executive Expansion of Transgender Rights: Electoral Incentives to Issue or Revoke Executive Orders." In *Transgender Rights and Politics: Groups, Issue Framing, and Policy Adoption*, edited by Jami K. Taylor and Donald P. Haider-Markel. Ann Arbor: University of Michigan Press.

Shafer, Byron E., and Richard Johnston. 2009. *The End of Southern Exceptionalism: Class, Race, and Partisan Change in the Postwar South.* Cambridge, MA: Harvard University Press.

Shaw, Russell. 1980. Letter to Bishop Kelly, February 21. Box 64, Folder "Pro-Life Activities, Jan—March 1980," NCCB Papers. Catholic University of America Archives, Washington, DC.

Sides, John, Michael Tesler, and Lynn Vavreck. 2019. *Identity Crisis: The 2016 Pres-*

idential Campaign and the Battle for the Meaning of America. Princeton, NJ: Princeton University Press.

Soble, Ron. 1992. "Elated Gallegly Plans to Erase East-West Split in County." *Los Angeles Times*, November 5.

Soble, Ron, and Alan C. Miller. 1992. "Campaign Fueled by Racial Charges." *Los Angeles Times*, October 11.

Southard, Helen. 1972. "Executive Meeting Minutes," January 14. Box 15, Folder 2, Lawrence Lader Papers, 1956–1986. New York Public Library Archives, New York, NY.

St. John, Jeffrey. 1975. "Is the Republican Party Doomed?" September 26. Box 19, Folder 8. Paul M. Weyrich Papers. American Heritage Center, Laramie, WY.

St. Martin, Thomas. 1973. Memo for MCCL Executive Committee, August 1. Box 11, Folder "MCCL 1973," ACCL Papers. Gerald R. Ford Presidential Library and Museum, Ann Arbor, MI.

Staggenborg, Suzanne. 1991. *The Pro-Choice Movement Organization and Activism in the Abortion Conflict*. Oxford: Oxford University Press.

Stanley, Timothy. 2010. *Kennedy vs. Carter: The 1980 Battle for the Democratic Party's Soul*. Lawrence: University Press of Kansas.

Stanton, Zack. 2020. "How 2020 Killed Off Democrats' Demographic Hopes." *Politico*, November 12. https://www.politico.com/news/magazine/2020/11/12/2020-election-analysis-democrats-future-david-shor-interview-436334.

Statistics Sweden. "Population by Country of Birth and Year." https://www.statistikdatabasen.scb.se/pxweb/en/ssd/START_BE_BE0101_BE0101E/FodelselandArK/table/tableViewLayout1/.

Stenner, Karen. 2005. *The Authoritarian Dynamic*. Cambridge: Cambridge University Press.

Stoker, Laura, and M. Kent Jennings. 2008. "Of Time and the Development of Partisan Polarization." *American Journal of Political Science* 52 (3): 619–35.

Sugrue, Thomas. 1996. *The Origins of the Urban Crisis: Race and Inequality in Postwar Detroit*. Princeton, NJ: Princeton University Press.

Sundquist, James L. 1983. *The Dynamics of the Party System: Alignment and Realignment of Political Parties in the United States*. Washington, DC: Brookings Institution.

Tadlock, Barry. 2015. "Issue Framing and Transgender Politics: An Examination of Interest Group Website and Media Coverage." In *Transgender Rights and Politics: Groups, Issue Framing, and Policy Adoption*, edited by Jami K. Taylor and Donald P. Haider-Markel. Ann Arbor: University of Michigan Press.

Tangner, Marc. 1975. Memo to the Committee, October 10. Box 19, Folder 9, Paul M. Weyrich Papers. American Heritage Center, Laramie, WY.

Tate, Katherine. 1993. *From Protest to Politics: The New Black Voters in American Elections*. Cambridge: Cambridge University Press.

Taylor, Jami K., and Donald P. Haider-Markel. 2014. "Conclusion and Future Directions in Transgender Politics and Policy." In *Transgender Rights and Politics:*

Groups, Issue Framing, and Policy Adoption, edited by Jami K. Taylor and Donald P. Haider-Markel, 273–82. Ann Arbor: University of Michigan Press.

Taylor, Jami K., Daniel Lewis, and Donald P. Haider-Markel, eds. 2018. *The Remarkable Rise of Transgender Rights*. Ann Arbor: University of Michigan Press.

Taylor, Jami K., Daniel Lewis, Donald P. Haider-Markel, Andrew Flores, Patrick Miller, and Barry Tadlock. 2018. "The Factors Underlying Public Opinion about Transgender Rights." In *The Remarkable Rise of Transgender Rights*, edited by Jami Taylor, Daniel Lewis, and Donald P. Haider-Markel, 87–106. Ann Arbor: University of Michigan Press.

Teeter, Robert. 1972a. Memo to H. R. Haldeman, January 6. Box 45, Folder 14, Contested Materials Collection. Richard Nixon Presidential Library.

Teeter, Robert. 1972b. Memo to H. R. Haldeman, August 11. Box 65, Folder "August 11, 1972 – H. R. Haldeman – Abortion," Robert Teeter Papers. Gerald R. Ford Presidential Library and Museum, Ann Arbor, MI.

Tesler, Michael. 2012. "The Spillover of Racialization into Health Care: How President Obama Polarized Public Opinion by Racial Attitudes and Race." *American Journal of Political Science* 56 (3): 690–704.

Tesler, Michael. 2016. *Post-Racial or Most-Racial? Race and Politics in the Obama Era*. Chicago: University of Chicago Press.

Time Magazine. 1976. "Time Soundings #8530." Roper Center for Public Opinion Research, Cornell University, Ithaca, NY. https://doi.org/10.25940/ROPER -31099134.

Time Magazine. 1977. "Time Soundings #8105, Yankelovich, Skelly & White." Roper Center for Public Opinion Research, Cornell University, Ithaca, NY. https://doi .org/10.25940/ROPER-31099140.

Tichenor, Daniel. 1994. "The Politics of Immigration Reform in the United States, 1981–1990." *Polity* 26 (3): 333–62.

Tichenor, Daniel. 2002. *Dividing Lines: The Politics of Immigration Control in America*. Princeton, NJ: Princeton University Press.

Tichenor, Daniel. 2009. "Navigating an American Minefield: The Politics of Illegal Immigration." *The Forum* 7 (3): 1–21.

Tichenor, Daniel. 2016. "Lyndon Johnson's Ambivalent Reform: The Immigration and National Act of 1965." *Presidential Studies Quarterly* 46 (3): 691–705.

Tolchin, Martin. 1979. "Carter, on Coast, Promises to Protect Human Rights of Illegal Aliens." *New York Times*, May 6, 1979. https://www.nytimes.com/1979/05/06/ archives/carter-on-coast-promises-to-protect-human-rights-of-illegal-aliens.html.

Tolchin, Martin. 1983. "Democrats Bar Action in House on Immigration." *New York Times*, October 2, 1983. https://www.nytimes.com/1983/10/02/us/democrats-bar -action-in-house-on-immigration.html.

Tolson, Mike. 2009. "Texas Politician Donald Yarborough Dies at 83." *Houston Chronicle*, September 23, 2009. https://www.chron.com/news/houston-texas/ article/Texas-politician-Donald-Yarborough-dies-at-83-1736099.php.

TRB from Washington. 1965a. "Who Should Enter." *New Republic*, February 20, EBSCOhost.

TRB from Washington. 1965b. "Minority Doubt." *New Republic*, October 2, 1965, EBSCOhost.

TRB from Washington. 1980. "Our Noble Experiment." *New Republic*, December 13, 1980, EBSCOhost.

Trounstine, Jessica. 2008. *Political Monopolies in American Cities: The Rise and Fall of Bosses and Reformers*. Chicago: University of Chicago Press.

UC Santa Barbara. The American Presidency Project. https://www.presidency.ucsb .edu/.

United Press International. 1968. "Wallace Critical of 'Anarchy' in U.S." *New York Times*, June 11, 1968. https://timesmachine.nytimes.com/timesmachine/1968/06/ 11/issue.html.

US Commission on Civil Rights. 1975. *The Voting Rights Act: Ten Years After*. https:// www.usccr.gov/files/pubs/msdelta/ch3.htm.

Valentine, Foy. 1978. Memo to Harry Hollis, December 18. Box 97, Folder 18, CLC 138-2. Southern Baptist Historical Library and Archives, Nashville, TN.

Valentino, Nicholas, Ted Brader, and Ashley Jardina. 2013. "Immigration Opposition among U.S. Whites: General Ethnocentrism or Media Priming of Attitudes about Latinos." *Political Psychology* 34 (2): 149–66.

Vargas, Zaragosa. 2005. *Labor Rights Are Civil Rights: Mexican American Workers in Twentieth-Century America*. Princeton, NJ: Princeton University Press.

Viguerie, Richard. 1980. "John Connally for President." *Conservative Digest*, February 1980. Box 4, Folder 3, Paul M. Weyrich Papers. American Heritage Center, Laramie, WY.

Ward, Jon. 2019. *Camelot's End: Kennedy vs. Carter and the Fight That Broke the Democratic Party*. New York: Twelve.

Weinger, Mackenzie. 2012. "Hannity: I've 'Evolved' on Immigration and Support a 'Pathway to Citizenship.'" *Politico*, November 8, 2012. https://www.politico .com/blogs/media/2012/11/hannity-ive-evolved-on-immigration-and-support-a -pathway-to-citizenship-149078.

Weyrich, Paul. 1971. Letter to Raymond Smith, April 29. Box 4, Folder 3, Paul M. Weyrich Scrapbooks, 1942–2009. Library of Congress, Washington, DC.

Weyrich, Paul. 1975a. Letter to the Committee, August 20. Box 19, Folder 7, Paul M. Weyrich Papers. American Heritage Center, Laramie, WY.

Weyrich, Paul. 1975b. Letter to Richard Viguerie, October 3. Box 43, Folder 13, Paul M. Weyrich Papers. American Heritage Center, Laramie, WY.

Weyrich, Paul. 1976. Letter to Terry Dolan, September 2. Box 1, Folder 21, Paul M. Weyrich Papers. American Heritage Center, Laramie, WY.

Weyrich, Paul. 1977. Letter to Cheryl Brown, March 30. Box 2, Folder 3, Paul M. Weyrich Papers. American Heritage Center, Laramie, WY.

Weyrich, Paul. 1979. Letter to Ed Feulner, April 10. Box 3, Folder 15, Paul M. Weyrich Papers. American Heritage Center, Laramie, WY.

Weyrich, Paul. 1981a. Letter to Rienk Kamer, July 16. Letter from the Coalitions
for America. Box 10, Folder 5, Paul M. Weyrich Scrapbooks, 1942–2009. Library
of Congress, Washington, DC.

Weyrich, Paul. 1981b. Memo to the Coalitions, July 22. Box 25, Folder 3, Paul M.
Weyrich Papers. American Heritage Center, Laramie, WY.

Weyrich, Paul. n.d. Memo: "Blue Collar or Blue Blood: The New Right Compared
with the Old Right." Box 16, Folder 30c, Conservative Caucus Papers. Jerry
Falwell Library, Liberty University, Lynchburg, VA.

Weyrich, Paul. n.d. Interview with Nathan Miller. Box 24, Folder 5, Paul M. Weyrich
Papers. American Heritage Center, Laramie, WY.

Wheatley, Jonathan, and Fernando Mendez. 2019. "Re-conceptualizing Dimensions
of Political Competition in Europe: A Demand-Side Approach." *British Journal
of Political Science*, 1–20.

Wiese, Arthur. 1979. "Study Disputes Voter 'Myths.'" *Houston Post*, September 12. Box 24, Folder 4, Paul M. Weyrich Papers. American Heritage Center,
Laramie, WY.

Wilcox, Clyde. 1992. *God's Warriors: The Christian Right in Twentieth-Century
America*. Baltimore: Johns Hopkins University Press.

Williams, Daniel. 2011. "The GOP's Abortion Strategy: Why Pro-Choice Republicans Became Pro-Life in the 1970s." *Journal of Policy History* 23 (4): 513–39.

Williams, Daniel. 2016. *Defenders of the Unborn: The Pro-Life Movement before
Roe v. Wade*. Oxford: Oxford University Press.

Wilson, Reid. 2019. "Legacy of California's Prop. 187 Foreshadows GOP's Path
Ahead." *The Hill*, November 10. https://thehill.com/homenews/state-watch/
469666-legacy-of-californias-prop-187-foreshadows-gops-path-ahead/.

Wolbrecht, Christina. 2000. *The Politics of Women's Rights: Parties, Positions, and
Change*. Princeton, NJ: Princeton University Press.

Wong, Carolyn. 2006. *Lobbying for Inclusion: Rights Politics and the Making of
Immigration Policy*. Palo Alto, CA: Stanford University Press.

Young, Lisa. 2000. *Feminists and Party Politics*. Vancouver: UBC Press.

Zaller, John. 1992. *The Nature and Origins of Mass Opinion*. New York: Cambridge
University Press.

Zaller, John. 2012. "What Nature and Origins Leaves Out." *Critical Review* 24 (4):
569–642.

Zhirkov, Kirill, and Nicholas Valentino. 2022. "The Origins and Consequences of
Racialized Schemas about U.S. Parties." *Journal of Race, Ethnicity and Politics*
7 (3): 484–504.

Ziegler, Mary. 2015. *After Roe: The Lost History of the Abortion Debate*. Cambridge,
MA: Harvard University Press.

Index

Chicago Studies in American Politics

A series edited by Susan Herbst, Lawrence R. Jacobs, Adam J. Berinsky, and Frances Lee; Benjamin I. Page, editor emeritus

Also in the series: